T0370420

ON PRACTICE
AND CONTRADICTION

This essential new series features classic texts by key figures that took center stage during a period of insurrection. Each book is introduced by a major contemporary radical writer who shows how these incendiary words still have the power to inspire, to provoke and maybe to ignite new revolutions . . .

ON PRACTICE
AND CONTRADICTION

MAO TSE-TUNG

INTRODUCTION BY SLAVOJ ŽIŽEK

VERSO

London • New York

First published by Verso 2007
Copyright © Verso 2007
Introduction © Slavoj Žižek 2007
Chapters 1, 3, 4, 5, 6, 7 and 10 published in *Selected Works of Mao Tse-tung*,
Foreign Languages Press, Peking 1967; copyright© Foreign Languages Press
1967. Chapters 2, 8, 9, 11 and 12 published in *Selected Works of Mao Tse-tung*, Kranti Publications, Secunderabad 1990; copyright © Kranti
Publications 1990.

3 5 7 9 10 8 6 4 2

Verso
UK: 6 Meard Street, London W1F 0EG
20 Jay Street, Suite 1010, Brooklyn, NY 11201
www.versobooks.com

Verso is the imprint of New Left Books

ISBN-13: 978-1-84467-587-6

British Library Cataloguing in Publication Data
A catalogue record for this book is available from the British Library

Library of Congress Cataloging-in-Publication Data
A catalog record for this book is available from the Library of Congress

Typeset in Bembo by Hewer Text UK Ltd, Edinburgh
Printed in the United States of America

CONTENTS

INTRODUCTION

MAO TSE-TUNG, THE
MARXIST LORD OF MISRULE

Slavoj Žižek

One of the most devious traps which lurk in wait for Marxists is the search for the moment of the Fall, when things took the wrong turn in the history of Marxism: was it already the late Engels with his more positivist-evolutionist understanding of historical materialism? Was it the revisionism *and* the orthodoxy of the Second International? Was it Lenin?[1] Or was it Marx himself in his late work, after he abandoned his youthful humanism (as some 'humanist Marxists' claimed decades ago)? This entire topic has to be rejected: there is no opposition here, the Fall is to be inscribed into the very origins. (To put it even more pointedly, such a search for the intruder who infected the original model and set in motion its degeneration cannot but reproduce the logic of anti-Semitism.) What this means is that, even if – or, rather, especially if – one submits the Marxist past to a ruthless critique, one has first to acknowledge it as 'one's own', taking full responsibility for it, not to comfortably get rid of the 'bad' turn of things by way of attributing it to a foreign intruder (the 'bad' Engels who was too stupid to understand Marx's dialectics, the 'bad' Lenin who didn't get the core of Marx's theory, the 'bad' Stalin who spoils the noble plans of the 'good' Lenin, etc.).

The first thing to do, then, is to fully endorse the displacement in the history of Marxism concentrated in two great passages (or, rather, violent cuts): the passage from Marx to Lenin, as well as the passage from Lenin to Mao. In each case, there is a displacement of the original constellation: from the most advanced country (as expected by Marx) to a relatively backward country – the revolution 'took place in a wrong country';

from workers to (poor) peasants as the main revolutionary agent, etc. In the same way as Christ needed Paul's 'betrayal' in order for Christianity to emerge as a universal church (recall that, among the twelve apostles, Paul occupies the place of Judas the traitor, replacing him!), Marx needed Lenin's 'betrayal' in order to enact the first Marxist revolution: it is an inner necessity of the 'original' teaching to submit to and survive this 'betrayal', to survive this violent act of being torn out of one's original context and thrown into a foreign landscape where it has to reinvent itself – *only in this way, universality is born.*

So, apropos the second violent transposition, that of Mao, it is too facile either to condemn his reinvention of Marxism as theoretically 'inadequate', as a regression with regard to Marx's standards (it is easy to show that peasants lack the substanceless proletarian subjectivity), but it is no less inadequate to blur the violence of the cut and to accept Mao's reinvention as a logical continuation or 'application' of Marxism (relying, as is usually the case, on the simple metaphoric expansion of class struggle: 'today's predominant class struggle is no longer between capitalists and proletariat in each country, it has shifted to the Third versus the First World, bourgeois versus proletarian nations'). The achievement of Mao is here tremendous: his name stands for the political mobilization of the hundreds of millions of anonymous Third World toilers whose labour provides the invisible 'substance', background, of historical development – the mobilization of all those whom even such a poet of 'otherness' as Lévinas dismissed as the 'yellow peril' – see, from what is arguably his weirdest text, 'The Russo-Chinese Debate and the Dialectic' (1960), a comment on the Soviet–Chinese conflict:

> The yellow peril! It is not racial, it is spiritual. It does not involve inferior values; it involves a radical strangeness, a stranger to the weight of its past, from where there does not filter any familiar voice or inflection, a lunar or Martian past.[2]

Does this not recall Heidegger's insistence, throughout the 1930s, that the main task of Western thought today is to defend the Greek breakthrough, the founding gesture of the 'West', the overcoming of the pre-philosophical, mythical, 'Asiatic' universe, to struggle against the renewed 'Asiatic' threat – the greatest antagonist of the West is 'the mythical in general and the Asiatic in particular?'[3] It is *this* Asiatic 'radical strangeness' which is mobilized, politicized, by Mao Tse-tung's communist movement.

In his *Phenomenology of Spirit*, Hegel introduces his notorious notion of womankind as 'the everlasting irony of the community': womankind

> changes by intrigue the universal end of the government into a private end, transforms its universal activity into a work of some particular individual, and perverts the universal property of the state into a possession and ornament for the family.[4]

In contrast to male ambition, a woman wants power in order to promote her own narrow family interests or, even worse, her personal caprice, incapable as she is of perceiving the universal dimension of state politics. How are we not to recall F. W. J. Schelling's claim that 'the same principle carries and holds us in its ineffectiveness which would consume and destroy us in its effectiveness'?[5] A power which, when it is kept at its proper place, can be benign and pacifying, turns into its radical opposite, into the most destructive fury, the moment it intervenes at a higher level, the level which is not its own: *the same* femininity which, within the closed circle of family life, is the very power of protective love, turns into obscene frenzy when displayed at the level of public and state affairs . . . In short, it is OK for a woman to protest against public state power on behalf of the rights of family and kinship; but woe betide a society in which women endeavour directly to influence decisions concerning the affairs of state, manipulating their weak male partners, effectively emasculating them . . . Is there not something similar in the terror aroused by the prospect of awakening the anonymous Asiatic masses? They are acceptable if they protest against their fate and allow us to help them (through large-scale humanitarian actions . . .), but not when they directly 'empower' themselves, to the horror of sympathetic liberals who are always ready to support the revolt of the poor and dispossessed, on condition that it is done with good manners?

Georgi M. Derluguian's *Bourdieu's Secret Admirer in the Caucasus*[6] tells the extraordinary story of Musa Shanib from Abkhazia, the leading intellectual of this turbulent region whose incredible career passed from Soviet dissident intellectual through democratic political reformer and Muslim fundamentalist warlord up to respected professor of philosophy, his entire career marked by the strange admiration for Pierre Bourdieu's thought. There are two ways to approach such a figure. The first reaction is to dismiss it as local eccentricity, to treat it with benevolent irony – 'what a strange choice, Bourdieu – who knows what this folkloric guy sees in Bourdieu . . .'. The second reaction is to directly assert the universal scope of theory – 'see how universal theory is: every intellectual from Paris to Chechnya and Abkhazia can debate Bourdieu's theories . . .' The true task, of course, is to avoid both these options and to assert the universality of a theory as the result of hard theoretical work and struggle, a struggle that is not external to theory: the point is not (only) that Shanib had to do a lot of work to break the constraints of his local context and grasp Bourdieu – this appropriation of Bourdieu by an Abkhazian intellectual also affects the substance of the theory itself, transposing it into a different universe. Did – *mutatis mutandis* – Lenin not do something similar with Marx? Mao's shift with regard to Lenin *and* Stalin concerns the relationship between the working class and peasantry: both Lenin and Stalin were deeply distrustful towards the peasantry, they saw as one of the main tasks of Soviet power to break the inertia of the peasants, their substantial attachment to the land, to 'proletarianize' them and thus fully expose them to the dynamics of modernization – in clear contrast to Mao who, in his critical notes on Stalin's *Economic Problems of Socialism in the USSR* (from 1958) remarked that 'Stalin's point of view . . . is almost completely wrong. The basic error is mistrust of the peasants.'[7] The theoretical and political consequences of this shift are properly shattering: they imply no less than a thorough reworking of Marx's Hegelian notion of the proletarian position as the position of 'substanceless subjectivity', of those who are reduced to the abyss of their subjectivity.

This is the movement of 'concrete universality', this radical 'transubstantiation' through which the original theory has to reinvent itself in a new context: only by way of surviving this transplant can it emerge as effectively universal. And, of course, the point is not that we are dealing here with the pseudo-Hegelian process of 'alienation' and 'disalienation', of how the original theory is 'alienated' and then has to incorporate the foreign context, reappropriate it, subordinate it to itself: what such a pseudo-Hegelian notion misses is the way this violent transplantation into a foreign context radically affects the original theory itself, so that, when this theory 'returns to itself in its otherness' (reinvents itself in the foreign context), its very substance changes – and yet this shift is not just the reaction to an external shock, it remains an inherent transformation of the *same* theory of the overcoming of capitalism. This is how capitalism is a 'concrete universality': it is not the question of isolating what all particular forms of capitalism have in common, their shared universal features, but of grasping this matrix as a positive force in itself, as something which all actual particular forms try to counteract, in order to contain its destructive effects.

The most reliable sign of capitalism's ideological triumph is the virtual disappearance of the very term in the last two or three decades: from the 1980s onwards,

> virtually no one, with the exception of a few allegedly archaic Marxists (an 'endangered species'), referred to capitalism any longer. The term was simply struck from the vocabulary of politicians, trade unionists, writers and journalists – not to mention social scientists, who had consigned it to historical oblivion.[8]

So what about the upsurge of the anti-globalization movement in the last years? Does it not clearly contradict this diagnostic? Not at all: a close look quickly shows how this movement also succumbs to 'the temptation to transform a critique of capitalism itself (centred on economic mechanisms, forms of work organization, and profit extraction) into a critique of "imperialism"'.[9] In this way, when one talks about 'globalization and its agents', the enemy is externalized (usually in the form of vulgar anti-Americanism). From this perspective, where the main task today is to fight 'the American empire', any ally is good if it is anti-American, and so unbridled Chinese 'communist' capitalism, violent Islamic anti-modernists, as well as the obscene Lukashenko regime in Belarus (see Chavez's visit to Belarus in July 2006), may appear as progressive anti-globalist comrades-in-arms . . . What we have here is thus another version of the ill-famed notion of 'alternate modernity': instead of the critique of capitalism as such, of confronting its basic mechanism, we get the critique of the imperialist 'excess', with the (silent) notion of mobilizing capitalist mechanisms within another, more 'progressive', framework.

This is how one should approach what is arguably Mao's central contribution to Marxist philosophy, his elaborations on the notion of contradiction: one should not dismiss them as a worthless philosophical regression (which, as one can easily demonstrate, relies on a vague notion of 'contradiction' which simply means 'struggle of opposite tendencies'). The main thesis of his great text 'On Contradiction' on the two facets of contradictions, 'the principal and the non-principal contradictions in a process, and the principal and the non-principal aspects of a contradiction', deserves a close reading. Mao's reproach to the 'dogmatic Marxists' is that they 'do not understand that it is precisely in the particularity of contradiction that the universality of contradiction resides':

> For instance, in capitalist society the two forces in contradiction, the proletariat and the bourgeoisie, form the principal contradiction. The other contradictions, such as those between the remnant feudal class and the bourgeoisie, between the peasant petty bourgeoisie and the bourgeoisie, between the proletariat and the peasant petty bourgeoisie, between the non-monopoly capitalists and the monopoly capitalists, between bourgeois democracy and bourgeois fascism, among the capitalist countries and between imperialism and the colonies, are all determined or influenced by this principal contradiction . . .
>
> When imperialism launches a war of aggression against such a country, all its various classes, apart from some traitors, can temporarily unite in a national war against imperialism. At such a time, the contradiction between imperialism and the country concerned becomes the principal contradiction, while all the contradictions among the various classes within the country (including what was the principal contradiction, between the feudal system and the great masses of the people) are temporarily relegated to a secondary and subordinate position.[10]

This is Mao's key point: the principal (universal) contradiction does not overlap with the contradiction which should be treated as dominant in a particular situation – the universal dimension literally *resides* in this particular contradiction. In each concrete situation, a different 'particular' contradiction is the predominant one, in the precise sense that, in order to win the fight for the resolution of the principal contradiction, one should treat a particular contradiction as the predominant one, to which all other struggles should be subordinated. In China under the Japanese occupation, patriotic unity against the Japanese was the predominant thing if Communists wanted to win the class struggle – *any direct focusing on class struggle in these conditions went against class struggle itself.* (Therein, perhaps, resides the main feature of 'dogmatic opportunism': to insist on the centrality of the principal contradiction at a wrong moment.) The further key point concerns the principal *aspect* of a contradiction; for example, with regard to the contradiction between the productive forces and the relations of production,

> the productive forces, practice and the economic base generally play the principal and decisive role; whoever denies this is not a materialist. But it must also be admitted that in certain conditions, such aspects as the relations of production, theory and the superstructure in turn manifest themselves in the principal and decisive role. When it is impossible for the productive forces to develop without a change in the relations of production, then the change in the relations of production plays the principal and decisive role.[11]

The political stakes of this debate are decisive: Mao's aim is to assert the key role, in the political struggle, of what the Marxist tradition usually refers to as the 'subjective factor' – theory, the superstructure. This is what, according to Mao, Stalin neglected:

> Stalin's [*Economic Problems of Socialism in the USSR*] from first to last says nothing about the superstructure. It is not concerned with people; it considers things, not people. . . . [He speaks] only of the relations of production, not of the superstructure or politics, or the role of the people. Communism cannot be reached unless there is a communist movement.[12]

Alain Badiou, a true Maoist here, applies this to today's constellation, avoiding the focus on the anti-capitalist struggle, even ridiculing its main form today (the anti-globalization movement), and defining the emancipatory struggle in strictly political terms as the struggle against (liberal) democracy, today's predominant ideologico-political form. 'Today the enemy is not called Empire or Capital. It's called Democracy.'[13] What, today, prevents the radical questioning of capitalism itself is precisely *the belief in the democratic form of the struggle against capitalism*. Lenin's stance against 'economism' as well as against 'pure' politics is crucial today, apropos of the split attitude towards economy in (what remains of) the Left: on the one hand, the 'pure politicians' who abandon economy as the site of struggle and intervention; on the other hand, the 'economists', fascinated by the functioning of today's global economy, who preclude any possibility of a political intervention proper. With regard to this split, today, more than ever, we should return to Lenin: yes, the economy is the key domain, the battle will be decided there, one has to break the spell of the global capitalism - *but* the intervention should be properly *political*, not economic. Today, when everyone is 'anti-capitalist', up to and including the Hollywood 'socio-critical' conspiracy movies (from *The Enemy of the State* to *The Insider*) in which the enemy is constituted by the big corporations with their ruthless pursuit of profit, the signifier 'anti-capitalism' has lost its subversive sting. What one should problematize is the self-evident opposite of this 'anti-capitalism': the faith in the democratic substance of honest Americans which will break up the conspiracy. *This* is the hard kernel of today's global capitalist universe, its true Master-Signifier: democracy.[14] Mao's further elaboration on the notion of contradiction in his 'On the Correct Handling of Contradictions Among the People' (1957) also cannot be reduced to its best-known feature, the rather commonsense point of distinguishing between the antagonistic and the non-antagonistic contradictions:

> The contradictions between ourselves and the enemy are antagonistic contradictions. Within the ranks of the people, the contradictions among the working people are non-antagonistic, while those between the exploited and the exploiting classes have a non-antagonistic as well as an antagonistic aspect. . . . Under the people's democratic dictatorship two different methods, one dictatorial and the other democratic, should be used to resolve the two types of contradictions which differ in nature – those between ourselves and the enemy and those among the people.[15]

One should always read this distinction together with its more 'ominous' supplement, a warning that the two aspects may overlap: 'In ordinary circumstances, contradictions among the people are not antagonistic. But if they are not handled properly, or if we relax our vigilance and lower our guard, antagonism may arise.' Democratic dialogue, the peaceful coexistence of different orientations among the working class, is not something simply given, a natural state of things, it is something gained and sustained by vigilance and struggle. Here, also, struggle has priority over unity: the very space of unity has to be won through struggle.

So what are we to do with these elaborations? One should be very precise in diagnosing, at the very abstract level of theory, where Mao was right and where he was wrong. Mao was right in rejecting the standard notion of 'dialectical synthesis' as the 'reconciliation' of the opposites, as a higher unity which encompasses their struggle; he was wrong in formulating this rejection, this insistence on the priority of struggle, division, over every synthesis or unity, in the terms of a general cosmology-ontology of the 'eternal struggle of opposites' – this is why he got caught in the simplistic, properly *non-dialectical*, notion of the 'bad infinity' of struggle. Mao clearly regresses here to primitive pagan wisdom regarding how every creature, every determinate form of life, sooner or later meets its end: 'One thing destroys another, things emerge, develop, and are destroyed, everywhere is like this. If things are not destroyed by others, then they destroy themselves.' One should give Mao his due at this level: he goes all the way in this direction, applying this principle not only to communism itself – see the following passage, in which Mao accomplishes a gigantic ontological 'leap forward' from the division of atomic nuclei into protons, anti-protons, etc., to the inevitable division of communism into stages:

> I don't believe that communism will not be divided into stages, and that there will be no qualitative changes. Lenin said that all things could be divided. He gave the atom as an example, saying that not only could it be divided, but the electron could, too. Formerly, however, it was held that the atom could not be divided; the branch of science devoted to splitting the atomic nucleus is still very young, only twenty or thirty years old. In recent decades, the scientists have resolved the atomic nucleus into its constituents, such as protons, anti-protons, neutrons, anti-neutrons, mesons and anti-mesons.[16]

He even goes a step further and moves beyond humanity itself, forecasting, in a proto-Nietzschean way, the 'overcoming' of man:

> The life of dialectics is the continuous movement towards opposites. Mankind will also finally meet its doom. When the theologians talk about doomsday, they are pessimistic and terrify people. We say the end of mankind is something which will produce something more advanced than mankind. Mankind is still in its infancy.[17]

And, further, the rise of (some) animals themselves to what we consider today as an exclusively human level of consciousness:

> In the future, animals will continue to develop. I don't believe that men alone are capable of having two hands. Can't horses, cows, sheep

evolve? Can only monkeys evolve? And can it be, moreover, that of all the monkeys only one species can evolve, and all the others are incapable of evolving? In a million years, ten million years, will horses, cows and sheep still be the same as those today? I think they will continue to change. Horses, cows, sheep and insects will all change.[18]

This 'cosmic perspective' is for Mao not just an irrelevant philosophical caveat; it has precise ethico-political consequences. When Mao high-handedly dismisses the threat of the atomic bomb, he is not downplaying the scope of the danger – he is fully aware that nuclear war may lead to the extinction of humanity as such, so, to justify his defiance, he has to adopt the 'cosmic perspective' from which the end of life on Earth 'would hardly mean anything to the universe as a whole':

The United States cannot annihilate the Chinese nation with its small stack of atom bombs. Even if the US atom bombs were so powerful that, when dropped on China, they would make a hole right through the earth, or even blow it up, that would hardly mean anything to the universe as a whole, though it might be a major event for the solar system.[19]

This 'cosmic perspective' also grounds Mao's dismissive attitude towards the human costs of economic and political endeavours. If one is to believe Mao's latest biography,[20] he caused the greatest famine in history by exporting food to Russia to buy nuclear and arms industries: 38 million people were starved and slave-driven to death in 1958-61. Mao knew exactly what was happening, saying: 'half of China may well have to die.' This is the instrumental attitude at its most radical: killing as part of a ruthless attempt to realize a goal, reducing people to a disposable means – and what one should bear in mind is that the Nazi Holocaust was *not* the same: the killing of the Jews was not part of a rational strategy, but an autotelic goal, a meticulously planned 'irrational' excess (recall the deportation of the last Jews from Greek islands in 1944, just before the German retreat, or the massive use of trains for transporting Jews instead of war materials in 1944). This is why Heidegger is wrong when he reduces the Holocaust to the industrial production of corpses: Stalinist communism was that, but *not* Nazism.[21]

The conceptual consequence of this 'bad infinity' that pertains to vulgar evolutionism is Mao's consistent rejection of the 'negation of negation' as a universal dialectical law. In explicit polemics against Engels (and, incidentally, following Stalin who, in his *On Dialectical and Historical Materialism*, also does not mention 'negation of negation' among the 'four main features of Marxist dialectics'):

> Engels talked about the three categories, but as for me I don't believe in two of those categories. (The unity of opposites is the most basic law, the transformation of quality and quantity into one another is the unity of the opposites quality and quantity, and the negation of the negation does not exist at all.) . . . There is no such thing as the negation of the negation. Affirmation, negation, affirmation, negation . . . in the development of things, every link in the chain of events is both affirmation and negation. Slave-holding society negated primitive society, but with reference to feudal society it constituted, in turn, the affirmation. Feudal society constituted the negation in relation to slave-holding society but it was in turn the affirmation with reference to capitalist society. Capitalist society was the negation in relation to feudal society, but it is, in turn, the affirmation in relation to socialist society.[22]

Along these lines, Mao scathingly dismisses the category of the 'dialectical synthesis' of opposites, promoting his own version of 'negative dialectics' – every synthesis is for him ultimately what Adorno in his critique of Lukács called '*erpresste Versöhnung*' (enforced reconciliation), at best a momentary pause in the ongoing struggle, which occurs not when the opposites are united, but when one side simply wins over the other:

> What is synthesis? You have all witnessed how the two opposites, the Kuomintang and the Communist Party, were synthesized on the mainland. The synthesis took place like this: their armies came, and we devoured them, we ate them bite by bite. . . . One thing eating another, big fish eating little fish, this is synthesis. It has never been put like this in books. I have never put it this way in my books either. For his part, Yang Hsien-chen believes that two combine into one, and that synthesis is the indissoluble tie between two opposites. What indissoluble ties are there in this world? Things may be tied, but in the end they must be severed. There is nothing which cannot be severed.[23]

(Note the tone of sharing a secret not to be rendered public, as if Mao is divulging his 'secret teaching', the cruel but realistic lesson that undermines the happy public optimism . . .) This was at the core of the famous debate, in the late 1950s, about the One and the Two (are the Two united into One, or is the One divided into Two?): 'In any given thing, the unity of opposites is conditional, temporary and transitory, and hence relative, whereas the struggle of opposites is absolute.' This brings us to what one is tempted to call Mao's ethico-political injunction – to paraphrase the last words of Beckett's *L'innommable*: 'in the silence you don't know, you must go on severing, I can't go on, I'll go on severing.'[24] This injunction should be located into its proper philosophical lineage. There are, roughly speaking, two philosophical approaches to an antagonistic constellation of either/or: either one opts for one pole against the other (Good against Evil, freedom against oppression, morality against hedonism, etc.), or one adopts a 'deeper' attitude of emphasizing the complicity of the opposites, and of advocating a proper measure or their unity. Although Hegel's dialectic seems a version of the second approach (the 'synthesis' of opposites), he opts for an unheard-of *third* version: the way to resolve the deadlock is to engage oneself neither in fighting for the 'good' side against the 'bad' one, nor in trying to bring them together in a balanced 'synthesis', but in opting for the *bad* side of the initial either/or. Of course, this 'choice of the worst' fails, but in this failure it undermines the entire field of alternatives and thus enables us to overcome its terms.

The first one to propose such a matrix of divisions was Gorgias. His *On Nature, or the Non-Existent* (the text survived only in summary form in Sextus Empiricus, and Aristotle's *On Melissus, Xenophanes and Gorgias*) can be summed up in three propositions: (a) Nothing exists; (b) If anything existed, it could not be known; (c) If anything did exist, and could be known, it could not be communicated to others. If there ever was a clear case of the Freudian logic of the borrowed kettle (providing mutually exclusive reasons), this is it:[25] (1) Nothing exists. (2) What exists, cannot be known. (3) What we know, cannot be communicated to others . . . But more interesting is the repeated 'diagonal' mode of division of the genus into species: Things exist or not. If they exist, they can be known or not. If they can be known, they can be communicated to others or not. Surprisingly, we find the same progressive differentiation at the opposite end of the history of Western philosophy, in the twentieth-century sophistry called 'dialectical materialism' (*Diamat*). In

Stalin's *On Dialectical and Historical Materialism*, when the four features of dialectics are enumerated:

> The principal features of the Marxist dialectical method are as follows:
>
> Contrary to metaphysics, dialectics does not regard nature as an accidental agglomeration of things, of phenomena, unconnected with, isolated from, and independent of, each other, but as a connected and integral whole . . .
>
> Contrary to metaphysics, dialectics holds that nature is not a state of rest and immobility, stagnation and immutability, but a state of continuous movement and change, of continuous renewal and development . . .
>
> Contrary to metaphysics, dialectics does not regard the process of development as a simple process of growth, where quantitative changes do not lead to qualitative changes, but as a development which passes from insignificant and imperceptible quantitative changes to open 'fundamental changes' to qualitative changes; a development in which the qualitative changes occur not gradually, but rapidly and abruptly, taking the form of a leap from one state to another . . .
>
> Contrary to metaphysics, dialectics holds that internal contradictions are inherent in all things and phenomena of nature, for they all have their negative and positive sides, a past and a future, something dying away and something developing; and that the struggle between these opposites . . . constitutes the internal content of the process of development.[26]

First, nature is not a conglomerate of dispersed phenomena, but a connected whole. Then, this Whole is not immobile, but in constant movement and change. Then, this change is not only a gradual quantitative drifting, but involves qualitative jumps and ruptures. Finally, this qualitative development is not a matter of harmonious deployment, but is propelled by the struggle of opposites . . . The trick here is that we are effectively *not* dealing merely with the Platonic dieresis, gradual subdivision of a genus into species and then species into subspecies: the underlying premise is that this 'diagonal' process of division is really vertical, i.e., that we are dealing with the different aspects of the *same* division. To put it in Stalinist jargon: an immobile Whole is not really a Whole, but just a conglomerate of elements; development which does not involve qualitative jumps is not really a development, but just stasis; a qualitative change which does not involve struggle of the opposites is not really a change, but just quantitative monotonous movement . . . Or, to put it in more ominous terms: those who advocate qualitative change without struggle of the opposites *really* oppose change and advocate the continuation of the same; those who advocate change without qualitative jumps *really* oppose change and advocate immobility . . . The political aspect of this logic is clearly discernible: 'those who advocate the transformation of capitalism into socialism without class struggle *really* reject socialism and want capitalism to continue', etc.

There are two famous quips of Stalin which are both grounded in this logic. When Stalin answered the question 'Which deviation is worse, the Rightist or the Leftist one?' by 'They are both worse!', the underlying premise is that the Leftist deviation is *really* ('objectively', as Stalinists liked to put it) not Leftist at all, but a concealed Rightist one! When Stalin wrote, in a report on a Party congress, that the delegates, with a majority of votes, unanimously approved the CC resolution, the underlying premise is, again, that there was in fact no minority within the Party: those who voted against thereby excluded themselves from the Party . . . In all these cases, *the genus repeatedly overlaps (fully coincides) with one of its species*. This is also what allows Stalin to read history retroactively, so that things 'become clear' retroactively: it was not that Trotsky was first fighting for the revolution with Lenin and Stalin and then, at a certain stage, opted for a different strategy from the one advocated by Stalin; this last opposition (Trotsky/Stalin) 'makes it clear' how, 'objectively', Trotsky was against revolution all the way back.

We find the same procedure in the classificatory impasse the Stalinist ideologists and political activists faced in their struggle for collectivization in the years 1928–33. In their attempt to account for their effort to crush the peasants' resistance in 'scientific' Marxist terms, they divided peasants into three categories (classes): the poor peasants (no land or minimal land, working for others), natural allies of the workers; the autonomous middle peasants, oscillating between the exploited and exploiters; the rich peasants, 'kulaks' (employing other workers, lending them money or seeds, etc.), the exploiting 'class enemy' which, as such, has to be 'liquidated'. However, in practice, this classification became more and more blurred and inoperative: in the state of generalized poverty, clear criteria no longer applied, and the other two categories often joined the kulaks in their resistance to forced collectivization. An additional category was thus introduced, that of a 'subkulak', a peasant who, although, with regard to his economic situation, was too poor to be considered a kulak proper, nonetheless shared the kulak 'counter-revolutionary' attitude. The 'subkulak' was thus

> a term without any real social content even by Stalinist standards, but merely rather unconvincingly masquerading as such. As was officially stated, 'by "kulak" we mean the carrier of certain political tendencies which are most frequently discernible in the subkulak, male and female.' By this means, any peasant whatever was liable to dekula-kization; and the 'subkulak' notion was widely employed, enlarging the category of victims greatly beyond the official estimate of kulaks proper even at its most strained.[27]

No wonder that the official ideologists and economists finally renounced the very effort to provide an 'objective' definition of kulak: 'The grounds given in one Soviet comment are that "the old attitudes of a kulak have almost disappeared, and the new ones do not lend themselves to recognition".'[28] The art of identifying a kulak was thus no longer a matter of objective social analysis; it became the matter of a complex 'hermeneutics of suspicion', of identifying one's 'true political attitudes' hidden beneath deceiving public proclamations, so that *Pravda* had to concede that 'even the best activists often cannot spot the kulak'.[29]

What all this points towards is the dialectical mediation of the 'subjective' and 'objective' dimension: the 'subkulak' no longer desig-nates an 'objective' social category; it designates the point at which objective social analysis breaks down and the subjective political attitude directly inscribes itself into the 'objective' order – in Lacanese, the *'subkulak' is the point of subjectivization of the 'objective' chain: poor peasant–middle peasant–kulak*. It is not an 'objective' subcategory (or subdivision) of the class of 'kulaks', but simply the name for the 'kulak' subjective political attitude – this accounts for the paradox that, although it appears as a subdivision of the class of 'kulaks', the class of 'subkulaks' is a species that overflows its own genus (that of kulaks), since 'subkulaks' are also to be found among middle and even poor peasants. In short, the 'subkulak' names political division as such, the Enemy whose presence traverses the *entire* social body of peasants, which is why he can be found everywhere, in all three peasant classes. This brings us back to the procedure of Stalinist diaeresis: the 'subkulak' names the excessive element that traverses all classes, the outgrowth which has to be eliminated.

And, to go back to Gorgias, one should read his argumentation in the same way. It may appear that Gorgias proceeds in three consistent divisions: first, things either exist or not; then, if they exist, they can be known or not; then, if they can be known, we can communicate this knowledge to others or not. However, the truth of this gradual sub-division is again the repetition of one and the same line of division: if we cannot communicate something to others, it means that we 'really' do not know it ourselves; if we cannot know something, it means that it 'really' does not exist in itself. There is a truth in this logic: as already Parmenides, Gorgias's teacher and reference, put it, thinking (knowing) is the same as being, and thinking (knowing) itself is rooted in language (communication) – 'The limits of my language are the limit of my world.'

The lesson of Hegel (and Lacan) is here that one should turn this diaeresis around: we can only speak about things that *do not* exist (Jeremy Bentham has an intuition of this in his theory of fictions) – or, more modestly and precisely, speech (presup)poses a lack/hole in the positive order of being. So not only can we think about non-existing things (which is why religion is consubstantial with 'human nature', its eternal temptation); we can also talk without thinking – not only in the vulgar sense of just inconsistently babbling, but in the Freudian sense of 'saying more than we intended', of producing a symptomatic slip of the tongue. So it is not that even if we know something, we cannot communicate it to others – we can communicate to others things we do not know (or, more precisely, to paraphrase Donald Rumsfeld, things we do not know we know, since, for Lacan, the unconscious as *une bévue* is *un savoir qui ne se sait pas*). This is why the Hegelo–Lacanian position is neither that of Plato nor that of his sophist opponents: against Plato, one should assert that we not only *can* talk about things that we do not understand–think, but that we ultimately talk *only* about them, about fictions. And, against sophists, one should assert that this in no way devalues truth, since, as Lacan put it, truth has the structure of a fiction.

So where does Mao fall short here? In the way he *opposes* this injunction to sever, to divide, to dialectical synthesis. When Mao mockingly refers to 'synthesizing' as the destruction of the enemy or his subordination, his mistake resides in this very mocking attitude – he does not see that this *is* the true Hegelian synthesis . . . What then, is the Hegelian 'negation of negation'? First, the old order is negated within its own ideologico-political form; then, this form itself has to be negated.

Those who oscillate, those who are afraid to take the second step of overcoming this form itself, are those who (to repeat Robespierre) want a 'revolution without revolution' – and Lenin displays all the strength of his 'hermeneutics of suspicion' in discerning the different forms of this retreat. The true victory (the true 'negation of negation') occurs when the enemy talks your language. In this sense, a true victory is a victory in defeat: it occurs when one's specific message is accepted as a universal ground, even by the enemy. (Say, in the case of rational science versus belief, the true victory of science takes place when the church starts to defend itself in the language of science.) Or, in the contemporary politics of the United Kingdom, as many a perspicuous commentator observed, the Thatcher revolution was in itself chaotic, impulsive, marked by unpredictable contingencies, and it was only the 'Third Way' Blairite government which was able to *institutionalize* it, to stabilize it into new institutional forms, or, to put it in Hegelese, to raise (what first appeared as) a contingency, a historical accident, into necessity. In this sense, Blair repeated Thatcherism, elevating it into a concept, in the same way that, for Hegel, Augustus repeated Caesar, transforming–sublating a (contingent) personal name into a concept, a title. Thatcher was not a Thatcherite, she was just herself – it was only Blair (more than John Major) who truly formed Thatcherism as a notion. The dialectical irony of history is that only a (nominal) ideologico-political enemy can do this to you, can elevate you into a concept – the empirical instigator has to be disposed of (Julius Caesar had to be murdered, Thatcher had to be ignominiously deposed).

There is a surprising lesson of the last decades, the lesson of West European Third Way social democracy, but also the lesson of the Chinese communists presiding over what is arguably the most explosive development of capitalism in the entire history: *we can do it better*. Recall the classical Marxist account of the overcoming of capitalism: capitalism unleashed the breathtaking dynamics of self-enhancing productivity – in capitalism, 'all that is solid melts into air', capitalism is the greatest revolutionizer in the entire history of humanity; on the other hand, this capitalist dynamic is propelled by its own inner obstacle or antagonism – the ultimate limit of capitalism (of the capitalist self-propelling productivity) is Capital itself, i.e. the capitalist incessant development and revolutionizing of its own material conditions, the mad dance of its unconditional spiral of productivity, is ultimately nothing but a desperate flight forward to escape its own debilitating inherent contradiction . . .

Marx's fundamental mistake was here to conclude, from these insights, that a new, higher social order (communism) is possible, an order that would not only maintain, but even raise to a higher degree and effectively fully release the potential of the self-increasing spiral of productivity which, in capitalism, on account of its inherent obstacle/contradiction, is again and again thwarted by socially destructive economic crises. In short, what Marx overlooked is that, to put it in the standard Derridean terms, this inherent obstacle/antagonism as the 'condition of impossibility' of the full deployment of the productive forces is simultaneously its 'condition of possibility': if we abolish the obstacle, the inherent contradiction of capitalism, we do not get the fully unleashed drive to productivity finally delivered of its impediment, but we lose precisely the productivity that seemed to be generated and simultaneously thwarted by capitalism – if we take away the obstacle, the very potential thwarted by this obstacle dissipates . . . And it is as if this logic of the 'obstacle as a positive condition' which underlay the failure of the socialist attempts to overcome capitalism is now returning with a vengeance in capitalism itself: capitalism can fully thrive not in the unencumbered reign of the market, but only when an obstacle (the minimal welfare-state interventions, up to the direct political rule of the Communist Party, as is the case in China) constrains its unimpeded reign.

So, ironically, *this* is the 'synthesis' of capitalism and communism in Mao's sense: in a unique example of the poetic justice of history, it was capitalism which 'synthesized' with Maoist communism. The key news from China over the last years is the emergence of large-scale workers' movements, protesting against the work conditions which are the price for China rapidly becoming the world's foremost manufacturing site, and the brutal way the authorities cracked down on it – a new proof, if one is still needed, that China is today the ideal capitalist state: freedom for capital, with the state doing the 'dirty job' of controlling the workers. China as the emerging superpower of the twenty-first century thus seems to embody a new kind of capitalism: disregard for ecological consequences, repression of workers' rights, everything subordinated to the ruthless drive to develop and become the new superpower. The great qustion is: what will the Chinese do with regard to the biogenetic revolution? Is it not a safe wager that they will throw themselves into unconstrained genetic manipulations of plants, animals and humans, bypassing all our 'Western' moral prejudices and limitations?

This is the ultimate price for Mao's theoretical mistake of the rejection of the 'negation of negation', of his failure to grasp how the 'negation of negation' is not a compromise between a position and its too radical negation, but, on the contrary, the only true negation.[30] And it is because Mao is unable to theoretically formulate this self-relating negation of form itself that he gets caught in the 'bad infinity' of endless negating, scissions into two, subdivision . . . In Hegelese, Mao's dialectic remains at the level of Understanding, of fixed notional oppositions; it is unable to formulate the properly dialectical self-relating of notional determinations. It is this 'serious mistake' (to use a Stalinist term) which led Mao, when he was courageous enough to draw all the consequences from his stances, to reach a properly nonsensical conclusion that, in order to invigorate class struggle, one should directly open up the field to the enemy:

> Let them go in for capitalism. Society is very complex. If one only goes in for socialism and not for capitalism, isn't that too simple? Wouldn't we then lack the unity of opposites, and be merely one-sided? Let them do it. Let them attack us madly, demonstrate in the streets, take up arms to rebel — I approve all of these things. Society is very complex, there is not a single commune, a single *hsien,* a single department of the Central Committee, which one cannot divide into two.[31]

Again, what Mao fails to do here is to proceed to the properly Hegelian 'identity of the opposites', and to recognize in the force the Revolution is fighting and trying to annihilate *its own essence,* as in G. K. Chesterton's *The Man Who Was Thursday*, in which the secret police chief organizing the search for the anarchist leader and this mysterious leader at the end appears to be one and the same person (God himself, incidentally). And did Mao himself ultimately not play a similar role, a role of secular God who is at the same time the greatest rebel against himself? What this Chestertonian identity of the good Lord with the anarchist Rebel enacts is the logic of the social *carnival* brought to the extreme of self-reflection: anarchist outbursts are not a transgression of the Law and Order; in our societies, anarchism already *is* in power wearing the mask of Law and Order – our Justice is the travesty of Justice, the spectacle of Law and order is an obscene carnival – the point made clear by the arguably greatest political poem in English, Shelley's 'The Mask of Anarchy', which describes the obscene parade of the figures of power:

And many more Destructions played
In this ghastly masquerade,
All disguised, even to the eyes,
Like Bishops, lawyers, peers, or spies.

Last came Anarchy: he rode
On a white horse, splashed with blood;
He was pale even to the lips,
Like Death in the Apocalypse.

And he wore a kingly crown;
And in his grasp a sceptre shone;
On his brow this mark I saw –
'I AM GOD, AND KING, AND LAW!'

And is not this Hegelian–Chestertonian shift from the criminal transgression of Law and Order to Law and Order itself as the highest criminal
transgression directly enacted by Mao himself? This is why, while setting
in motion and secretly pulling the strings of the self-destructive carnival,
Mao nonetheless remained exempt from its turbulence: at no moment
was there ever a serious threat that Stalin (or Mao) himself would be
ritualistically deposed, treated as 'yesterday a king, today a beggar' – he
was not the traditional Master, but the 'Lord of Misrule':

In the European Middle Ages it was customary for great households to
choose a 'Lord of Misrule'. The person chosen was expected to preside
over the revels that briefly reversed or parodied the conventional social
and economic hierarchies. . . . When the brief reign of misrule was
over, the customary order of things would be restored: the Lords of
Misrule would go back to their menial occupations, while their social
superiors resumed their wonted status. . . . Sometimes the idea of Lord
of Misrule would spill over from the realm of revel to the realm of
politics. . . . The apprentices took over from their guild masters for a
reckless day or two . . . gender roles were reversed for a day as the
women took over the tasks and airs normally associated only with
men. . . . Chinese philosophers also loved the paradoxes of status
reversed, the ways that wit or shame could deflate pretension and lead
to sudden shifts of insight. . . . It was Mao's terrible accomplishment to
seize on such insights from earlier Chinese philosophers, combine

them with elements drawn from Western socialist thought, and to use both in tandem to prolong the limited concept of misrule into a long-drawn-out adventure in upheaval. To Mao, the former lords and masters should never be allowed to return; he felt they were not his betters, and that society was liberated by their removal. He also thought the customary order of things should never be restored.[32]

Is, however, such a 'terrible accomplishment' not the elementary gesture of every true revolutionary? Why revolution at all, if we do not think that 'the customary order of things should never be restored'? What Mao does is to deprive the transgression of its ritualized, ludic character by taking it seriously: revolution is not just a temporary safety valve, a carnivalesque explosion destined to be followed by a sobering morning after. His problem was precisely the lack of the 'negation of negation', the failure of the attempts to transpose revolutionary negativity into a truly new positive Order: all temporary stabilizations of the revolution amounted to so many restorations of the old Order, so that the only way to keep the revolution alive was the 'spurious infinity' of endlessly repeated negation which reached its apex in the Great Cultural Revolution.[33] In his *Logiques des mondes*, Badiou elaborated two subjective attitudes of countering an event: the 'reactive subject' and the 'obscure subject'.[34] Insofar as one is ready to assume the risk of obscenely designating the reintroduction of capitalism into China a kind of event, one can claim that the Cultural Revolution and the Revisionism identified by the name 'Deng Xiaoping' stand, respectively, for the obscure and the reactive subject: Deng orchestrated the reintegration of capitalism into the new communist China, while the Cultural Revolution aimed at its total annihilation and was as such precisely what Badiou calls *un désastre obscur*. Badiou himself concedes that the final result of the Cultural Revolution was a negative one:

it all began when, between 1966 and 1968, saturating *in the Real* the previous hypotheses, the Red Guardist high-school pupils and students, and then the workers of Shanghai, prescribed for the decades to come the *affirmative realization* of this beginning, of which they themselves, since their fury remained caught up in what they were rising up against, explored only the face of pure negation.[35]

One should take a step further here: what if the Cultural Revolution was 'negative' not only in the sense of clearing the space and opening up the way for a new beginning, but *negative in itself*, negative as an index of its *incapacity* to generate the New? In this precise sense, there effectively *is* a parallel between the Cultural Revolution and the Stalinist purges at their decisive moment, when Stalin made the risky move of directly appealing to the lower rank-and-file members themselves, soliciting them to articulate their complaints against the arbitrary rule of the local Party bosses (a move similar to the Cultural Revolution) – their fury at the regime, unable to express itself directly, exploded all the more viciously against the personalized substitute targets. Since the upper nomenklatura at the same time retained its executive power also in the purges themselves, this set in motion a properly carnivalesque self-destructive vicious cycle in which virtually everyone was threatened. Another aspect of the spiralling vicious cycle was the very fluctuation of the directives from the top as to the thoroughness of the purges: the top demanded harsh measures, while at the same time warning against excesses, so the executors were put in an untenable position – ultimately, whatever they did was wrong. If they did not arrest enough traitors and discover enough conspiracies, they were considered too lenient and supporting counter-revolution; so, under this pressure, in order to meet the quota as it were, they had to fabricate evidence and invent plots – thereby exposing themselves to the criticism that they were themselves saboteurs, destroying thousands of honest communists on behalf of the foreign powers . . . Stalin's strategy of addressing directly the party masses, co-opting their anti-bureaucratic attitudes, was thus very dangerous:

> This not only threatened to open elite politics to public scrutiny but also risked discrediting the entire Bolshevik regime, of which Stalin himself was a part. . . . Finally, in 1937, Stalin broke all the rules of the game – indeed, destroyed the game completely – and unleashed a terror of all against all.[36]

One can discern very precisely the superego dimension of these events: this very violence inflicted by the communist Power on its own members bears witness to the radical self-contradiction of the regime, i.e. to the fact that, at the origins of the regime, there was an 'authentic' revolutionary project – incessant purges were necessary not only to erase the traces of the regime's own origins, but also as a kind of 'return of the repressed', a reminder of the radical negativity at the heart of the regime. The Stalinist purges of higher Party echelons relied on this fundamental betrayal: the accused were effectively guilty insofar as they, as the members of the new nomenklatura, betrayed the Revolution. The Stalinist terror is thus not simply the betrayal of the Revolution, i.e. the attempt to erase the traces of the authentic revolutionary past; it rather bears witness to a kind of 'imp of perversity' which compels the post-revolutionary new order to (re)inscribe its betrayal of the Revolution within itself, to 'reflect' it or 'remark' it in the guise of arbitrary arrests and killings which threatened all members of the nomenklatura – as in psychoanalysis, the Stalinist confession of guilt conceals the true guilt. (As is well known, Stalin wisely recruited into the NKVD people of lower social origins who were thus able to act out their hatred of the nomenklatura by arresting and torturing high apparatchiks.) This inherent tension between the stability of the rule of the new nomenklatura and the perverted 'return of the repressed' in the guise of the repeated purges of the ranks of the nomenklatura is at the very heart of the Stalinist phenomenon: purges are the very form in which the betrayed revolutionary heritage survives and haunts the regime . . .

This brings us back to the central weakness of Mao's thought and politics. Many a commentator has made ironic remarks about the apparent stylistic clumsiness of the titles of Soviet communist books and articles, such as their tautological character, or the repeated use of the same word (like 'revolutionary dynamics in the early stages of the Russian Revolution', or 'economic contradictions in the development of the Soviet economy'). However, what if this tautology points towards the awareness of the logic of betrayal best rendered by the classic reproach of Robespierre to the Dantonist opportunists: 'What you want is a revolution without revolution?' The tautological repetition thus signals the urge to repeat the negation, to relate it to itself – the true revolution is 'revolution with revolution', a revolution which, in its course, revolutionizes its own starting presuppositions. Hegel had a presentiment of this necessity when he wrote, 'It is a modern folly to alter a corrupt ethical system, its constitution and legislation, without changing the religion, to have a revolution without a reformation.'[37] He thereby announced the necessity of the Cultural Revolution as the condition of the successful social revolution. What this means is that the problem with hitherto revolutionary attempts was not that they were 'too extreme', but that they were *not radical enough*, that they did not question their own presuppositions. In a wonderful essay on *Chevengur*, Platonov's great peasant utopia written in 1927 and 1928 (just prior to forced collectivization), Fredric Jameson describes the two moments of the revolutionary process. It begins with the gesture of radical negativity:

> this first moment of world-reduction, of the destruction of the idols and the sweeping away of an old world in violence and pain, is itself the precondition for the reconstruction of something else. A first moment of absolute immanence is necessary, the blank slate of absolute peasant immanence or ignorance, before new and un-dreamed-of-sensations and feelings can come into being.[38]

Then follows the second stage, the invention of a new life – not only the construction of the new social reality in which our utopian dreams would be realized, but the (re)construction of these dreams themselves:

> a process that it would be too simple and misleading to call recon-struction or Utopian construction, since in effect it involves the very effort to find a way to begin imagining Utopia to begin with. Perhaps in a more Western kind of psychoanalytic language . . . we might think of the new onset of the Utopian process as a kind of desiring to desire, a learning to desire, the invention of the desire called Utopia in the first place, along with new rules for the fantasizing or daydreaming of such a thing – a set of narrative protocols with no precedent in our previous literary institutions.[39]

The reference to psychoanalysis is here crucial and very precise: in a radical revolution, people not only 'realize their old (emancipatory, etc.) dreams'; rather, they have to reinvent their very modes of dreaming. Is this not the exact formula of the link between death drive and sublimation? Therein resides the necessity of the Cultural Revolution clearly grasped by Mao: as Herbert Marcuse put it in another wonderful circular formula from the same epoch, *freedom* (from ideological constraints, from the predominant mode of dreaming) *is the condition of liberation*, i.e., if we only change reality in order to realize our dreams, and do not change these dreams themselves, we sooner or later regress to old reality. There is a Hegelian 'positing of presupposi-tions' at work here: the hard work of liberation retroactively forms its own presupposition.

It is *only* this reference to what happens *after* the revolution, to the 'morning after', that allows us to distinguish between libertarian pathetic outbursts and true revolutionary upheavals: the former outbursts lose their energy when one has to approach the prosaic work of social reconstruction – at this point, lethargy sets in. In contrast, recall the immense creativity of the Jacobins just prior to their fall, the numerous proposals about new civic religion, about how to sustain the dignity of old people, and so on. Therein also resides the interest of reading the reports about daily life in the Soviet Union in the early 1920s, with the enthusiastic urge to invent new rules for quotidian existence: What kind of marriage in the new society? What are the new rules of courting? How should birthdays be celebrated? What kind of burials? . . .[40]

At this point, the Cultural Revolution miserably failed. It is difficult to miss the irony of the fact that Badiou, who adamantly opposes the notion of the act as negative, locates the historical significance of the Maoist Cultural Revolution precisely in the negative gesture of signalling 'the end of the party-state as the central production of revolutionary political activity' – it is here that he should have been consistent and denied the evental status of the Cultural Revolution: far from being an Event, it was rather a supreme display of what Badiou likes to refer to as the 'morbid death drive'. Destroying old monuments was not a true negation of the past, it was rather an impotent *passage à l'acte* bearing witness to the failure to get rid of the past.

So, in a way, there is a kind of poetic justice in the fact that the final result of Mao's Cultural Revolution is today's unprecedented explosion of capitalist dynamism in China. That is to say, with the full deployment of capitalism, especially today's 'late capitalism', it is 'normal' life itself which, in a way, gets 'carnivalized', with its constant self-revolutionizing, with its reversals, crises, reinventions. Brian Massumi formulated clearly this deadlock, which is based on the fact that contemporary capitalism has already overcome the logic of totalizing normality and adopted the logic of the erratic excess:

> the more varied, and even erratic, the better. Normalcy starts to lose its hold. The regularities start to loosen. This loosening of normalcy is part of capitalism's dynamic. It's not a simple liberation. It's capitalism's own form of power. It's no longer disciplinary institutional power that defines everything, it's capitalism's power to produce variety – because markets get saturated. Produce variety and you produce a niche market. The oddest of affective tendencies are okay –

as long as they pay. Capitalism starts intensifying or diversifying affect, but only in order to extract surplus-value. It hijacks affect in order to intensify profit potential. It literally valorizes affect. The capitalist logic of surplus-value production starts to take over the relational field that is also the domain of political ecology, the ethical field of resistance to identity and predictable paths. It's very troubling and confusing, because it seems to me that there's been a certain kind of convergence between the dynamic of capitalist power and the dynamic of resistance.[41]

There *is* thus, beyond all cheap jibes and superficial analogies, a profound structural homology between Maoist permanent self-revolutionizing, the permanent struggle against the ossification of state structures, and the inherent dynamics of capitalism. One is tempted to paraphrase Brecht here – 'What is the robbing of a bank compared to the founding of a new bank?' – yet again: what are the violent and destructive outbursts of a Red Guardist caught in the Cultural Revolution compared to the true Cultural Revolution, the permanent dissolution of all life-forms necessitated by capitalist reproduction? It is the reign of today's global capitalism which is the true Lord of Misrule. This capitalist reappropriation of revolutionary dynamism is not without its comic side effects. It was recently made public that, in order to conceptualize the Israeli Defense Force's urban warfare against the Palestinians, the IDF military academies systematically refer to Deleuze and Guattari, especially to *A Thousand Plateaux*, using it as 'operational theory' – the catchwords used are 'Formless Rival Entities', 'Fractal Manoeuvre', 'Velocity vs Rhythms', 'The Wahhabi War Machine', 'Postmodern Anarchists', 'Nomadic Terrorists'. One of the key distinctions they rely on is the one between 'smooth' and 'striated' space, which reflect the organizational concepts of the 'war machine' and the 'state apparatus'. The IDF now often uses the term 'to smooth out space' when they want to refer to operation in a space as if it had no borders. Palestinian areas are thought of as 'striated' in the sense that they are enclosed by fences, walls, ditches, road blocks, and so on:

The attack conducted by units of the IDF on the city of Nablus in April 2002 was described by its commander, Brigadier-General Aviv Kokhavi, as 'inverse geometry', which he explained as 'the reorganization of the urban syntax by means of a series of micro-tactical actions'. During the battle soldiers moved within the city across hundreds of metres of overground tunnels carved out through a dense and contiguous urban structure. Although several thousand soldiers and Palestinian guerrillas were manoeuvring simultaneously in the city, they were so 'saturated' into the urban fabric that very few would have been visible from the air. Furthermore, they used none of the city's streets, roads, alleys or courtyards, or any of the external doors, internal stairwells and windows, but moved horizontally through walls and vertically through holes blasted in ceilings and floors. This form of movement, described by the military as 'infestation', seeks to redefine inside as outside, and domestic interiors as thoroughfares. The IDF's strategy of 'walking through walls' involves a conception of the city as not just the site but also the very medium of warfare: 'a flexible, almost liquid medium that is forever contingent and in flux'.[42]

So what follows from all this? Not, of course, the nonsensical accusation that Deleuze and Guattari were theorists of militaristic colonization – but the conclusion that the conceptual machine articulated by Deleuze and Guattari, far from being simply 'subversive', also fits the (military, economic and ideologico-political) operational mode of contemporary capitalism. How, then, are we to revolutionize an order whose very principle is constant self-revolutionizing? This, perhaps, is *the* question today, and this is the way one should *repeat* Mao, reinventing his message to the hundreds of millions of the anonymous downtrodden, a simple and touching message of courage: 'Bigness is nothing to be afraid of. The big will be overthrown by the small. The small will become big.' The same message of courage sustains also Mao's (in)famous stance towards a new atomic world war:

We stand firmly for peace and against war. But if the imperialists insist on unleashing another war, we should not be afraid of it. Our attitude on this question is the same as our attitude towards any disturbance: first, we are against it; second, we are not afraid of it. The First World War was followed by the birth of the Soviet Union with a population of 200 million. The Second World War was followed by the emergence of the socialist camp with a combined population of 900 million. If the imperialists insist on launching a third world war, it is certain that several hundred million more will turn to socialism, and then there will not be much room left on earth for the imperialists.[43]

It is all too easy to dismiss these lines as the empty posturing of a leader ready to sacrifice millions for his political goals (the extension *ad absurdum* of Mao's ruthless decision to starve tens of millions to death in the late 1950s) – the other side of this dismissive attitude is the basic message: 'we should not be afraid.' Is this not the *only* correct attitude apropos of war: 'first, we are against it; second, we are not afraid of it'? There is definitely something terrifying about this attitude – however, this terror is nothing less than the condition of freedom.

SUGGESTIONS FOR FURTHER READING

EDITIONS

Mao's Road to Power: Revolutionary Writings, 1912–1949, edited by Stuart R. Schram, Armonk, NY, M. E. Sharpe:

Volume I: The Pre-Marxist Period, 1912–1920 (1992);

Volume II: National Revolution and Social Revolution, December 1920 – June 1927 (1995);

Volume III: From the Jinggangshan to the Establishment of the Jiangxi Soviets, July 1927–December 1930 (1995);

Volume IV: The Rise and Fall of the Chinese Soviet Republic, 1931–1934 (1997);

Volume V: Toward the Second United Front, January 1935–July 1937 (1999);

Volume VI: The New Stage (August 1937–1938) (2004);

Volume VII: New Democracy (1939–1941) (2005).

Knight, Nick (ed.), *Mao Zedong on Dialectical Materialism: Writings on Philosophy, 1937,* Armonk, NY, M. E. Sharpe, 1990.

COMMENTARIES

Dirlik, Arif, Healy, Paul Michael, and Knight, Nick (eds), *Critical Perspectives on Mao Zedong's Thought,* Atlantic Highlands, NJ, Humanity Books, 1997.

Knight, Nick, *Marxist Philosophy in China: From Qu Qiubai to Mao Zedong, 1923–1945,* New York, Springer, 2005.

Meisner, Maurice, and Schott, Gareth, *Mao Zedong: A Political and Intellectual Portrait,* Cambridge, Polity Press, 2006.

Schram, Stuart, *The Thought of Mao Tse-Tung,* Cambridge, Cambridge University Press, 1989.

Spence, Jonathan, *Mao Zedong,* London, Penguin, 2006.

NOTE ON SOURCES

The editions of Mao's writings here are those available on the Marxist Internet Archive, www.marxists.org. We have chosen to retain the original Chinese editorial notes and transliteration for their evocative qualities. Many thanks to the Maoist Documentation Project and MIA teams for their hard work in digitalizing and proofing this material and for the additional notes.

Chapter 1 is from *Selected Works of Mao Tse-tung*, Foreign Languages Press, Peking, 1967 (first edition 1965, second printing 1967), volume I. Chapter 2 is from *Selected Works of Mao Tse-tung*, Kranti Publications, Secunderabad, 1990, volume VI. Chapter 3 is from *Selected Works of Mao Tse-tung*, Foreign Languages Press, Peking, 1967 (first edition 1965, second printing 1967), volume I. Chapter 4 is from *Selected Works of Mao Tse-tung*, Foreign Languages Press, Peking, 1967 (first edition 1965, second printing 1967), volume I. Chapter 5 is from *Selected Works of Mao Tse-tung*, Foreign Languages Press, Peking, 1967 (first edition 1965, second printing 1967), volume II. Chapter 6 is from *Selected Works of Mao Tse-tung*, Foreign Languages Press, Peking, 1967 (first edition 1965, second printing 1967), volume V. Chapter 7 is from *Selected Works of Mao Tse-tung*, Foreign Languages Press, Peking, 1967 (first edition 1965, second printing 1967), volume V. Chapter 8 is from *Selected Works of Mao Tse-tung*, Kranti Publications, Secunderabad, 1990, volume VIII. Chapter 9 is from *Selected Works of Mao Tse-tung*, Kranti Publications, Secunderabad, 1990, volume VIII. Chapter 10 is from *Selected Works of Mao Tse-tung*, Foreign Languages Press, Peking, 1967 (first edition 1965, second printing 1967), volume V. Chapter 11 is from *Selected Works of Mao Tse-tung*, Kranti Publications, Secunderabad, 1990, volume IX. Chapter 12 is from *Selected Works of Mao Tse-tung*, Kranti Publications, Secunderabad, 1990, volume IX.

I

A SINGLE SPARK CAN
START A PRAIRIE FIRE

5 January 1930

This was a letter written by Comrade Mao Tse-tung in criticism of certain pessimistic views then existing in the Party.

Some comrades in our Party still do not know how to appraise the current situation correctly and how to settle the attendant question of what action to take. Though they believe that a revolutionary high tide is inevitable, they do not believe it to be imminent. Therefore, they disapprove of the plan to take Kiangsi and only approve of roving guerrilla actions in the three areas on the borders of Fukien, Kwangtung and Kiangsi; at the same time, as they do not have a deep understanding of what it means to establish Red political power in the guerrilla areas, they do not have a deep understanding of the idea of accelerating the nation-wide revolutionary high tide through the consolidation and expansion of Red political power. They seem to think that, since the revolutionary high tide is still remote, it will be labour lost to attempt to establish political power by hard work. Instead, they want to extend our political influence through the easier method of roving guerrilla actions, and, once the masses throughout the country have been won over, or more or less won over, they want to launch a nation-wide armed insurrection which, with the participation of the Red Army, would become a great nation-wide revolution. Their theory that we must first win over the masses on a country-wide scale and in all regions and then establish political power does not accord with the actual state of the Chinese revolution. This theory derives mainly from the failure to understand clearly that China is a semi-colonial country for which many imperialist powers are contending. If one clearly understands this, one will understand first why the unusual phenomenon of prolonged and tangled warfare within the ruling classes is only to be found in China, why this warfare is steadily growing fiercer and spreading, and why there has never been a unified regime. Second, one will understand the gravity of the peasant problem and hence why rural uprisings have developed on the present country-wide scale. Third, one will understand the correctness of the slogan of workers' and peasants' democratic political power. Fourth, one will understand another unusual phenomenon, which is also absent outside China, and which follows from the first (that in China alone there is prolonged and tangled warfare within the ruling classes), namely, the existence and development of the Red Army and the guerrilla forces, and together with them, the existence and development of small Red areas encircled by the White regime. Fifth, one will understand that in semi-colonial China the establishment and expansion of the Red Army, the guerrilla forces and the Red areas is the highest form of peasant struggle under the leadership of the proletariat, the inevitable outcome of the growth of the semi-colonial peasant struggle, and undoubtedly the most important factor in accelerating the revolutionary high tide throughout the country. And sixth, one will also understand that the policy which merely calls for roving guerrilla actions cannot accomplish the task of accelerating this nation-wide revolutionary high tide, while the kind of policy adopted by Chu Teh and Mao Tse-tung and also by Fang Chih-min[1] is undoubtedly correct – that is, the policy of establishing base areas; of systematically setting up political power; of deepening the agrarian revolution; of expanding the people's armed forces by a comprehensive process of building up first the township Red Guards, then the district Red Guards, then the county Red Guards, then the local Red Army troops, all the way up to the regular Red Army troops; of spreading political power by advancing in a series of waves; etc., etc. Only thus is it possible to build the confidence of the revolutionary masses throughout the country, as the Soviet Union has built it throughout the world. Only thus is it possible to create tremendous difficulties for the reactionary ruling classes, shake their foundations and hasten their internal disintegration. Only thus is it really possible to create a Red Army which will become the chief weapon for the great revolution of the future. In short, only thus is it possible to hasten the revolutionary high tide.

Comrades who suffer from revolutionary impetuosity overestimate the subjective forces of the revolution[2] and underestimate the forces of the counter-revolution. Such an appraisal stems mainly from subjectivism. In the end, it undoubtedly leads to putschism. On the other hand, underestimating the subjective forces of the revolution and overestimating the forces of the counter-revolution would also constitute an improper appraisal and be certain to produce bad results of another kind. Therefore, in judging the political situation in China it is necessary to understand the following:

1. Although the subjective forces of the revolution in China are now weak, so also are all organizations (organs of political power, armed forces, political parties, etc.) of the reactionary ruling classes, resting as they do on the backward and fragile social and economic structure of China. This helps to explain why revolution cannot break out at once in the countries of Western Europe where, although the subjective forces of revolution are now perhaps somewhat stronger than in China, the forces of the reactionary ruling classes are many times stronger. In China the revolution will undoubtedly move towards a high tide more rapidly, for although the subjective forces of the revolution at present are weak, the forces of the counter-revolution are relatively weak too.

2. The subjective forces of the revolution have indeed been greatly weakened since the defeat of the revolution in 1927. The remaining forces are very small and those comrades who judge by appearances alone naturally feel pessimistic. But if we judge by essentials, it is quite another story. Here we can apply the old Chinese saying, 'A single spark can start a prairie fire'. In other words, our forces, although small at present, will grow very rapidly. In the conditions prevailing in China, their growth is not only possible but indeed inevitable, as the 30th May Movement and the Great Revolution which followed have fully proved. When we look at a thing, we must examine its essence and treat its appearance merely as an usher at the threshold, and once we cross the threshold, we must grasp the essence of the thing; this is the only reliable and scientific method of analysis.

3. Similarly, in appraising the counter-revolutionary forces, we must never look merely at their appearance, but should examine their essence. In the initial period of our independent regime in the Hunan–Kiangsi border area, some comrades genuinely believed the incorrect appraisal made by the Hunan Provincial Committee and regarded the class enemy

as not worth a rap; the two descriptive terms, 'terribly shaky' and 'extremely panicky', which are standing jokes to this day, were used by the Hunan Provincial Committee at the time (from May to June 1928) in appraising the Hunan ruler Lu Ti-ping.[3] Such an appraisal necessarily led to putschism in the political sphere. But during the four months from November of that year to February 1929 (before the war between Chiang Kai-shek and the Kwangsi warlords),[4] when the enemy's third 'joint suppression expedition'[5] was approaching the Chingkang Mountains, some comrades asked the question, 'How long can we keep the Red Flag flying?' As a matter of fact, the struggle in China between Britain, the United States and Japan had by then become quite open, and a state of tangled warfare between Chiang Kai-shek, the Kwangsi clique and Feng Yu-hsiang was taking shape; hence it was actually the time when the counter-revolutionary tide had begun to ebb and the revolutionary tide to rise again. Yet pessimistic ideas were to be found not only in the Red Army and local Party organizations; even the Central Committee was misled by appearances and adopted a pessimistic tone. Its February letter is evidence of the pessimistic analysis made in the Party at that time.

4. The objective situation today is still such that comrades who see only the superficial appearance and not the essence of what is before them are liable to be misled. In particular, when our comrades working in the Red Army are defeated in battle or encircled or pursued by strong enemy forces, they often unwittingly generalize and exaggerate their momentary, specific and limited situation, as though the situation in China and the world as a whole gave no cause for optimism and the prospects of victory for the revolution were remote. The reason they seize on the appearance and brush aside the essence in their observation of things is that they have not made a scientific analysis of the essence of the overall situation. The question whether there will soon be a revolutionary high tide in China can be decided only by making a detailed examination to ascertain whether the contradictions leading to a revolutionary high tide are really developing. Since contradictions are developing in the world between the imperialist countries, between the imperialist countries and their colonies, and between the imperialists and the proletariat in their own countries, there is an intensified need for the imperialists to contend for the domination of China. While the imperialist contention over China becomes more intense, both the contradiction

between imperialism and the whole Chinese nation and the contradictions among the imperialists themselves develop simultaneously on Chinese soil, thereby creating the tangled warfare which is expanding and intensifying daily and giving rise to the continuous development of the contradictions among the different cliques of China's reactionary rulers. In the wake of the contradictions among the reactionary ruling cliques – the tangled warfare among the warlords – comes heavier taxation, which steadily sharpens the contradiction between the broad masses of taxpayers and the reactionary rulers. In the wake of the contradiction between imperialism and China's national industry comes the failure of the Chinese industrialists to obtain concessions from the imperialists, which sharpens the contradiction between the Chinese bourgeoisie and the Chinese working class, with the Chinese capitalists trying to find a way out by frantically exploiting the workers and with the workers resisting. In the wake of imperialist commercial aggression, Chinese merchant-capitalist extortions, heavier government taxation, etc., comes the deepening of the contradiction between the landlord class and the peasantry, that is, exploitation through rent and usury is aggravated and the hatred of the peasants for the landlords grows. Because of the pressure of foreign goods, the exhaustion of the purchasing power of the worker and peasant masses, and the increase in government taxation, more and more dealers in Chinese-made goods and independent producers are being driven into bankruptcy. Because the reactionary government, though short of provisions and funds, endlessly expands its armies and thus constantly extends the warfare, the masses of soldiers are in a constant state of privation. Because of the growth in government taxation, the rise in rent and interest demanded by the landlords and the daily spread of the disasters of war, there are famine and banditry everywhere and the peasant masses and the urban poor are close to starvation. Because the schools have no money, many students fear that their education may be interrupted; because production is backward, many graduates have no hope of employment. Once we understand all these contradictions, we shall see in what a desperate situation, in what a chaotic state, China finds herself. We shall also see that the high tide of revolution against the imperialists, the warlords and the landlords is inevitable, and will come very soon. All China is littered with dry faggots which will soon be aflame. The saying 'A single spark can start a prairie fire' is an apt description of how the current situation will develop. We need only look at the strikes by the workers, the uprisings by the peasants, the mutinies of soldiers and the strikes of students which are developing in many places to see that it cannot be long before a 'spark' kindles 'a prairie fire'.

The gist of the above was already contained in the letter from the Front Committee to the Central Committee on 5 April 1929, which reads in part:

> The Central Committee's letter [dated 9 February 1929] makes too pessimistic an appraisal of the objective situation and our subjective forces. The Kuomintang's three 'suppression' campaigns against the Chingkang Mountains was the high water mark reached by the counter-revolutionary tide. But there it stopped, and since then the counter-revolutionary tide has gradually receded while the revolutionary tide has gradually risen. Although our Party's fighting capacity and organizational strength have been weakened to the extent described by the Central Committee, they will be rapidly restored, and the passivity among comrades in the Party will quickly disappear as the counter-revolutionary tide gradually ebbs. The masses will certainly come over to us. The Kuomintang's policy of massacre only serves to 'drive the fish into deep waters',[6] as the saying goes, and reformism no longer has any mass appeal. It is certain that the masses will soon shed their illusions about the Kuomintang. In the emerging situation, no other party will be able to compete with the Communist Party in winning over the masses. The political line and the organizational line laid down by the Party's Sixth National Congress[7] are correct, i.e. the revolution at the present stage is democratic and not socialist, and the present task of the Party [here the words 'in the big cities' should have been added][8] is to win over the masses and not to stage immediate insurrections. Nevertheless the revolution will develop swiftly, and we should take a positive attitude in our propaganda and preparations for armed insurrections. In the present chaotic situation we can lead the masses only by positive slogans and a positive attitude. Only by taking such an attitude can the Party recover its fighting capacity . . . Proletarian leadership is the sole key to victory in the revolution. Building a proletarian foundation for the Party and setting up Party branches in industrial enterprises in key districts are important organizational tasks for the Party at present; but at the same

time the major prerequisites for helping the struggle in the cities and hastening the rise of the revolutionary tide are specifically the development of the struggle in the countryside, the establishment of Red political power in small areas, and the creation and expansion of the Red Army. Therefore, it would be wrong to abandon the struggle in the cities, but in our opinion it would also be wrong for any of our Party members to fear the growth of peasant strength lest it should outstrip the workers' strength and harm the revolution. For in the revolution in semi-colonial China, the peasant struggle must always fail if it does not have the leadership of the workers, but the revolution is never harmed if the peasant struggle outstrips the forces of the workers.

The letter also contained the following reply on the question of the Red Army's operational tactics:

To preserve the Red Army and arouse the masses, the Central Committee asks us to divide our forces into very small units and disperse them over the countryside and to withdraw Chu Teh and Mao Tse-tung from the army, so concealing the major targets. This is an unrealistic view. In the winter of 1927–28, we did plan to disperse our forces over the countryside, with each company or battalion operating on its own and adopting guerrilla tactics in order to arouse the masses while trying not to present a target for the enemy; we have tried this out many times, but have failed every time. The reasons are: (1) most of the soldiers in the main force of the Red Army come from other areas and have a background different from that of the local Red Guards; (2) division into small units results in weak leadership and inability to cope with adverse circumstances, which easily leads to defeat; (3) the units are liable to be crushed by the enemy one by one; (4) the more adverse the circumstances, the greater the need for concentrating our forces and for the leaders to be resolute in struggle, because only thus can we have internal unity against the enemy. Only in favourable circumstances is it advisable to divide our forces for guerrilla operations, and it is only then that the leaders need not stay with the ranks all the time, as they must in adverse circumstances.

The weakness of this passage is that the reasons adduced against the division of forces were of a negative character, which was far from adequate. The positive reason for concentrating our forces is that only concentration will enable us to wipe out comparatively large enemy units and occupy towns. Only after we have wiped out comparatively large enemy units and occupied towns can we arouse the masses on a broad scale and set up political power extending over a number of adjoining counties. Only thus can we make a widespread impact (what we call 'extending our political influence') and contribute effectively to speeding the day of the revolutionary high tide. For instance, both the regime we set up in the Hunan–Kiangsi border area the year before last and the one we set up in western Fukien last year[9] were the product of this policy of concentrating our troops. This is a general principle. But are there not times when our forces should be divided up? Yes, there are. The letter from the Front Committee to the Central Committee says of guerrilla tactics for the Red Army, including the division of forces within a short radius:

> The tactics we have derived from the struggle of the past three years are indeed different from any other tactics, ancient or modern, Chinese or foreign. With our tactics, the masses can be aroused for struggle on an ever-broadening scale, and no enemy, however powerful, can cope with us. Ours are guerrilla tactics. They consist mainly of the following points:
>
> *Divide our forces to arouse the masses, concentrate our forces to deal with the enemy.*
>
> *The enemy advances, we retreat; the enemy camps, we harass; the enemy tires, we attack; the enemy retreats, we pursue.*
>
> *To extend stable base areas,[10] employ the policy of advancing in waves; when pursued by a powerful enemy, employ the policy of circling around. Arouse the largest numbers of the masses in the shortest possible time and by the best possible methods.*
>
> These tactics are just like casting a net; at any moment we should be able to cast it or draw it in. We cast it wide to win over the masses and draw it in to deal with the enemy. Such are the tactics we have used for the past three years.

Here, 'to cast the net wide' means to divide our forces within a short radius. For example, when we first captured the county town of Yunghsin in the Hunan–Kiangsi border area, we divided the forces of the 29th and 31st Regiments within the boundaries of Yunghsin

County. Again, when we captured Yunghsin for the third time, we once more divided our forces by dispatching the 28th Regiment to the border of Anfu County, the 29th to Lienhua, and the 31st to the border of Kian County. And, again, we divided our forces in the counties of southern Kiangsi last April and May, and in the counties of western Fukien last July. As to dividing our forces over a wide radius, it is possible only on the two conditions that circumstances are comparatively favourable and the leading bodies fairly strong. For the purpose of dividing up our forces is to put us in a better position for winning over the masses, for deepening the agrarian revolution and establishing political power, and for expanding the Red Army and the local armed units. It is better not to divide our forces when this purpose cannot be attained or the division of our forces would lead to defeat and to the weakening of the Red Army, as happened in August two years ago when our forces were divided on the Hunan–Kiangsi border for an attack on Chenchou. But there is no doubt that, given the two above-mentioned conditions, we should divide our forces, because division is then more advantageous than concentration. The Central Committee's February letter was not in the right spirit and had a bad effect on a number of Party comrades in the Fourth Army. At that time the Central Committee also issued a circular stating that war would not necessarily break out between Chiang Kai-shek and the Kwangsi warlords. Since then, however, the appraisals and directives of the Central Committee have in the main been correct. It has already issued another circular correcting the one containing the wrong appraisal. Although it has not made any correction of the letter to the Red Army, its subsequent directives have not been couched in the same pessimistic tone and its views on the Red Army's operations now coincide with ours. Yet the bad effect which this letter had on some comrades persists. Therefore, I feel that it is still necessary to give some explanation.

The plan to take Kiangsi Province within a year was also proposed last April by the Front Committee to the Central Committee, and a decision to that effect was later made at Yutu. The following reasons were given in the letter to the Central Committee:

> The armies of Chiang Kai-shek and the Kwangsi warlords are approaching each other in the vicinity of Kiukiang, and a big battle is imminent. The resumption of mass struggle, coupled with the

spread of contradictions among the ruling reactionaries, makes it probable that there will soon be a high tide of revolution. As for how our work should be arranged under these circumstances, we feel that, so far as the southern provinces are concerned, the armed forces of the compradors and landlords in Kwangtung and Hunan Provinces are too strong, and that in Hunan, moreover, we have lost almost all our mass following, inside as well as outside the Party, because of the Party's putschist mistakes. In the three provinces of Fukien, Kiangsi and Chekiang, however, the situation is different. First, militarily the enemy is weakest there. In Chekiang, there is only a small provincial force under Chiang Po-cheng.[11] In Fukien, although there are five groups of enemy troops totalling fourteen regiments in all, Kuo Fengming's troops have already been smashed; the troops under Chen Kuo-hui and Lu Hsing-pang[12] are bandits of small fighting capacity; the two brigades of marines stationed along the coast have never seen action and their fighting capacity is undoubtedly not high; Chang Chen[13] alone can put up some sort of a fight, but, according to an analysis made by the Fukien Provincial Committee, even he has only two relatively strong regiments. In addition, Fukien is now in a state of complete chaos, confusion and disunity. In Kiangsi, there are sixteen regiments under the two commands of Chu Pei-teh[14] and Hsiung Shih-hui;[15] they are stronger than the armed forces of either Fukien or Chekiang, but far inferior to those of Hunan. Secondly, fewer putschist mistakes have been made in these three provinces. We are not clear about the situation in Chekiang, but the Party's organizational and mass base is somewhat better in Kiangsi and Fukien than in Hunan. Take Kiangsi for example. In northern Kiangsi we still have some basis in Tehan, Hsiushui and Tungku; in western Kiangsi the Party and the Red Guards still have some strength in Ningkang, Yunghsin, Lienhua and Suichuan; in southern Kiangsi the prospects are still brighter, as the 2nd and 4th Regiments of the Red Army are steadily growing in strength in the counties of Kian, Yungfeng and Hsingkuo; and what is more, the Red Army under Fang Chih-min has by no means been wiped out. All this places us in a position to close in on Nanchang. We hereby recommend to the Central Committee that during the period of prolonged warfare among the Kuomintang warlords, we should contend with Chiang Kai-shek and the Kwangsi clique for Kiangsi Province and also for western Fukien and western Chekiang.

In these three provinces we should enlarge the Red Army and create an independent regime of the masses, with a time limit of one year for accomplishing this plan.

This proposal to contend for Kiangsi erred only in setting a time limit of one year. It was based not only on conditions within the province itself, but also on the prospect that a nation-wide high tide of revolution would soon arise. For unless we had been convinced that there would soon be a high tide of revolution, we could not possibly have concluded that we could take Kiangsi in a year. The only weakness in the proposal was that it set a time limit of one year, which it should not have done, and so gave a flavour of impetuosity to the word 'soon' in the statement, 'there will soon be a high tide of revolution'. As to the subjective and objective conditions in Kiangsi, they well deserve our attention. Besides the subjective conditions described in the letter to the Central Committee, three objective conditions can now be clearly pointed out. First, the economy of Kiangsi is mainly feudal, the merchant-capitalist class is relatively weak, and the armed forces of the landlords are weaker than in any other southern province. Second, Kiangsi has no provincial troops of its own and has always been garrisoned by troops from other provinces. Sent there for the 'suppression of Communists' or 'suppression of bandits', these troops are unfamiliar with local conditions, their interests are much less directly involved than if they were local troops, and they usually lack enthusiasm. And third, unlike Kwangtung which is close to Hong Kong and under British control in almost every respect, Kiangsi is comparatively remote from imperialist influence. Once we have grasped these three points, we can understand why rural uprisings are more widespread and the Red Army and guerrilla units more numerous in Kiangsi than in any other province.

How then should we interpret the word 'soon' in the statement 'there will soon be a high tide of revolution'? This is a common question among comrades. Marxists are not fortune-tellers. They should, and indeed can, only indicate the general direction of future developments and changes; they should not and cannot fix the day and the hour in a mechanistic way. But when I say that there will soon be a high tide of revolution in China, I am emphatically not speaking of something which in the words of some people 'is possibly coming', something illusory, unattainable and devoid of significance for action. It is like a ship far out at sea whose masthead can already be seen from the shore; it is like the morning sun in the east whose shimmering rays are visible from a high mountain top; it is like a child about to be born moving restlessly in its mother's womb.

2

OPPOSE BOOK WORSHIP

May 1930

I. NO INVESTIGATION, NO RIGHT TO SPEAK

Unless you have investigated a problem, you will be deprived of the right to speak on it. Isn't that too harsh? Not in the least. When you have not probed into a problem, into the present facts and its past history, and know nothing of its essentials, whatever you say about it will undoubtedly be nonsense. Talking nonsense solves no problems, as everyone knows, so why is it unjust to deprive you of the right to speak? Quite a few comrades always keep their eyes shut and talk nonsense, and for a communist that is disgraceful. How can a communist keep his eyes shut and talk nonsense?

It won't do!
It won't do!
You must investigate!
You must not talk nonsense!

II. TO INVESTIGATE A PROBLEM IS TO SOLVE IT

You can't solve a problem? Well, get down to investigating it, both the present situation and its past history! When you have investigated the problem thoroughly, you will know how to solve it. Conclusions invariably come after investigation, and not before. Only a blockhead cudgels his brains on his own or together with a group to 'find a solution' or 'evolve an idea' without first making some investigation. It must be stressed that this cannot possibly lead to an effective solution or a good idea. In other words, he is bound to arrive at a wrong solution and a wrong idea.

There are not a few comrades doing inspection work, as well as guerrilla leaders and cadres newly in office, who like to make political pronouncements the moment they arrive at a place and who strut about, criticizing this and condemning that when they have only seen the surface of things or minor details. Such purely subjective nonsensical talk is indeed detestable. These people are bound to make a mess of things, lose the confidence of the masses and prove incapable of solving any problem at all.

When they come across difficult problems, quite a number of people in leading positions simply heave a sigh without being able to solve them. They lose patience and ask to be transferred on the grounds that they 'have not the ability and cannot do the job'. These are cowards' words. Just get moving on your two legs, go the rounds of every section placed under your charge and 'inquire into everything',[1] as Confucius did. That way, you'll be able to solve the problems, however limited your ability. For although your head may be empty before you go outdoors, it won't be empty when you return but will contain all the material necessary for the solution of the problems. And that is how problems are solved. Must you go outdoors? Not necessarily. You can call a fact-finding meeting of people familiar with the situation in order to get at the source of what you call a difficult problem and come to know how it stands now, and then it will be easy to solve your difficult problem.

Investigation may be likened to the long months of pregnancy, and solving a problem to the day of birth. To investigate a problem is, indeed, to solve it.

III. OPPOSE BOOK WORSHIP

Whatever is written in a book is right – such is still the mentality of culturally backward Chinese peasants. Strangely enough, within the Communist Party there are also people who always say in a discussion, 'Show me where it's written in the book'. When we say that a directive of a higher organ of leadership is correct, that is not just because it comes from 'a higher organ of leadership' but because its contents conform with both the objective and subjective circumstances of the struggle and meet its requirements. It is quite wrong to take a formalistic attitude and blindly carry out directives without discussing and examining them in the light of actual conditions simply because they come from a higher organ. It is the mischief done by this formalism which explains why the line and tactics of the Party do not take deeper root among the masses. To carry out a directive of a higher organ blindly, and seemingly without any disagreement, is not really to carry it out but is the most artful way of opposing or sabotaging it.

The method of studying the social sciences exclusively from the book is likewise extremely dangerous and may even lead one onto the road of counter-revolution. Clear proof of this is provided by the fact that whole batches of Chinese communists who confined themselves to books in their study of the social sciences have turned into counter-revolutionaries. When we say Marxism is correct, it is certainly not because Marx was a 'prophet' but because his theory has been proved correct in our practice and in our struggle. We need Marxism in our struggle. In our acceptance of his theory no formalization of such mystical notions as 'prophecy' ever enters our minds. Many who have read Marxist books have become renegades from the revolution, whereas illiterate workers often grasp Marxism very well. Of course we should study Marxist books, but this study must be integrated with our country's actual conditions. We need books, but we must overcome book worship, which is divorced from the actual situation.

How can we overcome book worship? The only way is to investigate the actual situation.

IV. WITHOUT INVESTIGATING THE ACTUAL SITUATION, THERE IS BOUND TO BE AN IDEALIST APPRAISAL OF CLASS FORCES AND AN IDEALIST GUIDANCE IN WORK, RESULTING EITHER IN OPPORTUNISM OR IN PUTSCHISM

Do you doubt this conclusion? Facts will force you to accept it. Just try to appraise the political situation or guide the struggle without making any investigation, and you will see whether or not such appraisal or guidance is groundless and idealist and whether or not it will lead to opportunist or putschist errors. Certainly it will. This is not because of a failure to make careful plans before taking action but because of a failure to study the specific social situation carefully before making the plans, as often happens in our Red Army guerrilla units. Officers of the Li Kuei[2] type do not discriminate when they punish the men for offences. As a result, the offenders feel they have been unfairly treated, many disputes ensue, and the leaders lose all prestige. Does this not happen frequently in the Red Army?

We must wipe out idealism and guard against all opportunist and putschist errors before we can succeed in winning over the masses and defeating the enemy. The only way to wipe out idealism is to make the effort and investigate the actual situation.

V. THE AIM OF SOCIAL AND ECONOMIC INVESTIGATION IS TO ARRIVE AT A CORRECT APPRAISAL OF CLASS FORCES AND THEN TO FORMULATE CORRECT TACTICS FOR THE STRUGGLE

This is our answer to the question: Why do we have to investigate social and economic conditions? Accordingly, the object of our investigation is all the social classes and not fragmentary social phenomena. Of late, the comrades in the Fourth Army of the Red Army have generally given attention to the work of investigation,[3] but the method many of them employ is wrong. The results of their investigation are therefore as trivial as a grocer's accounts, or resemble the many strange tales a country bumpkin hears when he comes to town, or are like a distant view of a populous city from a mountain top. This kind of investigation is of little use and cannot achieve our main purpose. Our main purpose is to learn the political and economic situation of the various social classes. The outcome of our investigation should be a picture of the present situation of each class and the ups and downs of its development. For example, when we investigate the composition of the peasantry, not only must we know the number of owner-peasants, semi-owner peasants and tenant-peasants, who are differentiated according to landowning and land-holding relationships, but more especially we must know the number of rich peasants, middle peasants and poor peasants, who are differentiated according to class or stratum. When we investigate the composition of the merchants, not only must we know the number in each trade, such as grain, clothing, medicinal herbs, etc., but more especially we must know the number of small merchants, middle merchants and big merchants. We should investigate not only the state of each trade, but more especially the class relations within it. We should investigate the relationships not only between the different trades but more especially between the different classes. Our chief method of investigation must be to dissect the different social classes, the ultimate purpose being to understand their interrelations, to arrive at a correct appraisal of class forces and then to formulate the correct tactics for the struggle, defining which classes constitute the main force in the revolutionary struggle, which classes are to be won over as allies and which classes are to be overthrown. This is our sole purpose.

What are the social classes requiring investigation?

They are:

the industrial proletariat;
the handicraft workers;
the farm labourers;
the poor peasants;
the urban poor;
the lumpenproletariat;
the master handicraftsmen;
the small merchants;
the middle peasants;
the rich peasants;
the landlords;
the commercial bourgeoisie;
the industrial bourgeoisie.

In our investigation we should give attention to the state of all these classes or strata. Only the industrial proletariat and industrial bourgeoisie are absent in the areas where we are now working, and we constantly come across all the others. Our tactics of struggle are tactics in relation to all these classes and strata.

Another serious shortcoming in our past investigations has been the undue stress on the countryside to the neglect of the towns, so that many comrades have always been vague about our tactics towards the urban poor and the commercial bourgeoisie. The development of the struggle has enabled us to leave the mountains for the plains.[4] We have descended physically, but we are still up in the mountains mentally. We must understand the towns as well as the countryside, or we shall be unable to meet the needs of the revolutionary struggle.

VI. VICTORY IN CHINA'S REVOLUTIONARY STRUGGLE WILL DEPEND ON THE CHINESE COMRADES' UNDERSTANDING OF CHINESE CONDITIONS

The aim of our struggle is to attain socialism via the stage of democracy. In this task, the first step is to complete the democratic revolution by winning the majority of the working class and arousing the peasant masses and the urban poor for the overthrow of the landlord class, imperialism and the Kuomintang regime. The next step is to carry out the socialist revolution, which will follow on the development of this struggle. The fulfilment of this great revolutionary task is no simple or easy job and will depend entirely on correct and firm tactics on the part of the proletarian party. If its tactics of struggle are wrong, or irresolute and wavering, the revolution will certainly suffer temporary defeat. It must be borne in mind that the bourgeois parties, too, constantly discuss their tactics of struggle. They are considering how to spread reformist influences among the working class so as to mislead it and turn it away from the Communist Party leadership, how to get the rich peasants to put down the uprisings of the poor peasants, and how to organize gangsters to suppress the revolutionary struggles. In a situation whre the class struggle grows increasingly acute and is waged at close quarters, the proletariat has to depend for its victory entirely on the correct and firm tactics of struggle of its own party, the Communist Party. A Communist Party's correct and unswerving tactics of struggle can in no circumstance be created by a few people sitting in an office; they emerge in the course of mass struggle, that is, through actual experience. Therefore, we must at all times study social conditions and make practical investigations. Those comrades who are inflexible, conservative, formalistic and groundlessly optimistic think that the present tactics of struggle are perfect, that the 'book of documents'[5] of the Party's Sixth National Congress guarantees lasting victory, and that one can always be victorious merely by adhering to the established methods. These ideas are absolutely wrong and have nothing in common with the idea that communists should create favourable new situations through struggle; they represent a purely conservative line. Unless it is completely discarded, this line will cause great losses to the revolution and do harm to these comrades themselves. There are obviously some comrades in our Red Army who are content to leave things as they are, who do not seek to understand anything thoroughly and are groundlessly optimistic, and they spread the fallacy that 'this is proletarian'. They eat their fill and sit dozing in their offices all day long without ever moving a step and going out among the masses to investigate. Whenever they open their mouths, their platitudes make people sick. To awaken these comrades we must raise our voices and cry out to them:

Change your conservative ideas without delay!
Replace them by progressive and militant communist ideas!
Get into the struggle!
Go among the masses and investigate the facts!

VII. THE TECHNIQUE OF INVESTIGATION

1. HOLD FACT-FINDING MEETINGS AND UNDERTAKE INVESTIGATION THROUGH DISCUSSIONS

This is the only way to get near the truth, the only way to draw conclusions. It is easy to make mistakes if you do not hold fact-finding meetings for investigation through discussions but simply rely on one individual relating his own experience. You cannot possibly draw more or less correct conclusions at such meetings if you put questions casually instead of raising key questions for discussion.

2. WHAT KIND OF PEOPLE SHOULD ATTEND THE FACT-FINDING MEETINGS?

They should be people well acquainted with social and economic conditions. As far as age is concerned, older people are best, because they are rich in experience and not only know what is going on but understand the causes and effects. Young people with experience of struggle should also be included, because they have progressive ideas and sharp eyes. As far as occupation is concerned, there should be workers, peasants, merchants, intellectuals and occasionally soldiers – sometimes even vagrants. Naturally, when a particular subject is being looked into, those who have nothing to do with it need not be present. For example, workers, peasants and students need not attend when commerce is the subject of investigation.

3. WHICH IS BETTER, A LARGE FACT-FINDING MEETING OR A SMALL ONE?

That depends on the investigator's ability to conduct a meeting. If he is good at it, a meeting of as many as a dozen or even twenty or more people can be called. A large meeting has its advantages: the participants' answers to your questions can supply you with fairly accurate statistics (such as the percentage of poor peasants in the total peasant population) and enable you to come to fairly correct conclusions (such as whether equal or differentiated land redistribution is better). Of course, it has its disadvantages too: unless you are skilful in conducting meetings, you will find it difficult to keep order. So the number of people attending a meeting depends on the competence of the investigator. However, the minimum is three, or otherwise the information obtained will be too limited to correspond to the real situation.

4. PREPARE A DETAILED OUTLINE FOR THE INVESTIGATION

A detailed outline should be prepared beforehand, and the investigator should ask questions according to the outline, with those present at the meeting giving their answers. Any points which are unclear or doubtful should be put up for discussion. The detailed outline should include main subjects and subheadings and also detailed items. For instance, taking commerce as a main subject, it can have such subheadings as cloth, grain, other necessities and medicinal herbs; again, under cloth, there can be such detailed items as calico, home-spun and silk and satin.

5. PERSONAL PARTICIPATION

Everyone with responsibility for giving leadership – from the chairman of the township government to the chairman of the central government, from the detachment leader to the commander-in-chief, from the secretary of a Party branch to the general secretary – must personally undertake investigation into the specific social and economic conditions and not merely rely on reading reports. For investigation and reading reports are two entirely different things.

6. PROBE DEEPLY

Anyone new to investigation work should make one or two thorough investigations in order to gain full knowledge of a particular place (say, a village or a town) or a particular problem (say, the problem of grain or currency). Deep probing into a particular place or problem will make future investigation of other places or problems easier.

7. MAKE YOUR OWN NOTES

The investigator should not only preside at fact-finding meetings and give proper guidance to those present but should also make his own notes and record the results himself. To have others do it for him is no good.

3

ON PRACTICE

ON THE RELATION BETWEEN KNOWLEDGE
AND PRACTICE, BETWEEN KNOWING AND DOING

July 1937

There used to be a number of comrades in our Party who were dogmatists and who for a long period rejected the experience of the Chinese revolution, denying the truth that 'Marxism is not a dogma but a guide to action' and overawing people with words and phrases from Marxist works, torn out of context. There were also a number of comrades who were empiricists and who for a long period restricted themselves to their own fragmentary experience and did not understand the importance of theory for revolutionary practice or see the revolution as a whole, but worked blindly though industriously. The erroneous ideas of these two types of comrade, and particularly of the dogmatists, caused enormous losses to the Chinese revolution during 1931–34, and yet the dogmatists cloaking themselves as Marxists confused a great many comrades. 'On Practice' was written in order to expose the subjectivist errors of dogmatism and empiricism in the Party, and especially the error of dogmatism, from the standpoint of the Marxist theory of knowledge. It was entitled 'On Practice' because its stress was on exposing the dogmatist kind of subjectivism, which belittles practice. The ideas contained in this essay were presented by Comrade Mao Tse-tung in a lecture at the Anti-Japanese Military and Political College in Yenan.

Before Marx, materialism examined the problem of knowledge apart from the social nature of man and apart from his historical development, and was therefore incapable of understanding the dependence of knowledge on social practice, that is, the dependence of knowledge on production and the class struggle.

Above all, Marxists regard man's activity in production as the most fundamental practical activity, the determinant of all his other activities. Man's knowledge depends mainly on his activity in material production, through which he comes gradually to understand the phenomena, the properties and the laws of nature, and the relations between himself and nature; and through his activity in production he also gradually comes to understand, in varying degrees, certain relations that exist between man and man. None of this knowledge can be acquired apart from activity in production. In a classless society every person, as a member of society, joins in common effort with the other members, enters into definite relations of production with them and engages in production to meet man's material needs. In all class societies, the members of the different social classes also enter, in different ways, into definite relations of production and engage in production to meet their material needs. This is the primary source from which human knowledge develops.

Man's social practice is not confined to activity in production, but takes many other forms – class struggle, political life, scientific and artistic pursuits; in short, as a social being, man participates in all spheres of the practical life of society. Thus man, in varying degrees, comes to know the different relations between man and man, not only through his material life but also through his political and cultural life (both of which are intimately bound up with material life). Of these other types of social practice, class struggle in particular, in all its various forms, exerts a profound influence on the development of man's knowledge. In class society everyone lives as a member of a particular class, and every kind of thinking, without exception, is stamped with the brand of a class.

Marxists hold that in human society activity in production develops step by step from a lower to a higher level and that consequently man's knowledge, whether of nature or of society, also develops step by step from a lower to a higher level, that is, from the shallower to the deeper, from the one-sided to the many-sided. For a very long period in history, men were necessarily confined to a one-sided understanding of the history of society because, for one thing, the bias of the exploiting classes always distorted history and, for another, the small scale of production limited man's outlook. It was not until the modern proletariat emerged along with immense forces of production (large-scale industry) that man was able to acquire a comprehensive, historical understanding of the development of society and turn this knowledge into a science, the science of Marxism.

Marxists hold that man's social practice alone is the criterion of the truth of his knowledge of the external world. What actually happens is that man's knowledge is verified only when he achieves the anticipated results in the process of social practice (material production, class struggle or scientific experiment). If a man wants to succeed in his work, that is, to achieve the anticipated results, he must bring his ideas into correspondence with the laws of the objective external world; if they do not correspond, he will fail in his practice. After he fails, he draws his lessons, corrects his ideas to make them correspond to the laws of the external world, and can thus turn failure into success; this is what is meant by 'failure is the mother of success' and 'a fall into the pit, a gain in your wit'. The dialectical-materialist theory of knowledge places practice in the primary position, holding that human knowledge can in no way be separated from practice and repudiating all the erroneous theories which deny the importance of practice or separate knowledge from practice. Thus Lenin said, 'Practice is higher than (theoretical) knowledge, for it has not only the dignity of universality, but also of immediate actuality.'[1] The Marxist philosophy of dialectical materialism has two outstanding characteristics. One is its class nature: it openly avows that dialectical materialism is in the service of the proletariat. The other is its practicality: it emphasizes the dependence of theory on practice, emphasizes that theory is based on practice and in turn serves practice. The truth of any knowledge or theory is determined not by subjective feelings, but by objective results in social practice. Only social practice can be the criterion of truth. The standpoint of practice is the primary and basic standpoint in the dialectical materialist theory of knowledge.[2]

But how then does human knowledge arise from practice and in turn serve practice? This will become clear if we look at the process of the development of knowledge.

In the process of practice, man at first sees only the phenomenal side, the separate aspects, the external relations of things. For instance, some people from outside come to Yenan on a tour of observation. In the first day or two, they see its topography, streets and houses; they meet many people, attend banquets, evening parties and mass meetings, hear talk of various kinds and read various documents, all these being the phenomena, the separate aspects and the external relations of things. This is called the perceptual stage of cognition, namely, the stage of sense perceptions and impressions. That is, these particular things in Yenan act on the sense organs of the members of the observation group, evoke sense perceptions and give rise in their brains to many impressions together with a rough sketch of the external relations among these impressions: this is the first stage of cognition. At this stage, man cannot as yet form concepts, which are deeper, or draw logical conclusions.

As social practice continues, things that give rise to man's sense perceptions and impressions in the course of his practice are repeated many times; then a sudden change (leap) takes place in the brain in the process of cognition, and concepts are formed. Concepts are no longer the phenomena, the separate aspects and the external relations of things; they grasp the essence, the totality and the internal relations of things. Between concepts and sense perceptions there is not only a quantitative but also a qualitative difference. Proceeding further, by means of judgement and inference one is able to draw logical conclusions. The expression in *San Kuo Yen Yi*,[3] 'knit the brows and a stratagem comes to mind', or in everyday language, 'let me think it over', refers to man's use of concepts in the brain to form judgements and inferences. This is the second stage of cognition. When the members of the observation group have collected various data and, what is more, have 'thought them over', they are able to arrive at the judgement that 'the Communist Party's policy of the National United Front Against Japan is thorough, sincere and genuine'. Having made this judgement, they can, if they too are genuine about uniting to save the nation, go a step further and draw the following conclusion: 'The National United Front Against Japan can succeed'. This stage of conception, judgement and inference is the more important stage in the entire process of knowing a thing; it is the stage of rational knowledge. The real task of knowing is, through perception, to arrive at thought, to arrive step by step at the comprehension of the internal contradictions of objective things, of their laws and of the internal relations between one process and another, that is, to arrive at logical knowledge. To repeat, logical knowledge differs from perceptual knowledge in that perceptual knowledge pertains to the separate aspects, the phenomena and the external relations of things, whereas logical knowledge takes a big stride forward to reach the totality, the essence and the internal relations of things, and discloses the inner contradictions in the surrounding world. Therefore, logical knowledge is capable of grasping the development of the surrounding world in its totality, in the internal relations of all its aspects.

This dialectical-materialist theory of the process of the development of knowledge, basing itself on practice and proceeding from the shallower to the deeper, was never worked out by anybody before the rise of Marxism. Marxist materialism solved this problem correctly for the first time, pointing out both materialistically and dialectically the deepening movement of cognition, the movement by which man in society progresses from perceptual knowledge to logical knowledge in his complex, constantly recurring practice of production and class struggle. Lenin said, 'The abstraction of matter, of a law of nature, the abstraction of value, etc., in short, all scientific (correct, serious, not absurd) abstractions reflect nature more deeply, truly and completely.'[4] Marxism-Leninism holds that each of the two stages in the process of cognition has its own characteristics, with knowledge manifesting itself as perceptual at the lower stage and logical at the higher stage, but that both are stages in an integrated process of cognition. The perceptual and the rational are qualitatively different, but are not divorced from each other; they are unified on the basis of practice. Our practice proves that what is perceived cannot at once be comprehended and that only what is comprehended can be more deeply perceived. Perception only solves the problem of phenomena; theory alone can solve the problem of essence. The solving of both these problems is not separable in the slightest degree from practice. Whoever wants to know a thing has no way of doing so except by coming into contact with it, that is, by living (practising) in its environment. In feudal society it was impossible to know the laws of capitalist society in advance because capitalism had not yet emerged, the relevant practice was lacking. Marxism could be the product only of capitalist society. Marx, in the era of laissez-faire capitalism, could not concretely know certain laws peculiar to the era of imperialism beforehand, because imperialism, the last stage of capitalism, had not yet emerged and the relevant practice was lacking; only Lenin and Stalin could undertake this task. Leaving aside their genius, the reason why Marx, Engels, Lenin and Stalin could work out their theories was mainly that they personally took part in the practice of the class struggle and the scientific experimentation of their time; lacking this condition, no genius could have succeeded. The saying, 'without stepping outside his gate the scholar knows all the wide world's affairs', was mere empty talk in past times when technology was undeveloped. Even though this saying can be valid in the present age of developed technology, the people with real personal knowledge are those engaged in practice the wide world over. And it is only when these people have come to 'know' through their practice and when their knowledge has reached him through writing and technical media that the 'scholar' can indirectly 'know all the wide world's affairs'. If you want to know a certain thing or a certain class of things directly, you must personally participate in the practical struggle to change reality, to change that thing or class of things, for only thus can you come into contact with them as phenomena; only through personal participation in the practical struggle to change reality can you uncover the essence of that thing or class of things and comprehend them. This is the path to knowledge which every man actually travels, though some people, deliberately distorting matters, argue to the contrary. The most ridiculous person in the world is the 'know-all' who picks up a smattering of hearsay knowledge and proclaims himself 'the world's Number One authority'; this merely shows that he has not taken a proper measure of himself. Knowledge is a matter of science, and no dishonesty or conceit whatsoever is permissible. What is required is definitely the reverse – honesty and modesty. If you want knowledge, you must take part in the practice of changing reality. If you want to know the taste of a pear, you must change the pear by eating it yourself. If you want to know the structure and properties of the atom, you must make physical and chemical experiments to change the state of the atom. If you want to know the theory and methods of revolution, you must take part in revolution. All genuine knowledge originates in direct experience. But one cannot have direct experience of everything; as a matter of fact, most of our knowledge comes from indirect experience, for example, all knowledge from past times and foreign lands. To our ancestors and to foreigners, such knowledge was – or is – a matter of direct experience, and this knowledge is reliable if in the course of their direct experience the requirement of 'scientific abstraction', spoken of by Lenin, was – or is – fulfilled and objective reality scientifically reflected, otherwise it is not reliable. Hence a man's knowledge consists only of two parts, that which comes from direct experience and that which comes from indirect experience. Moreover, what is indirect experience for me is direct experience for other people. Consequently, considered as a whole, knowledge of any kind is inseparable from direct experience. All knowledge originates in perception of the objective external world through man's physical sense organs. Anyone who denies such perception, denies direct experience, or denies personal participation in the practice that changes reality, is not a materialist. That is why the 'know-all' is ridiculous. There is an old Chinese saying, 'How can you catch tiger cubs without entering the tiger's lair?' This saying holds true for man's practice and it also holds true for the theory of knowledge. There can be no knowledge apart from practice.

To make clear the dialectical-materialist movement of cognition arising on the basis of the practice which changes reality – to make clear the gradually deepening movement of cognition – a few additional concrete examples are given below.

In its knowledge of capitalist society, the proletariat was only in the perceptual stage of cognition in the first period of its practice, the period of machine-smashing and spontaneous struggle; it knew only some of the aspects and the external relations of the phenomena of capitalism. The proletariat was then still a 'class-in-itself'. But when it reached the second period of its practice, the period of conscious and organized economic and political struggles, the proletariat was able to comprehend the essence of capitalist society, the relations of exploitation between social classes and its own historical task; and it was able to do so because of its own practice and because of its experience of prolonged struggle, which Marx and Engels scientifically summed up in all its variety to create the theory of Marxism for the education of the proletariat. It was then that the proletariat became a 'class-for-itself'.

Similarly with the Chinese people's knowledge of imperialism. The first stage was one of superficial, perceptual knowledge, as shown in the indiscriminate anti-foreign struggles of the Movement of the Taiping Heavenly Kingdom, the Yi Ho Tuan Movement, and so on. It was only in the second stage that the Chinese people reached the stage of rational knowledge, saw the internal and external contradictions of imperialism and saw the essential truth that imperialism had allied itself with China's comprador and feudal classes to oppress and exploit the great masses of the Chinese people. This knowledge began about the time of the 4 May Movement of 1919.

Next, let us consider war. If those who lead a war lack experience of war, then at the initial stage they will not understand the profound laws pertaining to the directing of a specific war (such as our Agrarian

Revolutionary War of the past decade). At the initial stage they will merely experience a good deal of fighting and, what is more, suffer many defeats. But this experience (the experience of battles won and especially of battles lost) enables them to comprehend the inner thread of the whole war, namely, the laws of that specific war, to understand its strategy and tactics, and consequently to direct the war with confidence. If, at such a moment, the command is turned over to an inexperienced person, then he too will have to suffer a number of defeats (gain experience) before he can comprehend the true laws of the war.

'I am not sure I can handle it.' We often hear this remark when a comrade hesitates to accept an assignment. Why is he unsure of himself? Because he has no systematic understanding of the content and circumstances of the assignment, or because he has had little or no contact with such work, and so the laws governing it are beyond him. After a detailed analysis of the nature and circumstances of the assignment, he will feel more sure of himself and do it willingly. If he spends some time at the job and gains experience and if he is a person who is willing to look into matters with an open mind and not one who approaches problems subjectively, one-sidedly and superficially, then he can draw conclusions for himself as to how to go about the job and do it with much more courage. Only those who are subjective, one-sided and superficial in their approach to problems will smugly issue orders or directives the moment they arrive on the scene, without considering the circumstances, without viewing things in their totality (their history and their present state as a whole) and without getting to the essence of things (their nature and the internal relations between one thing and another). Such people are bound to trip and fall.

Thus it can be seen that the first step in the process of cognition is contact with the objects of the external world; this belongs to the stage of perception. The second step is to synthesize the data of perception by arranging and reconstructing them; this belongs to the stage of conception, judgement and inference. It is only when the data of perception are very rich (not fragmentary) and correspond to reality (are not illusory) that they can be the basis for forming correct concepts and theories.

Here two important points must be emphasized. The first, which has been stated before but should be repeated here, is the dependence of rational knowledge upon perceptual knowledge. Anyone who thinks that rational knowledge need not be derived from perceptual knowledge is an idealist. In the history of philosophy there is the 'rationalist' school that admits the reality only of reason and not of experience, believing that reason alone is reliable while perceptual experience is not; this school errs by turning things upside down. The rational is reliable precisely because it has its source in sense perceptions, otherwise it would be like water without a source, a tree without roots, subjective, self-engendered and unreliable. As to the sequence in the process of cognition, perceptual experience comes first; we stress the significance of social practice in the process of cognition precisely because social practice alone can give rise to human knowledge and it alone can start man on the acquisition of perceptual experience from the objective world. For a person who shuts his eyes, stops his ears and totally cuts himself off from the objective world there can be no such thing as knowledge. Knowledge begins with experience – this is the materialism of the theory of knowledge.

The second point is that knowledge needs to be deepened, that the perceptual stage of knowledge needs to be developed to the rational stage – this is the dialectics of the theory of knowledge.[5] To think that knowledge can stop at the lower, perceptual stage and that perceptual knowledge alone is reliable while rational knowledge is not, would be to repeat the historical error of 'empiricism'. This theory errs in failing to understand that, although the data of perception reflect certain realities in the objective world (I am not speaking here of idealist empiricism which confines experience to so-called introspection), they are merely one-sided and superficial, reflecting things incompletely and not reflecting their essence. Fully to reflect a thing in its totality, to reflect its essence, to reflect its inherent laws, it is necessary through the exercise of thought to reconstruct the rich data of sense perception, discarding the dross and selecting the essential, eliminating the false and retaining the true, proceeding from the one to the other and from the outside to the inside, in order to form a system of concepts and theories – it is necessary to make a leap from perceptual to rational knowledge. Such reconstructed knowledge is not more empty or more unreliable; on the contrary, whatever has been scientifically reconstructed in the process of cognition, on the basis of practice, reflects objective reality, as Lenin said, more deeply, more truly, more fully. As against this, vulgar 'practical men' respect experience but despise theory, and therefore cannot have a comprehensive view of an entire objective process, lack clear direction and long-range perspective, and are complacent over occasional successes and glimpses of the truth. If such persons direct a revolution, they will lead it up a blind alley.

Rational knowledge depends upon perceptual knowledge, and perceptual knowledge remains to be developed into rational knowledge – this is the dialectical-materialist theory of knowledge. In philosophy, neither 'rationalism' nor 'empiricism' understands the historical or the dialectical nature of knowledge, and although each of these schools contains one aspect of the truth (here I am referring to materialist, not to idealist, rationalism and empiricism), both are wrong on the theory of knowledge as a whole. The dialectical-materialist movement of knowledge from the perceptual to the rational holds true for a minor process of cognition (for instance, knowing a single thing or task) as well as for a major process of cognition (for instance, knowing a whole society or a revolution).

But the movement of knowledge does not end here. If the dialectical-materialist movement of knowledge were to stop at rational knowledge, only half the problem would be dealt with. And as far as Marxist philosophy is concerned, only the less important half at that. Marxist philosophy holds that the most important problem does not lie in understanding the laws of the objective world and thus being able to explain it, but in applying the knowledge of these laws actively to change the world. From the Marxist viewpoint, theory is important, and its importance is fully expressed in Lenin's statement, 'Without revolutionary theory there can be no revolutionary movement.'[6] But Marxism emphasizes the importance of theory precisely and only because it can guide action. If we have a correct theory but merely prate about it, pigeon-hole it and do not put it into practice, then that theory, however good, is of no significance. Knowledge begins with practice, and theoretical knowledge is acquired through practice and must then return to practice. The active function of knowledge manifests itself not only in the active leap from perceptual to rational knowledge, but – and this is more important – it must manifest itself in the leap from rational knowledge to revolutionary practice. The knowledge which grasps the laws of the world must be redirected to the practice of changing the world, must be applied anew in the practice of production, in the practice of revolutionary class struggle and revolutionary national struggle and in the practice of scientific experiment. This is the process of testing and developing theory, the continuation of the whole process of cognition. The problem of whether theory corresponds to objective reality is not, and cannot be, completely solved in the movement of knowledge from the perceptual to the rational, mentioned above. The only way to solve this problem completely is to redirect rational knowledge to social practice, apply theory to practice and see whether it can achieve the objectives one has in mind. Many theories of natural science are held to be true not only because they were so considered when natural scientists originated them, but because they have been verified in subsequent scientific practice. Similarly, Marxism-Leninism is held to be true not only because it was so considered when it was scientifically formulated by Marx, Engels, Lenin and Stalin but because it has been verified in the subsequent practice of revolutionary class struggle and revolutionary national struggle. Dialectical materialism is universally true because it is impossible for anyone to escape from its domain in his practice. The history of human knowledge tells us that the truth of many theories is incomplete and that this incompleteness is remedied through the test of practice. Many theories are erroneous and it is through the test of practice that their errors are corrected. That is why practice is the criterion of truth and why 'the standpoint of life, of practice, should be first and fundamental in the theory of knowledge'.[7] Stalin has well said, 'Theory becomes purposeless if it is not connected with revolutionary practice, just as practice gropes in the dark if its path is not illumined by revolutionary theory.'[8]

When we get to this point, is the movement of knowledge completed? Our answer is: it is and yet it is not. When men in society throw themselves into the practice of changing a certain objective process (whether natural or social) at a certain stage of its development, they can, as a result of the reflection of the objective process in their brains and the exercise of their subjective activity, advance their knowledge from the perceptual to the rational, and create ideas, theories, plans or programmes which correspond in general to the laws of that objective process. They then apply these ideas, theories, plans or programmes in practice in the same objective process. And if they can realize the aims they have in mind, that is, if in that same process of practice they can translate, or on the whole translate, those previously formulated ideas, theories, plans or programmes into fact, then the movement of knowledge may be considered completed with regard to this particular process. In the process of changing nature, take for example the fulfilment of an

engineering plan, the verification of a scientific hypothesis, the manu-
facture of an implement or the reaping of a crop; or in the process of
changing society, take for example the victory of a strike, victory in a war
or the fulfilment of an educational plan. All these may be considered the
realization of aims one has in mind. But generally speaking, whether in
the practice of changing nature or of changing society, men's original
ideas, theories, plans or programmes are seldom realized without any
alteration.

This is because people engaged in changing reality are usually subject
to numerous limitations; they are limited not only by existing scientific
and technological conditions but also by the development of the
objective process itself and the degree to which this process has become
manifest (the aspects and the essence of the objective process have not
yet been fully revealed). In such a situation, ideas, theories, plans or
programmes are usually altered partially and sometimes even wholly,
because of the discovery of unforeseen circumstances in the course of
practice. That is to say, it does happen that the original ideas, theories,
plans or programmes fail to correspond with reality either in full or in
part and are wholly or partially incorrect. In many instances, failures
have to be repeated many times before errors in knowledge can be
corrected and correspondence with the laws of the objective process
achieved, and consequently before the subjective can be transformed
into the objective, or in other words, before the anticipated results can
be achieved in practice. But when that point is reached, no matter
how, the movement of human knowledge regarding a certain objective process at a certain stage of its development may be considered
completed.

However, so far as the progression of the process is concerned, the
movement of human knowledge is not completed. Every process,
whether in the realm of nature or of society, progresses and develops
by reason of its internal contradiction and struggle, and the movement of
human knowledge should also progress and develop along with it. As far
as social movements are concerned, true revolutionary leaders must not
only be good at correcting their ideas, theories, plans or programmes
when errors are discovered, as has been indicated above; they must also
when a certain objective process has already progressed and changed
from one stage of development to another, be good at making themselves and all their fellow-revolutionaries progress and change in their
subjective knowledge along with it: that is to say, they must ensure that

the proposed new revolutionary tasks and new working programmes correspond to the new changes in the situation. In a revolutionary period the situation changes very rapidly; if the knowledge of revolutionaries does not change rapidly in accordance with the changed situation, they will be unable to lead the revolution to victory.

It often happens, however, that thinking lags behind reality; this is because man's cognition is limited by numerous social conditions. We are opposed to die-hards in the revolutionary ranks whose thinking fails to advance with changing objective circumstances and has manifested itself historically as Right opportunism. These people fail to see that the struggle of opposites has already pushed the objective process forward while their knowledge has stopped at the old stage. This is characteristic of the thinking of all die-hards. Their thinking is divorced from social practice, and they cannot march ahead to guide the chariot of society; they simply trail behind, grumbling that it goes too fast and trying to drag it back or turn it in the opposite direction.

We are also opposed to 'Left' phrase-mongering. The thinking of 'Leftists' outstrips a given stage of development of the objective process; some regard their fantasies as truth, while others strain to realize in the present an ideal which can only be realized in the future. They alienate themselves from the current practice of the majority of the people and from the realities of the day, and show themselves adventurist in their actions.

Idealism and mechanical materialism, opportunism and adventurism – all are characterized by the breach between the subjective and the objective, by the separation of knowledge from practice. The Marxist-Leninist theory of knowledge, characterized as it is by scientific social practice, cannot but resolutely oppose these wrong ideologies. Marxists recognize that in the absolute and general process of development of the universe, the development of each particular process is relative, and that hence, in the endless flow of absolute truth, man's knowledge of a particular process at any given stage of development is only relative truth. The sum total of innumerable relative truths constitutes absolute truth.[9] The development of an objective process is full of contradictions and struggles, and so is the development of the movement of human knowledge. All the dialectical movements of the objective world can sooner or later be reflected in human knowledge. In social practice, the process of coming into being, developing and passing away is infinite, and so is the process of coming into being, developing and passing away in human knowledge. As man's practice which changes objective reality in accordance with given ideas, theories, plans or programmes advances further and further, his knowledge of objective reality likewise becomes deeper and deeper. The movement of change in the world of objective reality is never-ending and so is man's cognition of truth through practice. Marxism-Leninism has in no way exhausted truth but ceaselessly opens up roads to the knowledge of truth in the course of practice. Our conclusion is the concrete, historical unity of the subjective and the objective, of theory and practice, of knowing and doing, and we are opposed to all erroneous ideologies, whether 'Left' or Right, which depart from concrete history.

In the present epoch of the development of society, the responsibility of correctly knowing and changing the world has been placed by history upon the shoulders of the proletariat and its party. This process, the practice of changing the world, which is determined in accordance with scientific knowledge, has already reached a historic moment in the world and in China, a great moment unprecedented in human history, that is, the moment for completely banishing darkness from the world and from China and for changing the world into a world of light such as never previously existed. The struggle of the proletariat and the revolutionary people to change the world comprises the fulfilment of the following tasks: to change the objective world and, at the same time, their own subjective world – to change their cognitive ability and change the relations between the subjective and the objective world. Such a change has already come about in one part of the globe, in the Soviet Union. There the people are pushing forward this process of change. The people of China and the rest of the world either are going through, or will go through, such a process. And the objective world which is to be changed also includes all the opponents of change, who, in order to be changed, must go through a stage of compulsion before they can enter the stage of voluntary, conscious change. The epoch of world communism will be reached when all mankind voluntarily and consciously changes itself and the world.

Discover the truth through practice, and again through practice verify and develop the truth. Start from perceptual knowledge and actively develop it into rational knowledge; then start from rational knowledge and actively guide revolutionary practice to change both the subjective and the objective world. Practice, knowledge, again practice, and again knowledge. This form repeats itself in endless cycles, and with each cycle the content of practice and knowledge rises to a higher level. Such is the whole of the dialectical-materialist theory of knowledge, and such is the dialectical-materialist theory of the unity of knowing and doing.

4

ON CONTRADICTION

August 1937

This essay on philosophy was written by Comrade Mao Tse-tung after his essay 'On Practice' and with the same object of overcoming the serious error of dogmatist thinking to be found in the Party at the time. Originally delivered as lectures at the Anti-Japanese Military and Political College in Yenan, it was revised by the author on its inclusion in his Selected Works.

The law of contradiction in things, that is, the law of the unity of opposites, is the basic law of materialist dialectics. Lenin said, 'Dialectics in the proper sense is the study of contradiction in the very essence of objects.'[1] Lenin often called this law the essence of dialectics; he also called it the kernel of dialectics.[2] In studying this law, therefore, we cannot but touch upon a variety of questions, upon a number of philosophical problems. If we can become clear on all these problems, we shall arrive at a fundamental understanding of materialist dialectics. The problems are: the two world outlooks, the universality of contradiction, the particularity of contradiction, the principal contradiction and the principal aspect of a contradiction, the identity and struggle of the aspects of a contradiction, and the place of antagonism in contradiction.

The criticism to which the idealism of the Deborin school has been subjected in Soviet philosophical circles in recent years has aroused great interest among us. Deborin's idealism has exerted a very bad influence in the Chinese Communist Party, and it cannot be said that the dogmatist thinking in our Party is unrelated to the approach of that school. Our present study of philosophy should therefore have the eradication of dogmatist thinking as its main objective.

I. THE TWO WORLD OUTLOOKS

Throughout the history of human knowledge, there have been two conceptions concerning the law of development of the universe, the metaphysical conception and the dialectical conception, which form two opposing world outlooks. Lenin said:

> The two basic (or two possible? or two historically observable?) conceptions of development (evolution) are: development as decrease and increase, as repetition, and development as a unity of opposites (the division of a unity into mutually exclusive opposites and their reciprocal relation).[3]

Here Lenin was referring to these two different world outlooks.

In China another name for metaphysics is *hsuan-hsueh*. For a long period in history, whether in China or in Europe, this way of thinking, which is part and parcel of the idealist world outlook, occupied a dominant position in human thought. In Europe, the materialism of the bourgeoisie in its early days was also metaphysical. As the social economy of many European countries advanced to the stage of highly developed capitalism, as the forces of production, the class struggle and the sciences developed to a level unprecedented in history, and as the industrial proletariat became the greatest motive force in historical development, there arose the Marxist world outlook of materialist dialectics. Then, in addition to open and barefaced reactionary idealism, vulgar evolutionism emerged among the bourgeoisie to oppose materialist dialectics.

The metaphysical or vulgar evolutionist world outlook sees things as isolated, static and one-sided. It regards all things in the universe, their forms and their species, as eternally isolated from one another and immutable. Such change as there is can only be an increase or decrease in quantity or a change of place. Moreover, the cause of such an increase or decrease or change of place is not inside things but outside them, that is, the motive force is external. Metaphysicians hold that all the different kinds of things in the universe and all their characteristics have been the same ever since they first came into being. All subsequent changes have simply been increases or decreases in quantity. They contend that a thing can only keep on repeating itself as the same kind of thing and cannot change into anything different. In their opinion, capitalist exploitation, capitalist competition, the individualist ideology of capitalist society, and so on, can all be found in ancient slave society, or even in primitive society, and will exist for ever unchanged. They ascribe the causes of social development to factors external to society, such as geography and climate. They search in an oversimplified way outside a thing for the causes of its development, and they deny the theory of materialist dialectics which holds that development arises from the contradictions inside a thing. Consequently they can explain neither the qualitative diversity of things, nor the phenomenon of one quality changing into another. In Europe, this mode of thinking existed as mechanical materialism in the seventeenth and eighteenth centuries and as vulgar evolutionism at the end of the nineteenth and the beginning of the twentieth centuries. In China, there was the metaphysical thinking exemplified in the saying 'Heaven changeth not, likewise the Tao changeth not',[4] and it was supported by the decadent feudal ruling classes for a long time. Mechanical materialism and vulgar evolutionism, which were imported from Europe in the last hundred years, are supported by the bourgeoisie.

As opposed to the metaphysical world outlook, the world outlook of materialist dialectics holds that in order to understand the development of a thing we should study it internally and in its relations with other things; in other words, the development of things should be seen as their internal and necessary self-movement, while each thing in its movement is interrelated to and interacts on the things around it. The fundamental cause of the development of a thing is not external but internal; it lies in the contradictoriness within the thing. There is internal contradiction in every single thing, hence its motion and development. Contradictoriness within a thing is the fundamental cause of its development, while its interrelations and interactions with other things are secondary causes. Thus materialist dialectics effectively combats the theory of external causes, or of an external motive force, advanced by metaphysical mechanical materialism and vulgar evolutionism. It is evident that purely external causes can only give rise to mechanical motion, that is, to changes in scale or quantity, but cannot explain why things differ qualitatively in thousands of ways and why one thing changes into another. As a matter of fact, even mechanical motion under external force occurs through the internal contradictoriness of things. Simple growth in plants and animals, their quantitative development, is likewise chiefly the result of their internal contradictions. Similarly, social development is due chiefly not to external but to internal causes. Countries with almost the same geographical and climatic conditions display great diversity and unevenness in their development. Moreover, great social changes may take place in one and the same country although its geography and climate remain unchanged. Imperialist Russia changed into the socialist Soviet Union, and feudal Japan, which had locked its doors against the world, changed into imperialist Japan, although no change occurred in the geography and climate of either country. Long dominated by feudalism, China has undergone great changes in the last hundred years and is now changing in the direction of a new China, liberated and free, and yet no change has occurred in her geography and climate. Changes do take place in the geography and climate of the earth as a whole and in every part of it, but they are insignificant when compared with changes in society; geographical and climatic changes manifest themselves in terms of tens of thousands of years, while social changes manifest themselves in thousands, hundreds or tens of years, and even in a few years or months in times of revolution. According to materialist dialectics, changes in nature are due chiefly to the development of the internal contradictions in nature. Changes in society are due chiefly to the development of the internal contradictions in society, that is, the contradiction between the productive forces and the relations of production, the contradiction between classes and the contradiction between the old and the new; it is the development of these contradictions that pushes society forward and gives the impetus for the supersession of the old society by the new. Does materialist dialectics exclude external causes? Not at all. It holds that external causes are the condition of change and internal causes are the basis of change, and that external causes become operative through internal causes. In a suitable temperature an egg changes into a chicken, but no temperature can change a stone into a chicken, because each has a different basis. There is constant interaction between the peoples of different countries. In the era of capitalism, and especially in the era of imperialism and proletarian revolution, the interaction and mutual impact of different countries in the political, economic and cultural spheres are extremely great. The October Socialist Revolution ushered in a new epoch in world history as well as in Russian history. It exerted influence on internal changes in the other countries in the world and, similarly and in a particularly profound way, on internal changes in China. These changes, however, were effected through the inner laws of development of these countries, China included. In battle, one army is victorious and the other is defeated; both the victory and the defeat are determined by internal causes. The one is victorious either because it is strong or because of its competent generalship, the other is vanquished either because it is weak or because of its incompetent generalship. It is through internal causes that external causes become operative. In China in 1927, the defeat of the proletariat by the big bourgeoisie came about through the opportunism then to be found within the Chinese proletariat itself (inside the Chinese Communist Party). When we liquidated this opportunism, the Chinese revolution resumed its advance. Later, the Chinese revolution again suffered severe setbacks at the hands of the enemy, because adventurism had risen within our Party. When we liquidated this adventurism, our cause advanced once again. Thus it can be seen that to lead the revolution to victory, a political party must depend on the correctness of its own political line and the solidity of its own organization.

The dialectical world outlook emerged in ancient times both in China and in Europe. Ancient dialectics, however, had a somewhat spontaneous and naive character. In the social and historical conditions then prevailing, it was not yet able to form a theoretical system, hence it could not fully explain the world and was supplanted by metaphysics. The famous German philosopher Hegel, who lived in the late eighteenth and early nineteenth centuries, made most important contributions to dialectics, but his dialectics was idealist. It was not until Marx and Engels, the great protagonists of the proletarian movement, had synthesized the positive achievements in the history of human knowledge and, in particular, critically absorbed the rational elements of Hegelian dialectics and created the great theory of dialectical and historical materialism that an unprecedented revolution occurred in the history of human knowledge. This theory was further developed by Lenin and Stalin. As soon as it spread to China, it wrought tremendous changes in the world of Chinese thought.

This dialectical world outlook teaches us primarily how to observe and analyse the movement of opposites in different things and, on the basis of such analysis, to indicate the methods for resolving contradictions. It is therefore most important for us to understand the law of contradiction in things in a concrete way.

II. THE UNIVERSALITY OF CONTRADICTION

For convenience of exposition, I shall deal first with the universality of contradiction and then proceed to the particularity of contradiction. The reason is that the universality of contradiction can be explained more briefly, for it has been widely recognized ever since the materialist-dialectical world outlook was discovered and materialist dialectics applied with outstanding success to analysing many aspects of human history and natural history and to changing many aspects of society and nature (as in the Soviet Union) by the great creators and continuers of Marxism – Marx, Engels, Lenin and Stalin – whereas the particularity of contradiction is still not clearly understood by many comrades, and especially by the dogmatists. They do not understand that it is precisely in the particularity of contradiction that the universality of contradiction resides. Nor do they understand how important is the study of the particularity of contradiction in the concrete things confronting us for guiding the course of revolutionary practice. Therefore, it is necessary to stress the study of the particularity of contradiction and to explain it at adequate length. For this reason, in our analysis of the law of contradiction in things, we shall first analyse the universality of contradiction, then place special stress on analysing the particularity of contradiction, and finally return to the universality of contradiction.

The universality or absoluteness of contradiction has a twofold meaning. One is that contradiction exists in the process of development of all things, and the other is that in the process of development of each thing a movement of opposites exists from beginning to end.

Engels said, 'Motion itself is a contradiction.'[5] Lenin defined the law of the unity of opposites as 'the recognition (discovery) of the contradictory, mutually exclusive, opposite tendencies in all phenomena and processes of nature (including mind and society)'.[6] Are these ideas correct? Yes, they are. The interdependence of the contradictory aspects present in all things and the struggle between these aspects determine the life of all things and push their development forward. There is nothing that does not contain contradiction; without contradiction nothing would exist.

Contradiction is the basis of the simple forms of motion (for instance, mechanical motion) and still more so of the complex forms of motion.

Engels explained the universality of contradiction as follows:

If simple mechanical change of place contains a contradiction, this is even more true of the higher forms of motion of matter, and especially of organic life and its development . . . life consists precisely and primarily in this – that a being is at each moment itself and yet something else. Life is therefore also a contradiction which is present in things and processes themselves, and which constantly originates and resolves itself; and as soon as the contradiction ceases, life, too, comes to an end, and death steps in. We likewise saw that also in the sphere of thought we could not escape contradictions, and that for example the contradiction between man's inherently unlimited capacity for knowledge and its actual presence only in men who are externally limited and possess limited cognition finds its solution in what is – at least practically, for us – an endless succession of generations, in infinite progress.

. . . one of the basic principles of higher mathematics is the contradiction that in certain circumstances straight lines and curves may be the same . . .

But even lower mathematics teems with contradictions.[7]

Lenin illustrated the universality of contradiction as follows:

In mathematics: + and – . Differential and integral.
In mechanics: action and reaction.
In physics: positive and negative electricity.
In chemistry: the combination and dissociation of atoms.
In social science: the class struggle.[8]

In war, offence and defence, advance and retreat, victory and defeat are all mutually contradictory phenomena. One cannot exist without the other. The two aspects are at once in conflict and in interdependence, and this constitutes the totality of a war, pushes its development forward and solves its problems.

Every difference in men's concepts should be regarded as reflecting an objective contradiction. Objective contradictions are reflected in subjective thinking, and this process constitutes the contradictory movement of concepts, pushes forward the development of thought, and ceaselessly solves problems in man's thinking.

Opposition and struggle between ideas of different kinds constantly occur within the Party; this is a reflection within the Party of contradictions between classes and between the new and the old in society. If there were no contradictions in the Party and no ideological struggles to resolve them, the Party's life would come to an end.

Thus it is already clear that contradiction exists universally and in all processes, whether in the simple or in the complex forms of motion, whether in objective phenomena or ideological phenomena. But does contradiction also exist at the initial stage of each process?

Is there a movement of opposites from beginning to end in the process of development of every single thing?

As can be seen from the articles written by Soviet philosophers criticizing it, the Deborin school maintains that contradiction appears not at the inception of a process but only when it has developed to a certain stage. If this were the case, then the cause of the development of the process before that stage would be external and not internal. Deborin thus reverts to the metaphysical theories of external causality and of mechanism. Applying this view in the analysis of concrete problems, the Deborin school sees only differences but not contradictions between the kulaks and the peasants in general under existing conditions in the Soviet Union, thus entirely agreeing with Bukharin. In analysing the French Revolution, it holds that before the Revolution there were likewise only differences but not contradictions within the Third Estate, which was composed of the workers, the peasants and the bourgeoisie. These views of the Deborin school are anti-Marxist. This school does not understand that each and every difference already contains contradiction and that difference itself is contradiction. Labour and capital have been in contradiction ever since the two classes came into being, only at first the contradiction had not yet become intense. Even under the social conditions existing in the Soviet Union, there is a difference between workers and peasants and this very difference is a contradiction, although, unlike the contradiction between labour and capital, it will not become intensified into antagonism or assume the form of class struggle; the workers and the peasants have established a firm alliance in the course of socialist construction and are gradually resolving this contradiction in the course of the advance from socialism to communism. The question is one of different kinds of contradiction, not of the presence or absence of contradiction. Contradiction is universal and absolute, it is present in the process of development of all things and permeates every process from beginning to end.

What is meant by the emergence of a new process? The old unity with its constituent opposites yields to a new unity with its constituent opposites, whereupon a new process emerges to replace the old. The old process ends and the new one begins. The new process contains new contradictions and begins its own history of the development of contradictions.

As Lenin pointed out, Marx in his *Capital* gave a model analysis of this movement of opposites which runs through the process of development of things from beginning to end. This is the method that must be employed in studying the development of all things. Lenin, too, employed this method correctly and adhered to it in all his writings.

In his *Capital*, Marx first analyses the simplest, most ordinary and fundamental, most common and everyday relation of bourgeois (commodity) society, a relation encountered billions of times – namely, the exchange of commodities. In this very simple phenomenon (in this 'cell' of bourgeois society) analysis reveals all the contradictions (or the germs of all the contradictions) of modern society. The subsequent exposition shows us the development (both growth and movement) of these contradictions and of this society in the [summation] of its individual parts, from its beginning to its end.

Lenin added, 'Such must also be the method of exposition (or study) of dialectics in general.'[9]

Chinese Communists must learn this method; only then will they be able correctly to analyse the history and the present state of the Chinese revolution and infer its future.

III. THE PARTICULARITY OF CONTRADICTION

Contradiction is present in the process of development of all things; it permeates the process of development of each thing from beginning to end. This is the universality and absoluteness of contradiction which we have discussed above. Now let us discuss the particularity and relativity of contradiction.

This problem should be studied on several levels.

First, the contradiction in each form of motion of matter has its particularity. Man's knowledge of matter is knowledge of its forms of motion, because there is nothing in this world except matter in motion and this motion must assume certain forms. In considering each form of motion of matter, we must observe the points which it has in common with other forms of motion. But what is especially important and necessary, constituting as it does the foundation of our knowledge of a thing, is to observe what is particular to this form of motion of matter, namely, to observe the qualitative difference between this form of motion and other forms. Only when we have done so can we distinguish between things. Every form of motion contains within itself its own particular contradiction. This particular contradiction constitutes the particular essence which distinguishes one thing from another. It is the internal cause or, as it may be called, the basis for the immense variety of things in the world. There are many forms of motion in nature, mechanical motion, sound, light, heat, electricity, dissociation, combination, and so on. All these forms are interdependent, but in its essence each is different from the others. The particular essence of each form of motion is determined by its own particular contradiction. This holds true not only for nature but also for social and ideological phenomena. Every form of society, every form of ideology, has its own particular contradiction and particular essence.

The sciences are differentiated precisely on the basis of the particular contradictions inherent in their respective objects of study. Thus the contradiction peculiar to a certain field of phenomena constitutes the object of study for a specific branch of science. For example, positive and negative numbers in mathematics; action and reaction in mechanics; positive and negative electricity in physics; dissociation and combination in chemistry; forces of production and relations of production, classes and class struggle, in social science; offence and defence in military science; idealism and materialism, the metaphysical outlook and the dialectical outlook, in philosophy; and so on – all these are the objects of study of different branches of science precisely because each branch has its own particular contradiction and particular essence. Of course, unless we understand the universality of contradiction, we have no way of discovering the universal cause or universal basis for the movement or development of things; however, unless we study the particularity of contradiction, we have no way of determining the particular essence of a thing which differentiates it from other things, no way of discovering the particular cause or particular basis for the movement or development of a thing, and no way of distinguishing one thing from another or of demarcating the fields of science.

As regards the sequence in the movement of man's knowledge, there is always a gradual growth from the knowledge of individual and particular things to the knowledge of things in general. Only after man knows the particular essence of many different things can he proceed to generalization and know the common essence of things.

When man attains the knowledge of this common essence, he uses it as a guide and proceeds to study various concrete things which have not yet been studied, or studied thoroughly, and to discover the particular essence of each; only thus is he able to supplement, enrich and develop his knowledge of their common essence and prevent such knowledge from withering or petrifying. These are the two processes of cognition: one, from the particular to the general, and the other, from the general to the particular. Thus cognition always moves in cycles and (so long as scientific method is strictly adhered to) each cycle advances human knowledge a step higher and so makes it more and more profound. Where our dogmatists err on this question is that, on the one hand, they do not understand that we have to study the particularity of contradiction and know the particular essence of individual things before we can adequately know the universality of contradiction and the common essence of things, and that, on the other hand, they do not understand that, after knowing the common essence of things, we must go further and study the concrete things that have not yet been thoroughly studied or have only just emerged. Our dogmatists are lazybones. They refuse to undertake any painstaking study of concrete things, they regard general truths as emerging out of the void, they turn them into purely abstract unfathomable formulae, and thereby completely deny and reverse the normal sequence by which man comes to know truth. Nor do they understand the interconnection of the two processes in cognition – from the particular to the general and then from the general to the particular. They understand nothing of the Marxist theory of knowledge.

It is necessary not only to study the particular contradiction and the essence determined thereby of every great system of the forms of motion of matter, but also to study the particular contradiction and the essence of each process in the long course of development of each form of motion of matter. In every form of motion, each process of development which is real (and not imaginary) is qualitatively different. Our study must emphasize and start from this point.

Qualitatively different contradictions can only be resolved by qualitatively different methods. For instance, the contradiction between the proletariat and the bourgeoisie is resolved by the method of socialist revolution; the contradiction between the great masses of the people and the feudal system is resolved by the method of democratic revolution; the contradiction between the colonies and imperialism is resolved by the method of national revolutionary war; the contradiction between the working class and the peasant class in socialist society is resolved by the method of collectivization and mechanization in agriculture; contradiction within the Communist Party is resolved by the method of criticism and self-criticism; the contradiction between society and nature is resolved by the method of developing the productive forces. Processes change, old processes and old contradictions disappear, new processes and new contradictions emerge, and the methods of resolving contradictions differ accordingly. In Russia, there was a fundamental difference between the contradiction resolved by the February Revolution and the contradiction resolved by the October Revolution, as well as between the methods used to resolve them. The principle of using different methods to resolve different contradictions is one which Marxist-Leninists must strictly observe. The dogmatists do not observe this principle; they do not understand that conditions differ in different kinds of revolution and so do not understand that different methods should be used to resolve different contradictions; on the contrary, they invariably adopt what they imagine to be an unalterable formula and arbitrarily apply it everywhere, which only causes setbacks to the revolution or makes a sorry mess of what was originally well done.

In order to reveal the particularity of the contradictions in any process in the development of a thing, in their totality or interconnections, that is, in order to reveal the essence of the process, it is necessary to reveal the particularity of the two aspects of each of the contradictions in that process; otherwise it will be impossible to discover the essence of the process. This likewise requires the utmost attention in our study.

There are many contradictions in the course of the development of any major thing. For instance, in the course of China's bourgeois-democratic revolution, where the conditions are exceedingly complex, there exist the contradiction between all the oppressed classes in Chinese society and imperialism, the contradiction between the great masses of the people and feudalism, the contradiction between the proletariat and the bourgeoisie, the contradiction between the pea-santry and the urban petty bourgeoisie on the one hand and the bourgeoisie on the other, the contradiction between the various reactionary ruling groups, and so on. These contradictions cannot be treated in the same way since each has its own particularity; moreover, the two aspects of each contradiction cannot be treated in the same way since each aspect has its own characteristics. We who are engaged in the Chinese revolution should not only understand the particularity of these contradictions in their totality, that is, in their interconnections, but should also study the two aspects of each contra-diction as the only means of understanding the totality. When we speak of understanding each aspect of a contradiction, we mean understanding what specific position each aspect occupies, what con-crete forms it assumes in its interdependence and in its contradiction with its opposite, and what concrete methods are employed in the struggle with its opposite, when the two are both interdependent and in contradiction, and also after the interdependence breaks down. It is of great importance to study these problems. Lenin meant just this when he said that the most essential thing in Marxism, the living soul of Marxism, is the concrete analysis of concrete conditions.[10] Our dogmatists have violated Lenin's teachings; they never use their brains to analyse anything concretely, and in their writings and speeches they always use stereotypes devoid of content, thereby creating a very bad style of work in our Party.

In studying a problem, we must shun subjectivity, one-sidedness and superficiality. To be subjective means not to look at problems objec-tively, that is, not to use the materialist viewpoint in looking at problems. I have discussed this in my essay 'On Practice' (this volume, Chapter 3). To be one-sided means not to look at problems all-sidedly, for example, to understand only China but not Japan, only the Communist Party but not the Kuomintang, only the proletariat but not the bourgeoisie, only the peasants but not the landlords, only the favourable conditions but not the difficult ones, only the past but not the future, only individual parts but not the whole, only the defects but not the achievements, only the plaintiff's case but not the defendant's, only underground revolutionary work but not open revolutionary work, and so on. In a word, it means not to understand the characteristics of both aspects of a contradiction. This is what we mean by looking at a problem one-sidedly. Or it may be called seeing the part but not the whole, seeing the trees but not the forest. That way it is impossible to find the method for resolving a contradiction, it is impossible to accomplish the tasks of the revolution, to carry out assignments well or to develop inner-Party ideological struggle correctly. When Sun Wu Tzu said in discussing military science, 'Know the enemy and know yourself, and you can fight a hundred battles with no danger of defeat',[11] he was referring to the two sides in a battle. Wei Chengi[12] of the Tang dynasty also understood the error of one-sidedness when he said, 'Listen to both sides and you will be enlightened, heed only one side and you will be benighted.' But our comrades often look at problems one-sidedly, and so they often run into snags. In the novel *Shui Hu Chuan*, Sung Chiang thrice attacked Chu Village.[13] Twice he was defeated because he was ignorant of the local conditions and used the wrong method. Later he changed his method: first he investigated the situation and familiarized himself with the maze of roads, then he broke up the alliance between the Li, Hu and Chu Villages and sent his men in disguise into the enemy camp to lie in wait, using a stratagem similar to that of the Trojan Horse in the foreign story. And on the third occasion he won. There are many examples of materialist dialectics in *Shui Hu Chuan*, of which the episode of the three attacks on Chu Village is one of the best. Lenin said:

> in order really to know an object we must embrace, study, all its sides, all connections and 'mediations'. We shall never achieve this com-
> pletely, but the demand for all-sidedness is a safeguard against mistakes
> and rigidity.[14]

We should remember his words. To be superficial means to consider neither the characteristics of a contradiction in its totality nor the characteristics of each of its aspects; it means to deny the necessity for probing deeply into a thing and minutely studying the characteristics of its contradiction, instead merely looking from afar and, after glimpsing the rough outline, immediately trying to resolve the contradiction (in order to answer a question, settle a dispute, handle work, or direct a military operation). This way of doing things is bound to lead to trouble. The reason the dogmatist and empiricist comrades in China have made mistakes lies precisely in their subjectivist, one-sided and superficial way of looking at things. To be one-sided and superficial is at the same time to be subjective. For all objective things are actually interconnected and are governed by inner laws. But instead of undertaking the task of reflecting things as they really are some people only look at things one-sidedly or superficially and so know neither their interconnections nor their inner laws. Their method is therefore subjectivist.

Not only does the whole process of the movement of opposites in the development of a thing, both in their interconnections and in each of the aspects, have particular features to which we must give attention, but each stage in the process has its particular features to which we must give attention too.

The fundamental contradiction in the process of development of a thing and the essence of the process determined by this fundamental contradiction will not disappear until the process is completed; but in a lengthy process the conditions usually differ at each stage. The reason is that, although the nature of the fundamental contradiction in the process of development of a thing and the essence of the process remain unchanged, the fundamental contradiction becomes more and more intensified as it passes from one stage to another in the lengthy process. In addition, among the numerous major and minor contradictions which are determined or influenced by the fundamental contradiction, some become more intense, some are temporarily or partially resolved or mitigated, and some new ones emerge: hence the process is marked by stages. If people do not pay attention to the stages in the process of development of a thing, they cannot deal with its contradictions properly.

For instance, when the capitalism of the era of free competition developed into imperialism, there was no change in the class nature of the two classes in fundamental contradiction, namely, the proletariat and the bourgeoisie, or in the capitalist essence of society. However, the contradiction between these two classes became intensified: the contradiction between monopoly and non-monopoly capital emerged, the contradiction between the colonial powers and the colonies deepened, the contradiction among the capitalist countries resulting from their uneven development manifested itself with particular sharpness: and thus there arose the special stage of capitalism, the stage of imperialism. Leninism is the Marxism of the era of imperialism and proletarian revolution precisely because Lenin and Stalin have correctly explained these contradictions and correctly formulated the theory and tactics of the proletarian revolution for their resolution.

Take the process of China's bourgeois-democratic revolution, which began with the Revolution of 1911: it, too, has several distinct stages. In particular, the revolution in its period of bourgeois leadership and the revolution in its period of proletarian leadership represent two vastly different historical stages. In other words, proletarian leadership has fundamentally changed the whole face of the revolution, has brought about a new alignment of classes, given rise to a tremendous upsurge in the peasant revolution, imparted thoroughness to the revolution against imperialism and feudalism, created the possibility of the transition from the democratic revolution to the socialist revolution, and so on. None of these was possible in the period when the revolution was under bourgeois leadership. Although no change has taken place in the nature of the fundamental contradiction in the process as a whole, i.e., in the anti-imperialist, anti-feudal, democratic-revolutionary nature of the process (the opposite of which is its semi-colonial and semi-feudal nature), nonetheless this process has passed through several stages of development in the course of more than twenty years. During this time many great events have taken place – the failure of the Revolution of 1911 and the establishment of the regime of the Northern warlords, the formation of the first national united front and the revolution of 1924–27, the break-up of the united front and the desertion of the bourgeoisie to the side of the counter-revolution, the wars among the new warlords, the Agrarian Revolutionary War, the establishment of the second national united front and the War of Resistance Against Japan. These stages are marked by particular features such as the intensification of certain contradictions (e.g., the Agrarian Revolutionary War and the Japanese invasion of the four north-eastern provinces), the partial or temporary resolution of other contradictions (e.g., the destruction of the Northern warlords and our confiscation of the land of the landlords), and the emergence of yet other contradictions (e.g., the conflicts among the new warlords, and the landlords' recapture of the land after the loss of our revolutionary base areas in the south).

In studying the particularities of the contradictions at each stage in the process of the development of a thing, we must not only observe them in their interconnections or their totality; we must also examine the two aspects of each contradiction.

For instance, consider the Kuomintang and the Communist Party. Take one aspect, the Kuomintang. In the period of the first united front, the Kuomintang carried out Sun Yat-sen's Three Great Policies of alliance with Russia, cooperation with the Communist Party and assistance to the peasants and workers. Hence it was revolutionary and vigorous, it was an alliance of various classes for the democratic revolution. After 1927, however, the Kuomintang changed into its opposite and became a reactionary bloc of the landlords and big bourgeoisie. After the Sian incident in December 1936, it began another change in the direction of ending the civil war and cooperating with the Communist Party for joint opposition to Japanese imperialism. Such have been the particular features of the Kuomintang in the three stages. Of course, these features have arisen from a variety of causes. Now take the other aspect, the Chinese Communist Party. In the period of the first united front, the Chinese Communist Party was in its infancy; it courageously led the revolution of 1924–27 but revealed its immaturity in its understanding of the character, the tasks and the methods of the revolution, and consequently it became possible for Chen Tu-hsiuism, which appeared during the latter part of this revolution, to assert itself and bring about the defeat of the revolution. After 1927, the Communist Party courageously led the Agrarian Revolutionary War and created the revolutionary army and revolutionary base areas; however, it committed adventurist errors which brought about very great losses both to the army and to the base areas. Since 1935 the Party has corrected these errors and has been leading the new united front for resistance to Japan; this great struggle is now developing. At the present stage, the Communist Party is a party that has gone through the test of two revolutions and acquired a wealth of experience. Such have been the particular features of the Chinese Communist Party in the three stages. These features, too, have arisen from a variety of causes. Without studying both these sets of features we cannot understand the particular relations between the two parties during the various stages of their development, namely, the establishment of a united front, the break-up of the united front, and the establishment of another united front. What is even more fundamental for the study of the particular features of the two parties is the examination of the class basis of the two parties and the resultant contradictions which have arisen between each party and other forces at different periods. For instance, in the period of its first cooperation with the Communist Party, the Kuomintang stood in contradiction to foreign imperialism and was therefore anti-imperialist; on the other hand, it stood in contradiction to the great masses of the people within the country – although in words it promised many benefits to the working people, in fact it gave them little or nothing. In the period when it carried on the anti-communist war, the Kuomintang collaborated with imperialism and feudalism against the great masses of the people and wiped out all the gains they had won in the revolution, and thereby intensified its contradictions with them. In the present period of the anti-Japanese war, the Kuomintang stands in contradiction to Japanese imperialism and wants cooperation with the Communist Party, without however relaxing its struggle against the Communist Party and the people or its oppression of them. As for the Communist Party, it has always, in every period, stood with the great masses of the people against imperialism and feudalism, but in the present period of the anti-Japanese war, it has adopted a moderate policy towards the Kuomintang and the domestic feudal forces because the Kuomintang has strongly favoured resisting Japan. The above circumstances have led sometimes to an alliance between the two parties, sometimes to struggle between them, and even during the periods of alliance there has been a complicated state of simultaneous alliance and struggle. If we do not study the particular features of both aspects of the contradiction, we shall fail to understand not only the relations of each party with the other forces, but also the relations between the two parties.

It can thus be seen that in studying the particularity of any kind of contradiction – the contradiction in each form of motion of matter, the contradiction in each of its processes of development, the two aspects of the contradiction in each process, the contradiction at each stage of a process, and the two aspects of the contradiction at each stage, in short, – in studying the particularity of all these contradictions – we must not be subjective and arbitrary but must analyse it concretely. Without concrete analysis there can be no knowledge of the particularity of any contradiction. We must always remember Lenin's insistence on the concrete analysis of concrete conditions.

Marx and Engels were the first to provide us with excellent models of such concrete analysis.

When Marx and Engels applied the law of contradiction in things to the study of the socio-historical process, they discovered the contradiction between the productive forces and the relations of production; they discovered the contradiction between the exploiting and exploited classes and also the resultant contradiction between the economic base and its superstructure (politics, ideology, etc.); and they discovered how these contradictions inevitably lead to different kinds of social revolution in different kinds of class society.

When Marx applied this law to the study of the economic structure of capitalist society, he discovered that the basic contradiction of this society is the contradiction between the social character of production and the private character of ownership. This contradiction manifests itself in the contradiction between the organized character of production in individual enterprises and the anarchic character of production in society as a whole. In terms of class relations, it manifests itself in the contradiction between the bourgeoisie and the proletariat.

Because the range of things is vast and there is no limit to their development, what is universal in one context becomes particular in another. Conversely, what is particular in one context becomes universal in another. The contradiction in the capitalist system between the social character of production and the private ownership of the means of production is common to all countries where capitalism exists and develops; as far as capitalism is concerned, this constitutes the universality of contradiction. But this contradiction of capitalism belongs only to a certain historical stage in the general development of class society; as far as the contradiction between the productive forces and the relations of production in class society as a whole is concerned, it constitutes the particularity of contradiction. However, in the course of dissecting the particularity of all these contradictions in capitalist society, Marx gave a still more profound, more pertinent and more complete elucidation of the universality of the contradiction between the productive forces and the relations of production in class society in general.

Since the particular is united with the universal and since the universality as well as the particularity of contradiction is inherent in everything – universality residing in particularity – we should, when studying an object, try to discover both the particular and the universal and their interconnection, to discover both particularity and universality and also their interconnection within the object itself, and to discover the interconnections of this object with the many objects outside it. When Stalin explained the historical roots of Leninism in his famous work *The Foundations of Leninism*, he analysed the international situation in which Leninism arose, analysed those contradictions of capitalism which reached their culmination under imperialism, and showed how these contradictions made proletarian revolution a matter for immediate action and created favourable conditions for a direct onslaught on capitalism. What is more, he analysed the reasons why Russia became the cradle of Leninism, why tsarist Russia became the focus of all the contradictions of imperialism, and why it was possible for the Russian proletariat to become the vanguard of the international revolutionary proletariat. Thus, Stalin analysed the universality of contradiction in imperialism, showing why Leninism is the Marxism of the era of imperialism and proletarian revolution, and at the same time analysed the particularity of tsarist Russian imperialism within this general contradiction, showing why Russia became the birthplace of the theory and tactics of proletarian revolution and how the universality of contradiction is contained in this particularity. Stalin's analysis provides us with a model for understanding the particularity and the universality of contradiction and their interconnection.

On the question of using dialectics in the study of objective phenomena, Marx and Engels, and likewise Lenin and Stalin, always enjoin people not to be in any way subjective and arbitrary but, from the concrete conditions in the actual objective movement of these phenomena, to discover their concrete contradictions, the concrete position of each aspect of every contradiction and the concrete interrelations of the contradictions. Our dogmatists do not have this attitude in study and therefore can never get anything right. We must take warning from their failure and learn to acquire this attitude, which is the only correct one in study.

The relationship between the universality and the particularity of contradiction is the relationship between the general character and the individual character of contradiction. By the former we mean that contradiction exists in and runs through all processes from beginning to end; motion, things, processes, thinking – all are contradictions. To deny contradiction is to deny everything. This is a universal truth for all times and all countries, which admits of no exception. Hence the general character, the absoluteness of contradiction. But this general character is contained in every individual character; without individual character there can be no general character. If all individual character were removed, what general character would remain? It is because each contradiction is particular that individual character arises. All individual character exists conditionally and temporarily, and hence is relative.

This truth concerning general and individual character, concerning absoluteness and relativity, is the quintessence of the problem of contradiction in things; failure to understand it is tantamount to abandoning dialectics.

IV. THE PRINCIPAL CONTRADICTION AND
THE PRINCIPAL ASPECT OF A CONTRADICTION

There are still two points in the problem of the particularity of contradiction which must be singled out for analysis, namely, the principal contradiction and the principal aspect of a contradiction.

There are many contradictions in the process of development of a complex thing, and one of them is necessarily the principal contradiction whose existence and development determines or influences the existence and development of the other contradictions.

For instance, in capitalist society the two forces in contradiction, the proletariat and the bourgeoisie, form the principal contradiction. The other contradictions, such as those between the remnant feudal class and the bourgeoisie, between the peasant petty bourgeoisie and the bourgeoisie, between the proletariat and the peasant petty bourgeoisie, between the non-monopoly capitalists and the monopoly capitalists, between bourgeois democracy and bourgeois fascism, among the capitalist countries and between imperialism and the colonies, are all determined or influenced by this principal contradiction.

In a semi-colonial country such as China, the relationship between the principal contradiction and the non-principal contradictions presents a complicated picture.

When imperialism launches a war of aggression against such a country, all its various classes, apart from some traitors, can temporarily unite in a national war against imperialism. At such a time, the contradiction between imperialism and the country concerned becomes the principal contradiction, while all the contradictions among the various classes within the country (including what was the principal contradiction, between the feudal system and the great masses of the people) are temporarily relegated to a secondary and subordinate position. So it was in China in the Opium War of 1840, the Sino-Japanese War of 1894 and the Yi Ho Tuan War of 1900, and so it is now in the present Sino-Japanese War.

But in another situation, the contradictions change position. When imperialism carries on its oppression not by war, but by milder means – political, economic and cultural – the ruling classes in semi-colonial countries capitulate to imperialism, and the two form an alliance for the joint oppression of the masses of the people. At such a time, the masses often resort to civil war against the alliance of imperialism and the feudal classes, while imperialism often employs indirect methods rather than direct action in helping the reactionaries in the semi-colonial countries to oppress the people, and thus the internal contradictions become particularly sharp. This is what happened in China in the Revolutionary War of 1911, the Revolutionary War of 1924–27, and the ten years of Agrarian Revolutionary War after 1927. Wars among the various reactionary ruling groups in the semi-colonial countries, e.g., the wars among the warlords in China, fall into the same category.

When a revolutionary civil war develops to the point of threatening the very existence of imperialism and its running dogs, the domestic reactionaries, imperialism often adopts other methods in order to maintain its rule: either it tries to split the revolutionary front from within or it sends armed forces to help the domestic reactionaries directly. At such a time, foreign imperialism and domestic reaction stand quite openly at one pole while the masses of the people stand at the other pole, thus forming the principal contradiction which determines or influences the development of the other contradictions. The assistance given by various capitalist countries to the Russian reactionaries after the October Revolution is an example of armed intervention. Chiang Kai-shek's betrayal in 1927 is an example of splitting the revolutionary front.

But whatever happens, there is no doubt at all that at every stage in the development of a process there is only one principal contradiction which plays the leading role.

Hence, if in any process there are a number of contradictions, one of them must be the principal contradiction playing the leading and decisive role, while the rest occupy a secondary and subordinate position. Therefore, in studying any complex process in which there are two or more contradictions, we must devote every effort to funding its principal contradiction. Once this principal contradiction is grasped, all problems can be readily solved. This is the method Marx taught us in his study of capitalist society. Likewise Lenin and Stalin taught us this method when they studied imperialism and the general crisis of capitalism and when they studied the Soviet economy. There are thousands of scholars and men of action who do not understand it, and the result is that, lost in a fog, they are unable to get to the heart of a problem and naturally cannot find a way to resolve its contradictions.

As we have said, one must not treat all the contradictions in a process as being equal but must distinguish between the principal and the secondary contradictions, and pay special attention to grasping the principal one. But, in any given contradiction, whether principal or secondary, should the two contradictory aspects be treated as equal? Again, no. In any contradiction the development of the contradictory aspects is uneven. Sometimes they seem to be in equilibrium, which is however only temporary and relative, while unevenness is basic. Of the two contradictory aspects, one must be principal and the other secondary. The principal aspect is the one playing the leading role in the contradiction. The nature of a thing is determined mainly by the principal aspect of a contradiction, the aspect which has gained the dominant position.

But this situation is not static; the principal and the non-principal aspects of a contradiction transform themselves into each other, and the nature of the thing changes accordingly. In a given process or at a given stage in the development of a contradiction, A is the principal aspect and B is the non-principal aspect; at another stage or in another process the roles are reversed – a change determined by the extent of the increase or decrease in the force of each aspect in its struggle against the other in the course of the development of a thing.

We often speak of 'the new superseding the old'. The supersession of the old by the new is a general, eternal and inviolable law of the universe. The transformation of one thing into another, through leaps of different forms in accordance with its essence and external conditions – this is the process of the new superseding the old. In each thing there is contradiction between its new and its old aspects, and this gives rise to a series of struggles with many twists and turns. As a result of these struggles, the new aspect changes from being minor to being major and rises to predominance, while the old aspect changes from being major to being minor and gradually dies out. And the moment the new aspect gains dominance over the old, the old thing changes qualitatively into a new thing. It can thus be seen that the nature of a thing is mainly determined by the principal aspect of the contradiction, the aspect which has gained predominance. When the principal aspect which has gained predominance changes, the nature of a thing changes accordingly.

In capitalist society, capitalism has changed its position from being a subordinate force in the old feudal era to being the dominant force, and the nature of society has accordingly changed from feudal to capitalist. In the new, capitalist era, the feudal forces changed from their former dominant position to a subordinate one, gradually dying out. Such was the case, for example, in Britain and France. With the development of the productive forces, the bourgeoisie changes from being a new class playing a progressive role to being an old class playing a reactionary role, until it is finally overthrown by the proletariat and becomes a class deprived of privately owned means of production and stripped of power, when it, too, gradually dies out. The proletariat, which is much more numerous than the bourgeoisie and grows simultaneously with it but under its rule, is a new force which, initially subordinate to the bourgeoisie, gradually gains strength, becomes an independent class playing the leading role in history, and finally seizes political power and becomes the ruling class. Thereupon the nature of society changes and the old capitalist society becomes the new socialist society. This is the path already taken by the Soviet Union, a path that all other countries will inevitably take.

Look at China, for instance. Imperialism occupies the principal position in the contradiction in which China has been reduced to a semi-colony; it oppresses the Chinese people, and China has been changed from an independent country into a semi-colonial one. But this state of affairs will inevitably change: in the struggle between the two sides, the power of the Chinese people which is growing under the leadership of the proletariat will inevitably change China from a semi-colony into an independent country, whereas imperialism will be overthrown and old China will inevitably change into New China.

The change of old China into New China also involves a change in the relation between the old feudal forces and the new popular forces within the country. The old feudal landlord class will be overthrown, and from being the ruler it will change into being the ruled; and this class, too, will gradually die out. From being the ruled, the people, led by the proletariat, will become the rulers. Thereupon, the nature of Chinese society will change and the old, semi-colonial and semi-feudal society will change into a new democratic society.

Instances of such reciprocal transformation are found in our past experience. The Ching dynasty which ruled China for nearly three hundred years was overthrown in the Revolution of 1911, and the revolutionary Tung Meng Hui under Sun Yat-sen's leadership was victorious for a time. In the Revolutionary War of 1924–27, the revolutionary forces of the Communist–Kuomintang alliance in the south changed from being weak to being strong and won victory in the Northern Expedition, while the Northern warlords who once ruled the roost were overthrown. In 1927, the people's forces led by the Communist Party were greatly reduced numerically under the attacks of Kuomintang reaction, but with the elimination of opportunism within their ranks they gradually grew again. In the revolutionary base areas under communist leadership, the peasants have been transformed from being the ruled to being the rulers, while the landlords have undergone a reverse transformation. It is always so in the world, the new displacing the old, the old being superseded by the new, the old being eliminated to make way for the new, and the new emerging out of the old.

At certain times in the revolutionary struggle, the difficulties outweigh the favourable conditions and so constitute the principal aspect of the contradiction and the favourable conditions constitute the secondary aspect. But through their efforts the revolutionaries can overcome the difficulties step by step and open up a favourable new situation; thus a difficult situation yields place to a favourable one. This is what happened after the failure of the revolution in China in 1927 and during the Long March of the Chinese Red Army. In the present Sino-Japanese War, China is again in a difficult position, but we can change this and fundamentally transform the situation as between China and Japan. Conversely, favourable conditions can be transformed into difficulty if the revolutionaries make mistakes. Thus the victory of the revolution of 1924–27 turned into defeat. The revolutionary base areas which grew up in the southern provinces after 1927 had all suffered defeat by 1934.

When we engage in study, the same holds good for the contradiction in the passage from ignorance to knowledge. At the very beginning of our study of Marxism, our ignorance of or scanty acquaintance with Marxism stands in contradiction to knowledge of Marxism. But by assiduous study, ignorance can be transformed into knowledge, scanty knowledge into substantial knowledge, and blindness in the application of Marxism into mastery of its application.

Some people think that this is not true of certain contradictions. For instance, in the contradiction between the productive forces and the relations of production, the productive forces are the principal aspect; in the contradiction between theory and practice, practice is the principal aspect; in the contradiction between the economic base and the superstructure, the economic base is the principal aspect; and there is no change in their respective positions. This is the mechanical materialist conception, not the dialectical materialist conception. True, the productive forces, practice and the economic base generally play the principal and decisive role; whoever denies this is not a materialist. But it must also be admitted that in certain conditions, such aspects as the relations of production, theory and the superstructure in turn manifest themselves in the principal and decisive role. When it is impossible for the productive forces to develop without a change in the relations of production, then the change in the relations of production plays the principal and decisive role. The creation and advocacy of revolutionary theory plays the principal and decisive role in those times of which Lenin said, 'Without revolutionary theory there can be no revolutionary movement.'[15] When a task, no matter which, has to be performed, but there is as yet no guiding line, method, plan or policy, the principal and decisive thing is to decide on a guiding line, method, plan or policy. When the superstructure (politics, culture, etc.) obstructs the development of the economic base, political and cultural changes become principal and decisive. Are we going against materialism when we say this? No. The reason is that while we recognize that in the general development of history the material determines the mental and social being determines social consciousness, we also – and indeed must – recognize the reaction of the mental on material things, of social consciousness on social being and of the superstructure on the economic base. This does not go against materialism; on the contrary, it avoids mechanical materialism and firmly upholds dialectical materialism.

In studying the particularity of contradiction, unless we examine these two facets – the principal and the non-principal contradictions in a process, and the principal and the non-principal aspects of a contradiction – that is, unless we examine the distinctive character of these two facets of contradiction, we shall get bogged down in abstractions, be unable to understand contradiction concretely and consequently be unable to find the correct method of resolving it. The distinctive character or particularity of these two facets of contradiction represents the unevenness of the forces that are in contradiction. Nothing in this world develops absolutely evenly; we must oppose the theory of even development or the theory of equilibrium. Moreover, it is these concrete features of a contradiction and the changes in the principal and non-principal aspects of a contradiction in the course of its development that manifest the force of the new superseding the old. The study of the various states of unevenness in contradictions, of the principal and non-principal contradictions and of the principal and the non-principal aspects of a contradiction constitutes an essential method by which a revolutionary political party correctly determines its strategic and tactical policies both in political and in military affairs. All communists must give it attention.

V. THE IDENTITY AND STRUGGLE OF THE ASPECTS OF A CONTRADICTION

When we understand the universality and the particularity of contradiction, we must proceed to study the problem of the identity and struggle of the aspects of a contradiction.

Identity, unity, coincidence, interpenetration, interpermeation, interdependence (or mutual dependence for existence), interconnection or mutual cooperation – all these different terms mean the same thing and refer to the following two points: first, the existence of each of the two aspects of a contradiction in the process of the development of a thing presupposes the existence of the other aspect, and both aspects coexist in a single entity; second, in given conditions, each of the two contradictory aspects transforms itself into its opposite. This is the meaning of identity.

Lenin said:

> Dialectics is the teaching which shows how opposites can be and how they happen to be (how they become) identical – under what conditions they are identical, transforming themselves into one another, – why the human mind should take these opposites not as dead, rigid, but as living, conditional, mobile, transforming themselves into one another.[16]

What does this passage mean?

The contradictory aspects in every process exclude each other, struggle with each other and are in opposition to each other. Without exception, they are contained in the process of development of all things and in all human thought. A simple process contains only a single pair of opposites, while a complex process contains more. And in turn, the pairs of opposites are in contradiction to one another.

That is how all things in the objective world and all human thought are constituted and how they are set in motion.

This being so, there is an utter lack of identity or unity. How then can one speak of identity or unity?

The fact is that no contradictory aspect can exist in isolation. Without its opposite aspect, each loses the condition for its existence. Just think, can any one contradictory aspect of a thing or of a concept in the human mind exist independently? Without life, there would be no death; without death, there would be no life. Without 'above', there would be no 'below', without 'below', there would be no 'above'. Without misfortune, there would be no good fortune; without good fortune, there would be no misfortune. Without facility, there would be no difficulty; without difficulty, there would be no facility. Without land-lords, there would be no tenant-peasants; without tenant-peasants, there would be no landlords. Without the bourgeoisie, there would be no proletariat; without the proletariat, there would be no bourgeoisie. Without imperialist oppression of nations, there would be no colonies or semi-colonies; without colonies or semi-colonies, there would be no imperialist oppression of nations. It is so with all opposites. Under given conditions, on the one hand they are opposed to each other, and on the other they are interconnected, interpenetrating, interpermeating and interdependent, and this character is described as identity. Under given conditions, all contradictory aspects possess the character of non-identity and hence are described as being in contradiction. But they also possess the character of identity and hence are interconnected. This is what Lenin means when he says that dialectics studies 'how opposites can be . . . identical'. How then can they be identical? Because each is the condition for the other's existence. This is the first meaning of identity.

But is it enough to say merely that each of the contradictory aspects is the condition for the other's existence, that there is identity between them and that consequently they can coexist in a single entity? No, it is not. The matter does not end with their dependence on each other for their existence; what is more important is their transformation into each other. That is to say, in given conditions, each of the contradictory aspects within a thing transforms itself into its opposite, changes its position to that of its opposite. This is the second meaning of the identity of contradiction.

Why is there identity here, too? You see, by means of revolution the proletariat, at one time the ruled, is transformed into the ruler, while the bourgeoisie, the erstwhile ruler, is transformed into the ruled and changes its position to that originally occupied by its opposite. This has already taken place in the Soviet Union, as it will take place throughout the world. If there were no interconnection and identity of opposites in given conditions, how could such a change take place?

The Kuomintang, which played a certain positive role at a certain stage in modern Chinese history, became a counter-revolutionary party after 1927 because of its inherent class nature and because of imperialist blandishments (these being the conditions); but it has been compelled to agree to resist Japan because of the sharpening of the contradiction between China and Japan and because of the Communist Party's policy of the united front (these being the conditions). Things in contradiction change into one another, and herein lies a definite identity.

Our agrarian revolution has been a process in which the landlord class owning the land is transformed into a class that has lost its land, while the peasants who once lost their land are transformed into smallholders who have acquired land, and such a process will occur yet again. Under given conditions having and not having, acquiring and losing, are interconnected; the two sides have a single identity. Under socialism, private peasant ownership is transformed into the public ownership of socialist agriculture; this has already taken place in the Soviet Union, as it will take place everywhere else. There is a bridge leading from private property to public property, which in philosophy is called identity, or transformation into each other, or interpenetration.

To consolidate the dictatorship of the proletariat or the dictatorship of the people is in fact to prepare the conditions for abolishing this dictatorship and advancing to the higher stage when all state systems are eliminated. To establish and build the Communist Party is in fact to prepare the conditions for the elimination of the Communist Party and all political parties. To build a revolutionary army under the leadership of the Communist Party and to carry on revolutionary war is in fact to prepare the conditions for the permanent elimination of war. These opposites are at the same time complementary.

War and peace, as everybody knows, transform themselves into each other. War is transformed into peace: for instance, the First World War was transformed into the post-war peace, and the civil war in China has now stopped, giving way to internal peace. Peace is transformed into war: for instance, the Kuomintang–Communist cooperation was transformed into war in 1927, and today's situation of world peace may be transformed into a second world war. Why is this so? Because in class society such contradictory things as war and peace share an identity under certain conditions.

All contradictory things are interconnected; not only do they coexist in a single entity under given conditions, but under other conditions, they also transform themselves into each other. This is the full meaning of the identity of opposites. This is what Lenin meant when he discussed 'how they happen to be (how they become) identical – under what conditions they are identical, transforming themselves into one another'.

Why is it that 'the human mind should take these opposites not as dead, rigid, but as living, conditional, mobile, transforming themselves into one another'? Because that is just how things are in objective reality. The fact is that the unity or identity of opposites in objective things is not dead or rigid, but is living, conditional, mobile, temporary and relative; in given conditions, every contradictory aspect transforms itself into its opposite. Reflected in man's thinking, this becomes the Marxist world outlook of materialist dialectics. It is only the reactionary ruling classes of the past and present and the metaphysicians in their service who regard opposites not as living, conditional, mobile and transforming themselves into one another, but as dead and rigid, and they propagate this fallacy everywhere to delude the masses of the people, thus seeking to perpetuate their rule. The task of communists is to expose the fallacies of the reactionaries and metaphysicians, to propagate the dialectics inherent in things, and so accelerate the transformation of things and achieve the goal of revolution.

In speaking of the identity of opposites in given conditions, what we are referring to is real and concrete opposites and the real and concrete transformations of opposites into one another. There are innumerable transformations in mythology, for instance, Kua Fu's race with the sun in *Shan Hai Ching*,[17] Yi's shooting down of nine suns in *Huai Nan Tzu*,[18] the Monkey King's seventy-two metamorphoses in *Hsi Yu Chi*,[19] the numerous episodes of ghosts and foxes metamorphosed into human beings in the *Strange Tales of Liao Chai*,[20] etc. But these legendary transformations of opposites are not concrete changes reflecting concrete contradictions. They are naive, imaginary, subjectively conceived transformations conjured up in men's minds by innumerable real and complex transformations of opposites into one another. Marx said, 'All mythology masters and dominates and shapes the forces of nature in and through the imagination; hence it disappears as soon as man gains mastery over the forces of nature.'[21] The myriads of changes in mythology (and also in fairy tales) delight people because they imaginatively picture man's conquest of the forces of nature, and the best myths possess 'eternal charm', as Marx put it; but myths are not built out of the concrete contradictions existing in given conditions and therefore are not a scientific reflection of reality. That is to say, in myths or fairy tales the aspects constituting a contradiction have only an imaginary identity, not a concrete identity. The scientific reflection of the identity in real transformations is Marxist dialectics.

Why can an egg but not a stone be transformed into a chicken? Why is there identity between war and peace and none between war and a stone? Why can human beings give birth only to human beings and not to anything else? The sole reason is that the identity of opposites exists only in necessary given conditions. Without these necessary given conditions there can be no identity whatsoever.

Why is it that in Russia in 1917 the bourgeois-democratic February Revolution was directly linked with the proletarian socialist October Revolution, while in France the bourgeois revolution was not directly linked with a socialist revolution and the Paris Commune of 1871 ended in failure? Why is it, on the other hand, that the nomadic system of Mongolia and Central Asia has been directly linked with socialism? Why is it that the Chinese revolution can avoid a capitalist future and be directly linked with socialism without taking the old historical road of the Western countries, without passing through a period of bourgeois dictatorship? The sole reason is the concrete conditions of the time. When certain necessary conditions are present, certain contradictions arise in the process of development of things and, moreover, the opposites contained in them are interdependent and become transformed into one another; otherwise none of this would be possible.

Such is the problem of identity. What then is struggle? And what is the relation between identity and struggle?

Lenin said:

The unity (coincidence, identity, equal action) of opposites is conditional, temporary, transitory, relative. The struggle of mutually exclusive opposites is absolute, just as development and motion are absolute.[22]

What does this passage mean?

All processes have a beginning and an end, all processes transform themselves into their opposites. The constancy of all processes is relative, but the mutability manifested in the transformation of one process into another is absolute.

There are two states of motion in all things, that of relative rest and that of conspicuous change. Both are caused by the struggle between the two contradictory elements contained in a thing. When the thing is in the first state of motion, it is undergoing only quantitative and not qualitative change and consequently presents the outward appearance of being at rest. When the thing is in the second state of motion, the quantitative change of the first state has already reached a culminating point and gives rise to the dissolution of the thing as an entity and thereupon a qualitative change ensues, hence the appearance of a conspicuous change. Such unity, solidarity, combination, harmony, balance, stalemate, deadlock, rest, constancy, equilibrium, solidity, attraction, etc., as we see them in daily life, are all the appearances of things in the state of quantitative change. On the other hand, the dissolution of unity — that is, the destruction of this solidarity, combination, harmony, balance, stalemate, deadlock, rest, constancy, equilibrium, solidity and attraction, and the change of each into its opposite — are all the appearances of things in the state of qualitative change, the transformation of one process into another. Things are constantly transforming themselves from the first into the second state of motion; the struggle of opposites goes on in both states but the contradiction is resolved through the second state. That is why we say that the unity of opposites is conditional, temporary and relative, while the struggle of mutually exclusive opposites is absolute.

When we said above that two opposite things can coexist in a single entity and can transform themselves into each other because there is identity between them, we were speaking of conditionality, that is to say, in given conditions two contradictory things can be united and can transform themselves into each other, but in the absence of these conditions, they cannot constitute a contradiction, cannot coexist in the same entity and cannot transform themselves into one another. It is because the identity of opposites obtains only in given conditions that we have said identity is conditional and relative. We may add that the struggle between opposites permeates a process from beginning to end and makes one process transform itself into another, that it is ubiquitous, and that struggle is therefore unconditional and absolute.

The combination of conditional, relative identity and unconditional, absolute struggle constitutes the movement of opposites in all things.

We Chinese often say, 'Things that oppose each other also complement each other.'[23] That is, things opposed to each other have identity [are identical to one another]. This saying is dialectical and contrary to metaphysics. 'Oppose each other' refers to the mutual exclusion or the struggle of two contradictory aspects. 'Complement each other' means that in given conditions the two contradictory aspects unite and achieve identity. Yet struggle is inherent in identity and without struggle there can be no identity.

In identity there is struggle, in particularity there is universality, and in individuality there is generality. To quote Lenin, 'there is an absolute in the relative'.[24]

VI. THE PLACE OF ANTAGONISM IN CONTRADICTION

The question of the struggle of opposites includes the question of what is antagonism. Our answer is that antagonism is one form, but not the only form, of the struggle of opposites.

In human history, antagonism between classes exists as a particular manifestation of the struggle of opposites. Consider the contradiction between the exploiting and the exploited classes. Such contradictory classes coexist for a long time in the same society, be it slave society, feudal society or capitalist society, and they struggle with each other; but it is not until the contradiction between the two classes develops to a certain stage that it assumes the form of open antagonism and develops into revolution. The same holds for the transformation of peace into war in class society.

Before it explodes, a bomb is a single entity in which opposites coexist under given conditions. The explosion takes place only when a new condition, ignition, is present. An analogous situation arises in all those natural phenomena which finally assume the form of open conflict to resolve old contradictions and produce new things.

It is highly important to grasp this fact. It enables us to understand that revolutions and revolutionary wars are inevitable in class society and that, without them, it is impossible to accomplish any leap in social development and to overthrow the reactionary ruling classes and therefore impossible for the people to win political power. Communists must expose the deceitful propaganda of the reactionaries, such as the assertion that social revolution is unnecessary and impossible. They must firmly uphold the Marxist-Leninist theory of social revolution and enable the people to understand that social revolution is not only entirely necessary but also entirely practicable, and that the whole history of mankind and the triumph of the Soviet Union have confirmed this scientific truth.

However, we must make a concrete study of the circumstances of each specific struggle of opposites and should not arbitrarily apply the formula discussed above to everything. Contradiction and struggle are universal and absolute, but the methods of resolving contradictions, that is, the forms of struggle, differ according to the differences in the nature of the contradictions. Some contradictions are characterized by open antagonism, others are not. In accordance with the concrete development of things, some contradictions which were originally non-antagonistic develop into antagonistic ones, while others which were originally antagonistic develop into non-antagonistic ones.

As already mentioned, so long as classes exist, contradictions between correct and incorrect ideas in the Communist Party are reflections within the Party of class contradictions. At first, with regard to certain issues, such contradictions may not manifest themselves as antagonistic. But with the development of the class struggle, they may grow and become antagonistic. The history of the Communist Party of the Soviet Union shows us that the contradictions between the correct thinking of Lenin and Stalin and the fallacious thinking of Trotsky, Bukharin and others did not at first manifest themselves in an antagonistic form, but that later they did develop into antagonism. There are similar cases in the history of the Chinese Communist Party. At first the contradictions between the correct thinking of many of our Party comrades and the fallacious thinking of Chen Tu-hsiu, Chang Kuo-tao and others also did not manifest themselves in an antagonistic form, but later they did develop into antagonism. At present the contradiction between correct and incorrect thinking in our Party does not manifest itself in an antagonistic form, and if comrades who have committed mistakes can correct them, it will not develop into antagonism. Therefore, the Party must on the one hand wage a serious struggle against erroneous thinking, and on the other give the comrades who have committed errors ample opportunity to wake up. This being the case, excessive struggle is obviously inappropriate. But if the people who have committed errors persist in them and aggravate them, there is the possibility that this contradiction will develop into antagonism.

Economically, the contradiction between town and country is an extremely antagonistic one both in capitalist society, where under the rule of the bourgeoisie the towns ruthlessly plunder the countryside, and in the Kuomintang areas in China, where under the rule of foreign imperialism and the Chinese big comprador bourgeoisie the towns most rapaciously plunder the countryside. But in a socialist country and in our revolutionary base areas, this antagonistic contradiction has changed into one that is non-antagonistic; and when communist society is reached it will be abolished.

Lenin said, 'Antagonism and contradiction are not at all one and the same. Under socialism, the first will disappear, the second will remain.'[25] That is to say, antagonism is one form, but not the only form, of the struggle of opposites; the formula of antagonism cannot be arbitrarily applied everywhere.

VII. CONCLUSION

We may now say a few words to sum up. The law of contradiction in things, that is, the law of the unity of opposites, is the fundamental law of nature and of society and therefore also the fundamental law of thought. It stands opposed to the metaphysical world outlook. It represents a great revolution in the history of human knowledge. According to dialectical materialism, contradiction is present in all processes of objectively existing things and of subjective thought and permeates all these processes from beginning to end; this is the universality and absoluteness of contradiction. Each contradiction and each of its aspects have their respective characteristics; this is the particularity and relativity of contradiction. In given conditions, opposites possess identity, and consequently can coexist in a single entity and can transform themselves into each other; this again is the particularity and relativity of contradiction. But the struggle of opposites is ceaseless, it goes on both when the opposites are coexisting and when they are transforming themselves into each other, and becomes especially conspicuous when they are transforming themselves into one another; this again is the universality and absoluteness of contradiction. In studying the particularity and relativity of contradiction, we must give attention to the distinction between the principal contradiction and the non-principal contradictions and to the distinction between the principal aspect and the non-principal aspect of a contradiction; in studying the universality of contradiction and the struggle of opposites in contradiction, we must give attention to the distinction between the different forms of struggle. Otherwise we shall make mistakes. If, through study, we achieve a real understanding of the essentials explained above, we shall be able to demolish dogmatist ideas which are contrary to the basic principles of Marxism-Leninism and detrimental to our revolutionary cause, and our comrades with practical experience will be able to organize their experience into principles and avoid repeating empiricist errors. These are a few simple conclusions from our study of the law of contradiction.

COMBAT LIBERALISM

7 September 1937

We stand for active ideological struggle because it is the weapon for ensuring unity within the Party and the revolutionary organizations in the interest of our fight. Every communist and revolutionary should take up this weapon.

But liberalism rejects ideological struggle and stands for unprincipled peace, thus giving rise to a decadent, philistine attitude and bringing about political degeneration in certain units and individuals in the Party and the revolutionary organizations.

Liberalism manifests itself in various ways.

To let things slide for the sake of peace and friendship when a person has clearly gone wrong, and refrain from principled argument because he is an old acquaintance, a fellow townsman, a schoolmate, a close friend, a loved one, an old colleague or old subordinate; or to touch on the matter lightly instead of going into it thoroughly, so as to keep on good terms – the result is that both the organization and the individual are harmed: this is one type of liberalism.

To indulge in irresponsible criticism in private instead of actively putting forward one's suggestions to the organization; to say nothing to people to their faces but to gossip behind their backs, or to say nothing at a meeting but to gossip afterwards; to show no regard at all for the principles of collective life but to follow one's own inclination: this is a second type.

To let things drift if they do not affect one personally; to say as little as possible while knowing perfectly well what is wrong, to be worldly wise and play safe and seek only to avoid blame: this is a third type.

Not to obey orders but to give pride of place to one's own opinions. To demand special consideration from the organization but to reject its discipline: this is a fourth type.

To indulge in personal attacks, pick quarrels, vent personal spite or seek revenge instead of entering into an argument and struggling against incorrect views for the sake of unity or progress or getting the work done properly: this is a fifth type.

To hear incorrect views without rebutting them and even to hear counter-revolutionary remarks without reporting them, but instead to take them calmly as if nothing had happened: this is a sixth type.

To be among the masses and fail to conduct propaganda and agitation or speak at meetings or conduct investigations and inquiries among them, and instead to be indifferent to them and show no concern for their well-being, forgetting that one is a communist and behaving as if one were an ordinary non-communist: this is a seventh type.

To see someone harming the interests of the masses and yet not feel indignant, or dissuade or stop him or reason with him, but to allow him to continue: this is an eighth type.

To work half-heartedly without a definite plan or direction; to work perfunctorily and muddle along – 'So long as one remains a monk, one goes on tolling the bell': this is a ninth type.

To regard oneself as having rendered great service to the revolution, to pride oneself on being a veteran, to disdain minor assignments while being quite unequal to major tasks, to be slipshod in work and slack in study: this is a tenth type.

To be aware of one's own mistakes and yet make no attempt to correct them, taking a liberal attitude towards oneself: this is an eleventh type.

We could name more. But these eleven are the principal types.

They are all manifestations of liberalism.

Liberalism is extremely harmful in a revolutionary collective. It is a corrosive which eats away unity, undermines cohesion, causes apathy and creates dissension. It robs the revolutionary ranks of compact organization and strict discipline, prevents policies from being carried through and alienates the Party organizations from the masses which the Party leads. It is an extremely bad tendency.

Liberalism stems from petty-bourgeois selfishness, it places personal interests first and the interests of the revolution second, and this gives rise to ideological, political and organizational liberalism.

People who are liberals look upon the principles of Marxism as abstract dogma. They approve of Marxism, but are not prepared to practise it or to practise it in full; they are not prepared to replace their liberalism by Marxism. These people have their Marxism, but they have their liberalism as well – they talk Marxism but practise liberalism; they apply Marxism to others but liberalism to themselves. They keep both kinds of goods in stock and find a use for each. This is how the minds of certain people work.

Liberalism is a manifestation of opportunism and conflicts fundamentally with Marxism. It is negative and objectively has the effect of helping the enemy; that is why the enemy welcomes its preservation in our midst. Such being its nature, there should be no place for it in the ranks of the revolution.

We must use Marxism, which is positive in spirit, to overcome liberalism, which is negative. A communist should have largeness of mind and he should be staunch and active, looking upon the interests of the revolution as his very life and subordinating his personal interests to those of the revolution; always and everywhere he should adhere to principle and wage a tireless struggle against all incorrect ideas and actions, so as to consolidate the collective life of the Party and strengthen the ties between the Party and the masses; he should be more concerned about the Party and the masses than about any private person, and more concerned about others than about himself. Only thus can he be considered a communist.

All loyal, honest, active and upright communists must unite to oppose the liberal tendencies shown by certain people among us, and set them on the right path. This is one of the tasks on our ideological front.

6

THE CHINESE PEOPLE CANNOT BE COWED BY THE ATOM BOMB

28 January 1955

*Main points of a conversation with Ambassador Carl-Johan (Cay) Sundstrom,
the first Finnish envoy to China, when he presented his credentials.*

China and Finland are friendly countries. Our relations are based on the
Five Principles of Peaceful Coexistence.

China and Finland have never come into conflict. In the past, China's
wars with European countries were only with Britain, France, Germany,
tsarist Russia, Italy, the Austro-Hungarian Empire and Holland. These
countries all came from afar to commit aggressions against China, as in
the invasions by the Anglo-French allied forces and by the allied forces of
the eight powers, including the United States and Japan. Sixteen
countries took part in the war of aggression against Korea, including
Turkey and Luxembourg. All these aggressor countries claimed to be
peace-loving while branding Korea and China as aggressors.

Today, the danger of a world war and the threats to China come
mainly from the warmongers in the United States. They have occupied
our Taiwan and the Taiwan Straits and are contemplating an atomic war.
We have two principles: first, we don't want war; second, we will strike
back resolutely if anyone invades us. This is what we teach the members
of the Communist Party and the whole nation. The Chinese people are
not to be cowed by US atomic blackmail. Our country has a population
of 600 million and an area of 9,600,000 square kilometres. The United
States cannot annihilate the Chinese nation with its small stack of atom
bombs. Even if the US atom bombs were so powerful that, when
dropped on China, they would make a hole right through the earth, or

even blow it up, that would hardly mean anything to the universe as a whole, though it might be a major event for the solar system.

We have an expression, millet plus rifles. In the case of the United States, it is planes plus the A-bomb. However, if the United States with its planes plus the A-bomb is to launch a war of aggression against China, then China with its millet plus rifles is sure to emerge the victor. The people of the whole world will support us. As a result of the First World War, the tsar, the landlords and the capitalists in Russia were wiped out; as a result of the Second World War, Chiang Kai-shek and the landlords were overthrown in China and the East European countries and a number of countries in Asia were liberated. Should the United States launch a third world war and were it to last eight or ten years, the result would be the elimination of the ruling classes in the United States, Britain and the other accomplice countries and the transformation of most of the world into countries led by the Communist Parties. World wars end not in favour of the warmongers but in favour of the Communist Parties and the revolutionary people in all lands. If the warmongers are to make war, then they mustn't blame us for making revolution or engaging in 'subversive activities' as they keep saying all the time. If they desist from war, they can survive a little longer on this earth. But the sooner they make war the sooner they will be wiped from the face of the earth. Then a people's united nations would be set up, maybe in Shanghai, maybe somewhere in Europe, or it might be set up again in New York, provided the US warmongers had been wiped out.

7

US IMPERIALISM IS A PAPER TIGER

14 July 1956

Part of a talk with two Latin American public figures.

The United States is flaunting the anti-communist banner everywhere in order to perpetrate aggression against other countries.

The United States owes debts everywhere. It owes debts not only to the countries of Latin America, Asia and Africa, but also to the countries of Europe and Oceania. The whole world, Britain included, dislikes the United States. The masses of the people dislike it. Japan dislikes the United States because it oppresses her. None of the countries in the East is free from US aggression. The United States has invaded our Taiwan Province. Japan, Korea, the Philippines, Vietnam and Pakistan all suffer from US aggression, although some of them are allies of the United States. The people are dissatisfied and in some countries so are the authorities.

All oppressed nations want independence.

Everything is subject to change. The big decadent forces will give way to the small new-born forces. The small forces will change into big forces because the majority of the people demand this change. The US imperialist forces will change from big to small because the American people, too, are dissatisfied with their government.

In my own lifetime I myself have witnessed such changes. Some of us present were born in the Ching dynasty and others after the 1911 Revolution.

The Ching dynasty was overthrown long ago. By whom? By the party led by Sun Yat-sen, together with the people. Sun Yat-sen's forces were so small that the Ching officials didn't take him seriously. He led many uprisings which failed each time. In the end, however, it was Sun Yat-sen who brought down the Ching dynasty. Bigness is nothing to be afraid of. The big will be overthrown by the small. The small will become big. After overthrowing the Ching dynasty, Sun Yat-sen met with defeat. For he failed to satisfy the demands of the people, such as their demands for land and for opposition to imperialism. Nor did he understand the necessity of suppressing the counter-revolutionaries who were then moving about freely. Later, he suffered defeat at the hands of Yuan Shih-kai, the chieftain of the Northern warlords. Yuan Shih-kai's forces were larger than Sun Yat-sen's. But here again this law operated: small forces linked with the people become strong, while big forces opposed to the people become weak. Subsequently Sun Yat-sen's bourgeois-democratic revolutionaries cooperated with us communists and together we defeated the warlord set-up left behind by Yuan Shih-kai.

Chiang Kai-shek's rule in China was recognized by the governments of all countries and lasted twenty-two years, and his forces were the biggest. Our forces were small, 50,000 Party members at first but only a few thousand after counter-revolutionary suppressions. The enemy made trouble everywhere. Again this law operated: the big and strong end up in defeat because they are divorced from the people, whereas the small and weak emerge victorious because they are linked with the people and work in their interest. That's how things turned out in the end.

During the anti-Japanese war, Japan was very powerful, the Kuomintang troops were driven to the hinterland, and the armed forces led by the Communist Party could only conduct guerrilla warfare in the rural areas behind the enemy lines. Japan occupied large Chinese cities such as Peking, Tientsin, Shanghai, Nanking, Wuhan and Canton. Nevertheless, like Germany's Hitler the Japanese militarists collapsed in a few years, in accordance with the same law.

We underwent innumerable difficulties and were driven from the south to the north, while our forces fell from several hundred thousand strong to a few tens of thousands. At the end of the 25,000–li Long March we had only 25,000 men left.

In the history of our Party many erroneous 'Left' and Right lines have occurred. Gravest of all were the Right deviationist line of Chen Tu-hsiu and the 'Left' deviationist line of Wang Ming. Besides, there were the Right deviationist errors committed by Chang Kuo-tao, Kao Kang and others.

There is also a good side to mistakes, for they can educate the people and the Party. We have had a good many teachers by negative example, such as Japan, the United States, Chiang Kai-shek, Chen Tu-hsiu, Li Li-san, Wang Ming, Chang Kuo-tao and Kao Kang. We paid a very high price to learn from these teachers by negative example. In the past, Britain made war on us many times. Britain, the United States, Japan, France, Germany, Italy, tsarist Russia and Holland were all very interested in this land of ours. They were all our teachers by negative example and we were their pupils.

During the War of Resistance, our troops grew and became 900,000 strong through fighting against Japan. Then came the War of Liberation. Our arms were inferior to those of the Kuomintang. The Kuomintang troops then numbered four million, but in three years of fighting we wiped out eight million of them all told. The Kuomintang, though aided by US imperialism, could not defeat us. The big and strong cannot win, it is always the small and weak who win out.

Now US imperialism seems quite powerful, but in reality it isn't. It is very weak politically because it is divorced from the masses of the people and is disliked by everybody and by the American people too. In appearance it is very powerful but in reality it is nothing to be afraid of: it is a paper tiger. Outwardly a tiger, it is made of paper, unable to withstand the wind and the rain. I believe the United States is nothing but a paper tiger.

History as a whole, the history of class society for thousands of years, has proved this point: the strong must give way to the weak. This holds true for the Americas as well.

Only when imperialism is eliminated can peace prevail. The day will come when the paper tigers will be wiped out. But they won't become extinct of their own accord: they need to be battered by the wind and the rain.

When we say US imperialism is a paper tiger, we are speaking in terms of strategy. Regarding it as a whole, we must despise it. But regarding each part, we must take it seriously. It has claws and fangs. We have to destroy it piecemeal. For instance, if it has ten fangs, knock off one the first time, and there will be nine left, knock off another, and there will be eight left. When all the fangs are gone, it will still have claws. If we deal with it step by step and in earnest, we shall certainly succeed in the end.

Strategically, we must utterly despise US imperialism. Tactically, we must take it seriously. In struggling against it, we must take each battle, each encounter, seriously. At present, the United States is powerful, but when looked at in a broader perspective, as a whole and from a long-term viewpoint, it has no popular support, its policies are disliked by the people, because it oppresses and exploits them. For this reason, the tiger is doomed. Therefore, it is nothing to be afraid of and can be despised. But today the United States still has strength, turning out more than 100 million tons of steel a year and hitting out everywhere. That is why we must continue to wage struggles against it, fight it with all our might and wrest one position after another from it. And that takes time.

It seems that the countries of the Americas, Asia and Africa will have to go on quarrelling with the United States till the very end, till the paper tiger is destroyed by the wind and the rain.

To oppose US imperialism, people of European origin in the Latin-American countries should unite with the indigenous Indians. Perhaps the white immigrants from Europe can be divided into two groups, one composed of rulers and the other of ruled. This should make it easier for the group of oppressed white people to get close to the local people, for their position is the same.

Our friends in Latin America, Asia and Africa are in the same position as we and are doing the same kind of work, doing something for the people to lessen their oppression by imperialism. If we do a good job, we can root out imperialist oppression. In this we are comrades.

We are of the same nature as you in our opposition to imperialist oppression, differing only in geographical position, nationality and language. But we are different in nature from imperialism, and the very sight of it makes us sick.

What use is imperialism? The Chinese people will have none of it, nor will the people in the rest of the world. There is no reason for the existence of imperialism.

8

CONCERNING STALIN'S *ECONOMIC PROBLEMS OF SOCIALISM IN THE USSR*

November 1958

Provincial and regional committees must study this book.[1] In the past everyone read it without gaining a deep impression. It should be studied in conjunction with China's actual circumstances. The first three chapters contain much that is worth paying attention to, much that is correct, although there are places where perhaps Stalin himself did not make things clear enough. For example, in chapter 1 he says only a few things about objective laws and how to go about planning the economy, without unfolding his ideas; or, it may be that to his mind Soviet planning of the economy already reflected objective governing principles. On the question of heavy industry, light industry and agriculture, the Soviet Union did not lay enough emphasis on the latter two and had losses as a result. In addition, they did not do a good job of combining the immediate and the long-term interests of the people. In the main they walked on one leg. Comparing the planning, which of us after all had the better-adapted 'planned proportionate development'? Another point: Stalin emphasized only technology, technical cadre. He wanted nothing but technology, nothing but cadre; no politics, no masses. This too is walking on one leg! And in industry they walk on one leg when they pay attention to heavy industry but not to light industry. Furthermore, they did not point out the main aspects of the contradictions in the relationships between the departments of heavy industry. They exaggerated the importance of heavy industry, claiming that steel was the foundation, machinery the heart and soul. Our position is that grain is the mainstay of agriculture, steel of industry, and that if steel is taken as the mainstay, then once we have the raw material the machine industry will follow along. Stalin raised questions in chapter 1: he suggested the objective governing principles, but he failed to provide satisfactory answers.

In chapter 2 he discusses commodities, in chapter 3 the law of value. Relatively speaking, I favour many of the views expressed. To divide production into two major departments and to say that the means of production are not commodities – these points deserve study. In Chinese agriculture there are still many means of production that should be commodities. My view is that the last of the three appended letters[2] is entirely wrong. It expresses a deep uneasiness, a belief that the peasantry cannot be trusted to release agricultural machinery but would hang on to it. On the one hand Stalin says that the means of production belong to state ownership. On the other, he says that the peasants cannot afford them. The fact is that he is deceiving himself. The state controlled the peasantry very, very tightly, inflexibly. For the two transitions Stalin failed to find the proper ways and means, a vexing matter for him.

Capitalism leaves behind it the commodity form, which we must still retain for the time being. Commodity exchange laws governing value play no regulating role in our production. This role is played by planning, by the great leap forward under planning, by politics-in-command. Stalin speaks only of the production relations, not of the superstructure, nor of the relationship between superstructure and economic base. Chinese cadres participate in production; workers participate in management. Sending cadres down to lower levels to be tempered, discarding old rules and regulations – all these pertain to the superstructure, to ideology. Stalin mentions economics only, not politics. He may speak of selfless labour, but in reality even an extra hour's labour is begrudged. There is no selflessness at all. The role of people, the role of the labourer – these are not mentioned. If there were no communist movement it is hard to imagine making the transition to communism. 'All people are for me, I for all people.' This does not belong. It ends up with everything being connected to the self. Some say Marx said it. If he did let's not make propaganda out of it. 'All people for me' means everybody for me, the individual. 'I am for all.' Well, how many can you be for?

Bourgeois right is manifested as bourgeois law and education. We want to destroy a part of the ideology of bourgeois right, the lordly pose, the three styles [the bureaucratic, the sectarian and the subjective] and the five airs [the officious, the arrogant, the apathetic, the extravagant, and the precious]. But commodity circulation, the commodity form, the law of value, these, on the other hand, cannot be destroyed summarily, despite the fact that they are bourgeois categories. If we now carry on propaganda for the total elimination of the ideology of bourgeois right it would not be a reasonable position, bear in mind.

There are a few in socialist society – landlords, rich peasants, Right-wingers – who are partial to capitalism and advocate it. But the vast majority are thinking of crossing over to communism. This, however, has to be done by steps. You cannot get to heaven in one step. Take the people's communes: on the one hand, they have to develop self-sufficient production, on the other, commodity exchange. We use commodity exchange and the law of value as tools for developing production and facilitating the transition. We are a nation whose commodity production is very underdeveloped. Last year we produced 3.7 trillion catties of food grains.[3] Of that number, commodity grains amounted to about 800 or 900 billion catties. Apart from grain, industrial crops like cotton and hemp are also underdeveloped. Therefore we have to have this [commodity] stage of development. At present there are still a good many counties where there is no charge for food but they cannot pay wages. In Hopei there are three such counties, and another that can pay wages, but not much: three or five yuan. So we still have to develop production, to develop things that can be sold other than food grains. At the Sian Agricultural Conference this point was insufficiently considered. In sum, we are a nation whose commerce is underdeveloped, and yet in many respects we have entered socialism. We must eliminate a part of bourgeois right, but commodity production and exchange must still be kept. Now there is a tendency to feel that the sooner communism comes the better. Some suggest that in only three or five years we will be making the transition. In Fan County, Shantung, it was suggested that four years might be a little slow!

At present there are some economists who do not enjoy economics – Yaroshenko[4] for one. For now and until some time in the future we shall have to expand allocation and delivery to the communes. And we shall have to expand commodity production. Otherwise we won't be able to pay wages or improve life. Some of our comrades are guilty of a misapprehension when, coming upon commodities and commodity production, they want to destroy bourgeois rule every single day, e.g., they say wages, grades, etc., are detrimental to the free-supply system. In 1953 we changed the free-supply system into a wage system.[5] This approach was basically correct. We had to take one step backward. But there was a problem: we also took a step backward in the matter of grades. As a result there was a furor over this matter. After a period of rectification grades were scaled down. The grade system is a father–son relation, a cat-and-mouse relation. It has to be attacked day after day. Sending down the cadres to lower levels, running the experimental fields[6] – these are ways of changing the grade system; otherwise, no great leaps!

In urban people's communes capitalists can enter and serve as personnel. But the capitalist label should stay on them. With respect to socialism and communism, what is meant by constructing socialism? We raise two points: (1) the concentrated manifestation of constructing socialism is making socialist, all-embracing public ownership[7] a reality; (2) constructing socialism means turning commune-level collective ownership into public ownership. Some comrades disapprove of drawing such a hard-and-fast line between these two types of ownership system, seeing the communes as being already completely publicly owned. In reality, however, there are two distinct systems. One type is public ownership, as in the Anshan Iron and Steel Works; the other is commune-level collective ownership. If we do not recognize this, what is the use of socialist construction? Stalin admitted the distinction when he spoke of three conditions. These three basic conditions make sense and may be summarized as follows: (1) increase social output; (2) raise collective ownership to public ownership; (3) go from exchange of commodities to exchange of products, from exchange value to use value.

On these two above-mentioned points we Chinese are (1) expanding and striving to increase output, concurrently promoting industry and agriculture with preference given to developing heavy industry; and (2) raising small collective ownership to public ownership, and then further to all-embracing public ownership. Those who do not admit these distinctions [between types of ownership] would seem to hold the view that we have already arrived at public ownership. This is wrong. Stalin was speaking of culture when he proposed the three conditions, the physical development and education of the whole people. For this he proposed four conditions: (a) six hours' work per day; (b) combining technical education with work; (c) improving residential conditions; (d) raising wages. Raising wages and lowering prices are particularly helpful here, but the political conditions are missing.

All these conditions are basically to increase production. Once output is plentiful it will be easier to solve the problem of turning collective ownership into public ownership. To increase production we need 'More! Faster! Better! More economically!' And for this we need politics-in-command, the four concurrent promotions, the rectification campaigns, the smashing of the ideology of bourgeois right. Add to this the people's communes and it becomes all the easier to achieve 'More! Faster! Better! More economically!'

What are the implications of all-embracing public ownership? There are two: (1) the means of production are owned by the whole people; and (2) the output is owned by the whole people.

The characteristic of the people's commune is that it is the basic level at which industry, agriculture, the military, education and commerce are to be integrated in our social structure. At the present time it is the basic-level administrative organization. The militia deals with foreign threats, especially from the imperialists. The commune is the best organizational form for carrying out the two transitions, first from socialist (the present) to all-embracing public, and then from all-embracing public to communist ownership. In future, when the transitions have been completed, the commune will be the basic mechanism of communist society.

9

CRITIQUE OF STALIN'S
ECONOMIC PROBLEMS OF
SOCIALISM IN THE USSR

[1958]

Stalin's book from first to last says nothing about the superstructure. It is not concerned with people; it considers things, not people. Does the kind of supply system for consumer goods help spur economic development or not? He should at least have touched on this. Is it better to have commodity production or is it better not to? Everyone has to study this. Stalin's point of view in his last letter[1] is almost completely wrong. The basic error is mistrust of the peasants.

Parts of the first, second and third chapters are correct; other parts could have been clearer. For example, the discussion of the planned economy is not complete. The rate of development of the Soviet economy is not high enough, although it is faster than the capitalists' rate. Relations between agriculture and industry, as well as between light and heavy industry, are not clearly explained.

It looks as if they have had serious losses. The relationship between long- and short-term interests has not seen any spectacular developments. They walk on one leg, we walk on two. They believe that technology decides everything, that cadres decide everything, speaking only of 'expert', never of 'Red', only of the cadres, never of the masses. This is walking on one leg. As far as heavy industry goes, they have failed to find the primary contradiction, calling steel the foundation, machinery the heart and guts, coal the food . . . For us steel is the mainstay, the primary contradiction in industry, while food grains are the mainstay in agriculture. Other things develop proportionally.

In the first chapter he discusses grasping the laws, but without proposing a method. On commodity production and the law of value he has a number of views that we approve of ourselves, but there are problems as well. Limiting commodity production to the means of subsistence is really rather doubtful. Mistrust of the peasants is the basic viewpoint of the third letter. Essentially, Stalin did not discover a way to make the transition from collective to public ownership. Commodity production and exchange are forms we have kept, while in connection with the law of value we must speak of planning and at the same time politics-in-command. He speaks only of the relations of production, not of the superstructure or politics, or the role of the people. Communism cannot be reached unless there is a communist movement.[2]

1.

These comrades . . . it is evident . . . confuse laws of science, which reflect objective processes in nature or society, processes which take place independently of the will of man, with the laws which are issued by governments, which are made by the will of man, and which have only juridical validity. But they must not be confused.

This principle is basically correct, but two things are wrong: first, the conscious activity of the Party and the masses is not sufficiently brought out; second, it is not comprehensive enough in that it fails to explain that what makes government decrees correct is not only that they emerge from the will of the working class but also the fact that they faithfully reflect the imperatives of objective economic laws.

2.

Leaving aside astronomical, geological, and other similar processes, which man really is powerless to influence, even if he has come to know the laws of their development . . .

This argument is wrong. Human knowledge and the capability to transform nature have no limit. Stalin did not consider these matters developmentally. What cannot now be done, may be done in the future.

3.

> *The same must be said of the laws of economic development, the laws of political economy – whether in the period of capitalism or in the period of socialism. Here, too, the laws of economic development, as in the case of natural science, are objective laws, reflecting processes of economic development which take place independently of the will of man.*

How do we go about planning the economy? There is not enough attention given to light industry, to agriculture.

4.

> *That is why Engels says in the same book: 'The laws of his own social action, hitherto standing face to face with man as laws of nature foreign to, and dominating, him, will then be used with full understanding, and so mastered by him' (Anti-Dühring).*

Freedom is necessary objective law understood by people. Such law confronts people, is independent of them. But once people understand it, they can control it.

5.

> *The specific role of Soviet government was due to two circumstances: first, that what Soviet government had to do was not to replace one form of exploitation by another, as was the case in earlier revolutions, but to abolish exploitation altogether; second, that in view of the absence in the country of any ready-made rudiments of a socialist economy, it had to create new, socialist forms of economy, 'starting from scratch,' so to speak.*

The inevitability of socialist economic laws – that is something that needs to be studied. At the Ch'engtu Conference I said that we would have to see whether or not our general programme ('More! Faster! Better! More economically!' the three concurrent promotions, and the mass line) would flop;[3] or if it could succeed. This cannot be demonstrated for several or even as many as ten years. The laws of the revolution, which used to be doubted by some, have now been proved correct because the enemy has been overthrown. Can socialist construction work? People still have doubts. Does our Chinese practice conform to the economic laws of China? This has to be studied. My view is that if the practice conforms generally, things will be all right.

6.

> *This [creating new, socialist forms of economy 'from scratch'] was undoubtedly a difficult, complex, and unprecedented task.*

With respect to the creating of socialist economic forms we have the precedent of the Soviet Union and for this reason should do a bit better than they. If we ruin things it will show that Chinese Marxism does not work. As to the difficulty and complexity of the tasks, things are no different from what the Soviet Union faced.

7.

> *It is said that the necessity for balanced (proportionate) development of the national economy in our country enables the Soviet government to abolish existing economic laws and to create new ones. That is absolutely untrue. Our yearly and five-yearly plans must not be confused with the objective economic law of balanced, proportionate development of the national economy.*

This is the crux of the matter.

8.

> *That means that the law of balanced development of the national economy makes it possible for our planning bodies to plan social production correctly. But possibility must not be confused with actuality. They are two different things. In order to turn the possibility into actuality, it is necessary to study this economic law, to master it, to learn to apply it with full understanding, and to compile such plans as fully reflect the requirements of this law. It cannot be said that the requirements of this economic law are fully reflected by our yearly and five-yearly plans.*

The central point of this passage is that we must not confuse the objective law of planned proportionate development with planning. In the past we too devised plans, but they frequently caused a storm. Too much! Too little! Blindly we bumped into things, never sure of the best way. Only after suffering tortuous lessons, moving in U-shaped patterns, everyone racking their brains to think of answers, did we hit upon the forty-article agricultural programme which we are now putting into effect. And we are in the midst of devising a new forty articles. After another three years' bitter struggle we will develop further; after full and sufficient discussions we will again proceed. Can we make it a reality? It remains to be proved in objective practice. We worked on industry for eight years but did not realize that we had to take steel as the mainstay. This was the principal aspect of the contradiction in industry. It was monism. Among the large, the medium and the small, we take the large as the mainstay; between the centre and the regions, the centre. Of the two sides of any contradiction one is the principal side. As important as eight years' achievements are, we were feeling our way along, nonetheless. It cannot be said that our planning of production was entirely correct, that it entirely reflected the objective laws. Planning is done by the whole Party, not simply the planning committee or the economics committee, but by all levels; everyone is involved. In this passage Stalin is theoretically correct. But there is not yet a finely detailed analysis, nor even the beginnings of a clear explanation. The Soviets did not distinguish among the large, the medium and the small, the region and the centre; nor did they promote concurrently industry and agriculture. They have not walked on two legs at all. Their rules and regulations hamstrung people. But we have not adequately studied and grasped our situation, and as a result our plans have not fully reflected objective laws either.

9.

> Let us examine Engels's formula. Engels's formula cannot be considered fully clear and precise, because it does not indicate whether it is referring to the seizure by society of all or only part of the means of production; that is, whether all or only part of the means of production are converted into public property. Hence, this formula of Engels's may be understood either way.

This analysis touches the essentials! The problem is dividing the means of production into two parts. To say the means of production are not commodities deserves study.

10.

In this section, 'Commodity Production under Socialism', Stalin has not comprehensively set forth the conditions for the existence of commodities. The existence of two kinds of ownership is the main premise for commodity production. But ultimately commodity production is also related to the productive forces. For this reason, even under completely socialized public ownership, commodity exchange will still have to be operative in some areas.

11.

> *It follows from this that Engels has in mind countries where capitalism and the concentration of production have advanced far enough both in industry and agriculture to permit the expropriation of all the means of production in the country and their conversion into public property. Engels, consequently, considers that in such countries, parallel with the socialization of all the means of production, commodity production should be put an end to. And that, of course, is correct.*

Stalin's analysis of Engels's formula is correct. At present there is a strong tendency to do away with commodity production. People get upset the minute they see commodity production, taking it for capitalism itself. But it looks as if commodity production will have to be greatly developed and the money supply increased for the sake of the solidarity of several hundred million peasants. This poses a problem for the ideology of several hundred thousand cadres as well as for the solidarity of several hundred million peasants. We now possess only a part of the means of production. But it appears that there are those who wish to declare at once ownership by the whole people, divesting the small and medium producers. But they fail to declare the category of ownership! Is it to be commune-owned or county-owned? To abolish commodities and commodity production in this way, merely by declaring public ownership, is to strip the peasantry. At the end of 1955, procurement and purchase got us almost 90 billion catties of grain, causing us no little trouble. Everyone was talking about food, and household after household was talking about unified purchase. But it was purchase, after all, not allocation. Only later did the crisis ease when we made the decision to make this 83 billion catties of grain. I cannot understand why people have forgotten these things so promptly.

12.

> *I leave aside in this instance the question of the importance of foreign trade to Britain and the vast part it plays in her national economy. I think that only after an investigation of this question can it be finally decided what would be the future [fate] of commodity production in Britain after the proletariat had assumed power and all the means of production had been nationalized.*

Fate depends on whether or not commodity production is abolished.

13.

> *But here is a question: What are the proletariat and its party to do in countries, ours being a case in point, where the conditions are favorable for the assumption of power by the proletariat and the overthrow of capitalism [where capitalism has so concentrated the means of production in industry that they may be expropriated and made the property of society, but where agriculture, notwithstanding the growth of capitalism, is divided up among numerous small and medium owner-producers to such an extent as to make it impossible to consider the expropriation of these producers?]*[4] . . . *[This] would throw the peasantry into the camp of the enemies of the proletariat for a long time.*

In sum, the principle governing commodity production was not grasped. Chinese economists are Marxist-Leninist as far as book learning goes. But when they encounter economic practice Marxism–Leninism gets short-changed. Their thinking is confused. If we make mistakes we will lead the peasantry to the enemy side.

14.–18.

> Lenin's answer may be briefly summed up as follows:
> 14. *Favorable conditions for the assumption of power should not be missed – the proletariat should assume power without waiting until capitalism has succeeded in ruining the millions of small and medium individual producers.*
> 15. *The means of production in industry should be expropriated and converted into public property.*

16. *As to the small and medium individual producers, they should be gradually united in producers' cooperatives, i.e., in large agricultural enterprises, collective farms.*

17. *Industry should be developed to the utmost and the collective farms should be placed on the modern technical basis of large-scale production, not expropriating them, but on the contrary generously supplying them with first-class tractors and other machines.*

18. *In order to ensure an economic bond between town and country, between industry and agriculture, commodity production (exchange through purchase and sale) should be preserved for a certain period, it being the form of economic tie with the town which is alone acceptable to the peasants, and Soviet trade − state, cooperative, and collective-farm − should be developed to the full and the capitalists of all types and descriptions ousted from trading activity.*

The history of socialist construction in our country has shown that this path of development, mapped out by Lenin, has fully justified itself.

These five points are all correct.

14. This passage has a correct analysis. Take conditions in China. There is development.

15. Our policy towards the national bourgeoisie has been to redeem their property.

16. We are developing the people's communes on an ever larger scale.

17. This is precisely what we are doing now.

18. There are those who want no commodity production, but they are wrong. On commodity production we still have to take it from Stalin, who, in turn, got it from Lenin. Lenin had said to devote the fullest energies to developing commerce. We would rather say, devote the fullest energies to developing industry, agriculture and commerce. The essence of the problem is the peasant question. There are those who regard the peasant as even more conscious than the workers. We have carried through or are in the process of carrying through on these five items. Some areas still have to be developed, such as commune-run industry or concurrent promotion of industry and agriculture.

19.

> *There can be no doubt that in the case of all capitalist countries with a more or less numerous class of small and medium producers, this path of development is the only possible and expedient one for the victory of socialism.*

Lenin said the same thing.

20.

> *Commodity production must not be regarded as something sufficient unto itself, something independent of the surrounding economic conditions. Commodity production is older than capitalist production. It existed in slave-owning society, and served it, but did not lead to capitalism. It existed in feudal society and served it, yet, although it prepared some of the conditions for capitalist production, it did not lead to capitalism.*
>
> *Bearing in mind that in our country commodity production is not so boundless and all-embracing as it is under capitalist conditions, being confined within strict bounds thanks to such decisive economic conditions as social ownership of the means of production, the abolition of the system of wage labor, and the elimination of the system of exploitation, why then, one asks, cannot commodity production similarly serve our socialist society for a certain period without leading to capitalism?*

This statement is a little exaggerated. But it is true that commodity production was not a capitalist institution exclusively.

The second plenary session of the Central Committee suggested policies of utilizing, restricting and transforming (commodity production).

This condition is fully operative in China.

This point is entirely correct. We no longer have such circumstances and conditions. There are those who fear commodities. Without exception they fear capitalism, not realizing that with the elimination of capitalists it is allowable to expand commodity production vastly. We are still backward in commodity production, behind Brazil and India. Commodity production is not an isolated thing. Look at the context: capitalism or socialism. In a capitalist context it is capitalist commodity production. In a socialist context it is socialist commodity production. Commodity production has existed since ancient times. Buying and selling began in what history calls the Shang ['commerce'] dynasty. The last king of the Shang dynasty, Chou, was competent in civil and military matters, but he was turned into a villain along with the first emperor of the Ch'in[5] and Ts'ao Ts'ao.[6] This is wrong. 'Better to have no books than complete faith in them.'[7] In capitalist society there are no socialist institutions considered as social institutions, but the working class and socialist ideology do exist in capitalist society. The thing that determines commodity production is the surrounding economic conditions. The question is, can commodity production be regarded as a useful instrument for furthering socialist production? I think commodity production will serve socialism quite tamely. This can be discussed among the cadres.

21.

> *It is said that, since the domination of social ownership of the means of production has been established in our country, and the system of wage labor and exploitation has been abolished, commodity production has lost all meaning and should therefore be done away with.*

Change 'our country' to 'China' and it becomes most intriguing.

22.

> *Today there are two basic forms of socialist production in our country: state, or publicly owned production, and collective farm production, which cannot be said to be publicly owned.*

'Today' refers to 1952, thirty-five years after their revolution. We stand but nine years from ours.

He refers to two basic forms. In the communes not only land and machinery but labour, seeds and other means of production as well are commune-owned. Thus the output is so owned. But don't think the Chinese peasants are so wonderfully advanced. In Hsiuwu County, Honan, the Party secretary was concerned whether or not, in the event of flood or famine, the state would pay wages after public ownership was declared and the free-supply system instituted. He was also concerned that in times of bumper harvests the state would appropriate public grain but fail to pay wages, leaving the peasants to suffer whether the harvest succeeds or fails. This represents the concerns of the peasants. Marxists should be concerned with these problems. Our commodity production should be developed to the fullest, but it is going to take fifteen years or more and patience as well. We have waged war for decades. Now we still have to have patience, to wait for Taiwan's liberation, to wait for socialist construction to be going well. Don't hope for early victories!

23.

[How the two basic forms of ownership will ultimately become one] is a special question which requires separate discussion.

Stalin is avoiding the issue, having failed to find a method or suitable formulation [on the transition from collective to public ownership].

24.

Consequently, our commodity production is not of the ordinary type, but is a special kind of commodity production, commodity production without capitalists, which is concerned mainly with the goods of associated socialist producers (the state, the collective farms, the cooperatives), the sphere of action of which is confined to items of personal consumption, which obviously cannot possibly develop into capitalist production, and which, together with its 'money economy,' is designed to serve the development and consolidation of socialist production.

The 'sphere of action' is not limited to items of individual consumption. Some means of production have to be classed as commodities. If agricultural output consists of commodities but industrial output does not, then how is exchange to be carried out? If 'our country' is changed to 'China', the paragraph becomes all the more interesting to read. In China not only consumer goods but the agricultural means of production have to be supplied. Stalin never sold the means of production to the peasants. Khrushchev changed that.

[Chairman Mao commented on page 13 of the original text:] Let us not confuse the problem of the dividing line between socialism and communism with the problem of the dividing line between collective and public ownership. The collective ownership system leaves us with the problem of commodity production, the goal of which is consolidating the worker–peasant alliance and developing production. Today there are those who say that the communism of the peasants is glorious. After one trip to the rural areas they think the peasantry is simply wonderful, that they are about to enter paradise, that they are better than the workers. This is the surface phenomenon. We shall have to see if the peasants really have a communist spirit, and more than that, we shall have to examine the commune ownership system, including the extent to which the means of production and subsistence belong to communal collective ownership. As the county Party committee secretary of Hsiuwu, Honan, said, we still have to develop commodity production, and not charge blindly ahead.

25.

Further, I think that we must also discard certain other concepts taken from Marx's Capital *– where Marx was concerned with an analysis of capitalism – and artificially applied to our socialist relations . . . It is natural that Marx used concepts (categories) which fully corresponded to capitalist relations. But it is strange, to say the least, to use these concepts now, when the working class is not only not bereft of power and means of production, but, on the contrary, is in possession of the power and controls the means of production. Talk of labor power being a commodity, and of 'hiring' of workers sounds rather absurd now, under our system, as though the working class, which possesses means of production, hires itself and sells its labor power to itself.*

In particular, the means of production in the industrial sector.

Commodity production has to be vastly developed, not for profits but for the peasantry, the agricultural–industrial alliance, and the development of production.

Especially after rectification. After the rectification and anti-Rightist campaigns labour-power was no longer a commodity. It was in the service of the people, not the dollar. The labour-power question is not resolved until labour-power is no longer a commodity.

26.

It is sometimes asked whether the law of value exists and operates in our country, under the socialist system.

The law of value does not have a regulative function. Planning and politics-in-command play that role.

27.

True, the law of value has no regulating function in our socialist production.

In our society the law of value has no regulative function, that is, has no determinative function. Planning determines production, e.g., for pigs or steel we do not use the law of value; we rely on planning.

10

ON THE CORRECT HANDLING OF CONTRADICTIONS AMONG THE PEOPLE

27 February 1957

Speech at the Eleventh Session (Enlarged) of the Supreme State Conference. Comrade Mao Tse-tung went over the verbatim record and made certain additions before its publication in the People's Daily *on 19 June 1957.*

Our general subject is the correct handling of contradictions among the people. For convenience, let us discuss it under twelve subheadings. Although reference will be made to contradictions between ourselves and the enemy, this discussion will centre on contradictions among the people.

I. TWO TYPES OF CONTRADICTIONS DIFFERING IN NATURE

Never before has our country been as united as it is today. The victories of the bourgeois-democratic revolution and of the socialist revolution and our achievements in socialist construction have rapidly changed the face of the old China. A still brighter future lies ahead for our motherland. The days of national disunity and chaos which the people detested are gone, never to return. Led by the working class and the Communist Party, our 600 million people, united as one, are engaged in the great task of building socialism. The unification of our country, the unity of our people and the unity of our various nationalities – these are the basic guarantees for the sure triumph of our cause. However, this does not mean that contradictions no longer exist in our society. To imagine that none exist is a naive idea which is at variance with objective reality. We are confronted with two types of social contradictions – those between ourselves and the enemy and those among the people. The two are totally different in nature.

To understand these two different types of contradictions correctly, we must first be clear about what is meant by 'the people' and what is meant by 'the enemy'. The concept of 'the people' varies in content in different countries and in different periods of history in a given country. Take our own country for example. During the War of Resistance Against Japan, all those classes, strata and social groups opposing Japanese aggression came within the category of the people, while the Japanese imperialists, their Chinese collaborators and the pro-Japanese elements were all enemies of the people. During the War of Liberation, the US imperialists and their running dogs – the bureaucrat-capitalists, the landlords and the Kuomintang reactionaries who represented these two classes – were the enemies of the people, while the other classes, strata and social groups which opposed them all came within the category of the people. At the present stage, the period of building socialism, the classes, strata and social groups which favour, support and work for the cause of socialist construction all come within the category of the people, while the social forces and groups which resist the socialist revolution and are hostile to or sabotage socialist construction are all enemies of the people.

The contradictions between ourselves and the enemy are antagonistic contradictions. Within the ranks of the people, the contradictions among the working people are non-antagonistic, while those between the exploited and the exploiting classes have a non-antagonistic as well as an antagonistic aspect. There have always been contradictions among the people, but they are different in content in each period of the revolution and in the period of building socialism. In the conditions prevailing in China today, the contradictions among the people comprise the contradictions within the working class, the contradictions within the peasantry, the contradictions within the intelligentsia, the contradictions between the working class and the peasantry, the contradictions between the workers and peasants on the one hand and the intellectuals on the other, the contradictions between the working class and other sections of the working people on the one hand and the national bourgeoisie on the other, the contradictions within the national bourgeoisie, and so on. Our

People's Government is one that genuinely represents the people's interests, it is a government that serves the people. Nevertheless, there are still certain contradictions between this government and the people. These include the contradictions between the interests of the state and the interests of the collective on the one hand and the interests of the individual on the other, between democracy and centralism, between the leadership and the led, and the contradictions arising from the bureaucratic style of work of some of the state personnel in their relations with the masses. All these are also contradictions among the people. Generally speaking, the fundamental identity of the people's interests underlies the contradictions among the people.

In our country, the contradiction between the working class and the national bourgeoisie comes under the category of contradictions among the people. By and large, the class struggle between the two is a class struggle within the ranks of the people, because the Chinese national bourgeoisie has a dual character. In the period of the bourgeois-democratic revolution, it had both a revolutionary and a conciliationist side to its character. In the period of the socialist revolution, exploitation of the working class for profit constitutes one side of the character of the national bourgeoisie, while its support of the Constitution and its willingness to accept socialist transformation constitute the other. The national bourgeoisie differs from the imperialists, the landlords and the bureaucrat-capitalists. The contradiction between the national bourgeoisie and the working class is one between exploiter and exploited, and is by nature antagonistic. But in the concrete conditions of China, this antagonistic contradiction between the two classes, if properly handled, can be transformed into a non-antagonistic one and be resolved by peaceful methods. However, the contradiction between the working class and the national bourgeoisie will change into a contradiction between ourselves and the enemy if we do not handle it properly and do not follow the policy of uniting with, criticizing and educating the national bourgeoisie, or if the national bourgeoisie does not accept this policy of ours.

Since they are different in nature, the contradictions between ourselves and the enemy and the contradictions among the people must be resolved by different methods. To put it briefly, the former entail drawing a clear distinction between ourselves and the enemy, and the latter entail drawing a clear distinction between right and wrong. It is of course true that the distinction between ourselves and the enemy is also one of right and wrong. For example, the question of who is in the right, we or the domestic and foreign reactionaries, the imperialists, the feudalists and bureaucrat-capitalists, is also one of right and wrong, but it is in a different category from questions of right and wrong among the people.

Our state is a people's democratic dictatorship led by the working class and based on the worker–peasant alliance. What is this dictatorship for? Its first function is internal, namely, to suppress the reactionary classes and elements and those exploiters who resist the socialist revolution, to suppress those who try to wreck our socialist construction, or in other words, to resolve the contradictions between ourselves and the internal enemy. For instance, to arrest, try and sentence certain counter-revolutionaries, and to deprive landlords and bureaucrat-capitalists of their right to vote and their freedom of speech for a certain period of time – all this comes within the scope of our dictatorship. To maintain public order and safeguard the interests of the people, it is necessary to exercise dictatorship as well over thieves, swindlers, murderers, arsonists, criminal gangs and other scoundrels who seriously disrupt public order. The second function of this dictatorship is to protect our country from subversion and possible aggression by external enemies. In such con-tingencies, it is the task of this dictatorship to resolve the contradiction between ourselves and the external enemy. The aim of this dictatorship is to protect all our people so that they can devote themselves to peaceful labour and make China a socialist country with modern industry, modern agriculture, and modern science and culture. Who is to exercise this dictatorship? Naturally, the working class and the entire people under its leadership. Dictatorship does not apply within the ranks of the people. The people cannot exercise dictatorship over themselves, nor must one section of the people oppress another. Law-breakers among the people will be punished according to law, but this is different in principle from the exercise of dictatorship to suppress enemies of the people. What applies among the people is democratic centralism. Our Constitution lays it down that citizens of the People's Republic of China enjoy freedom of speech, the press, assembly, association, procession, demonstration, religious belief, and so on. Our Constitution also provides that the organs of state must practise democratic centralism, that they must rely on the masses and that their personnel must serve the people. Our socialist democracy is the broadest kind of democracy, such as is not to be found in any bourgeois state. Our dictatorship is the people's democratic dictatorship led by the working class and based on the worker–peasant alliance. That is to say, democracy operates within the ranks of the people, while the working class, uniting with all others enjoying civil rights, and in the first place with the peasantry, enforces dictatorship over the reactionary classes and elements and all those who resist socialist transformation and oppose socialist construction. By civil rights, we mean, politically, the rights of freedom and democracy.

But this freedom is freedom with leadership and this democracy is democracy under centralized guidance, not anarchy. Anarchy does not accord with the interests or wishes of the people.

Certain people in our country were delighted by the Hungarian incident. They hoped that something similar would happen in China, that thousands upon thousands of people would take to the streets to demonstrate against the People's Government. Their hopes ran counter to the interests of the masses and therefore could not possibly win their support. Deceived by domestic and foreign counter-revolutionaries, a section of the people in Hungary made the mistake of resorting to violence against the People's Government, with the result that both the state and the people suffered. The damage done to the country's economy in a few weeks of rioting will take a long time to repair. In our country there were some others who wavered on the question of the Hungarian incident because they were ignorant of the real state of affairs in the world. They think that there is too little freedom under our People's Democracy and that there is more freedom under Western parliamentary democracy. They ask for a two-party system as in the West, with one party in office and the other in opposition. But this so-called two-party system is nothing but a device for maintaining the dictatorship of the bourgeoisie; it can never guarantee freedoms to the working people. As a matter of fact, freedom and democracy exist not in the abstract, but only in the concrete. In a society where class struggle exists, if there is freedom for the exploiting classes to exploit the working people, there is no freedom for the working people not to be exploited. If there is democracy for the bourgeoisie, there is no democracy for the proletariat and other working people. The legal existence of the Communist Party is tolerated in some capitalist countries, but only to the extent that it does not endanger the fundamental interests of the bourgeoisie; it is not tolerated beyond that. Those who demand freedom and democracy in the abstract regard democracy as an end and not as a means. Democracy as such sometimes seems to be an end, but it is in fact only a means. Marxism teaches us that democracy is part of the super-structure and belongs to the realm of politics. That is to say, in the last analysis, it serves the economic base. The same is true of freedom. Both democracy and freedom are relative, not absolute, and they come into being and develop in specific historical conditions. Within the ranks of the people, democracy is correlative with centralism and freedom with discipline. They are the two opposites of a single entity, contradictory as well as united, and we should not one-sidedly emphasize one to the exclusion of the other. Within the ranks of the people, we cannot do without freedom, nor can we do without discipline; we cannot do without democracy, nor can we do without centralism. This unity of democracy and centralism, of freedom and discipline, constitutes our democratic centralism. Under this system, the people enjoy broad democracy and freedom, but at the same time they have to keep within the bounds of socialist discipline. All this is well understood by the masses.

In advocating freedom with leadership and democracy under cen-tralized guidance, we in no way mean that coercive measures should be taken to settle ideological questions or questions involving the distinction between right and wrong among the people. All attempts to use administrative orders or coercive measures to settle ideological questions or questions of right and wrong are not only ineffective but harmful. We cannot abolish religion by administrative order or force people not to believe in it. We cannot compel people to give up idealism, any more than we can force them to embrace Marxism. The only way to settle questions of an ideological nature or controversial issues among the people is by the democratic method, the method of discussion, criticism, persuasion and education, and not by the method of coercion or repression. To be able to carry on their production and studies effectively and to lead their lives in peace and order, the people want their government and those in charge of production and of cultural and educational organizations to issue appropriate administrative regulations of an obligatory nature. It is common sense that without them the maintenance of public order would be impossible. Administrative regulations and the method of persuasion and education complement each other in resolving contradictions among the people. In fact, administrative regulations for the maintenance of public order must be accompanied by persuasion and education, for in many cases regula-tions alone will not work.

This democratic method of resolving contradictions among the people was epitomized in 1942 in the formula 'unity–criticism–unity'. To elaborate, that means starting from the desire for unity, resolving contradictions through criticism or struggle, and arriving at a new unity on a new basis. In our experience this is the correct method of resolving contradictions among the people. In 1942 we used it to resolve contradictions inside the Communist Party, namely, the contradictions between the dogmatists and the great majority of the membership, and between dogmatism and Marxism. The 'Left' dogmatists had resorted to the method of 'ruthless struggle and merciless blows' in inner-Party struggle. It was the wrong method. In criticizing 'Left' dogmatism, we did not use this old method but adopted a new one, that is, one of starting from the desire for unity, distinguishing between right and wrong through criticism or struggle, and arriving at a new unity on a new basis. This was the method used in the rectification movement of 1942. Within a few years, by the time the Chinese Communist Party held its Seventh National Congress in 1945, unity was achieved throughout the Party as anticipated, and consequently the people's revolution triumphed. Here, the essential thing is to start from the desire for unity. For without this desire for unity, the struggle, once begun, is certain to throw things into confusion and get out of hand. Wouldn't this be the same as 'ruthless struggle and merciless blows'? And what Party unity would there be left? It was precisely this experience that led us to the formula 'unity–criticism–unity'. Or, in other words, 'learn from past mistakes to avoid future ones and cure the sickness to save the patient'. We extended this method beyond our Party. We applied it with great success in the anti-Japanese base areas in dealing with the relations between the leadership and the masses, between the army and the people, between officers and men, between the different units of the army, and between the different groups of cadres. The use of this method can be traced back to still earlier times in our Party's history. Ever since 1927 when we built our revolutionary armed forces and base areas in the south, this method had been used to deal with the relations between the Party and the masses, between the army and the people, between officers and men, and with other relations among the people. The only difference was that during the Anti-Japanese War we employed this method much more consciously. And since the liberation of the whole country, we have employed this same method of 'unity–criticism–unity' in our relations with the democratic parties and with industrial and commercial circles. Our task now is to continue to extend and make still better use of this method throughout the ranks of the people; we want all our factories, cooperatives, shops, schools, offices and people's organizations, in a word, all our 600 million people, to use it in resolving contradictions among themselves.

In ordinary circumstances, contradictions among the people are not antagonistic. But if they are not handled properly, or if we relax our vigilance and lower our guard, antagonism may arise. In a socialist country, a development of this kind is usually only a localized and temporary phenomenon. The reason is that the system of exploitation of man by man has been abolished and the interests of the people are fundamentally identical. The antagonistic actions which took place on a fairly wide scale during the Hungarian incident were the result of the operations of both domestic and foreign counter-revolutionary elements. This was a particular as well as a temporary phenomenon. It was a case of the reactionaries inside a socialist country, in league with the imperialists, attempting to achieve their conspiratorial aims by taking advantage of contradictions among the people to foment dissension and stir up disorder. The lesson of the Hungarian incident merits attention.

Many people seem to think that the use of the democratic method to resolve contradictions among the people is something new. Actually it is not. Marxists have always held that the cause of the proletariat must depend on the masses of the people and that communists must use the democratic method of persuasion and education when working among the labouring people and must on no account resort to commandism or coercion. The Chinese Communist Party faithfully adheres to this Marxist-Leninist principle. It has been our consistent view that under the people's democratic dictatorship two different methods, one dictatorial and the other democratic, should be used to resolve the two types of contradictions which differ in nature – those between ourselves and the enemy and those among the people. This idea has been explained again and again in many Party documents and in speeches by many leading comrades of our Party. In my article 'On the People's Democratic Dictatorship', written in 1949, I said, 'The combination of these two aspects, democracy for the people and dictatorship over the reactionaries, is the people's democratic dictatorship.' I also pointed out that in order to settle problems within the ranks of the people 'the method we employ is democratic, the method of persuasion, not of compulsion'. Again, in addressing the second session of the First

National Committee of the Political Consultative Conference on 2 June, I said:

> The people's democratic dictatorship uses two methods. Towards the enemy, it uses the method of dictatorship, that is, for as long a period of time as is necessary it does not permit them to take part in political activity and compels them to obey the law of the People's Government, to engage in labour and, through such labour, be transformed into new men. Towards the people, on the contrary, it uses the method of democracy and not of compulsion, that is, it must necessarily let them take part in political activity and does not compel them to do this or that but uses the method of democracy to educate and persuade. Such education is self-education for the people, and its basic method is criticism and self-criticism.

Thus, on many occasions we have discussed the use of the democratic method for resolving contradictions among the people; furthermore, we have in the main applied it in our work, and many cadres and many other people are familiar with it in practice. Why then do some people now feel that it is a new issue? Because, in the past, the struggle between ourselves and the enemy, both internal and external, was most acute, and contradictions among the people therefore did not attract as much attention as they do today.

Quite a few people fail to make a clear distinction between these two different types of contradictions – those between ourselves and the enemy and those among the people – and are prone to confuse the two. It must be admitted that it is sometimes quite easy to do so. We have had instances of such confusion in our work in the past. In the course of cleaning out counter-revolutionaries good people were sometimes mistaken for bad, and such things still happen today. We are able to keep mistakes within bounds because it has been our policy to draw a sharp line between ourselves and the enemy and to rectify mistakes whenever discovered.

Marxist philosophy holds that the law of the unity of opposites is the fundamental law of the universe. This law operates universally, whether in the natural world, in human society, or in man's thinking. Between the opposites in a contradiction there is at once unity and struggle, and it is this that impels things to move and change. Contradictions exist everywhere, but their nature differs in accordance with the different nature of different things. In any given thing, the unity of opposites is conditional, temporary and transitory, and hence relative, whereas the struggle of opposites is absolute. Lenin gave a very clear exposition of this law. It has come to be understood by a growing number of people in our country. But for many people it is one thing to accept this law and quite another to apply it in examining and dealing with problems. Many dare not openly admit that contradictions still exist among the people of our country, while it is precisely these contradictions that are pushing our society forward. Many do not admit that contradictions still exist in socialist society, with the result that they become irresolute and passive when confronted with social contradictions; they do not understand that socialist society grows more united and consolidated through the ceaseless process of correctly handling and resolving contradictions. For this reason, we need to explain things to our people, and to our cadres in the first place, in order to help them understand the contradictions in socialist society and learn to use correct methods for handling them.

Contradictions in socialist society are fundamentally different from those in the old societies, such as capitalist society. In capitalist society contradictions find expression in acute antagonisms and conflicts, in sharp class struggle; they cannot be resolved by the capitalist system itself and can only be resolved by socialist revolution. The case is quite different in socialist society: there, the contradictions are not antagonistic and can be ceaselessly resolved by the socialist system itself.

In socialist society the basic contradictions are still those between the relations of production and the productive forces and between the superstructure and the economic base. However, they are fundamentally different in character and have different features from the contradictions between the relations of production and the productive forces and between the superstructure and the economic base in the old societies. The present social system of our country is far superior to that of the old days. If it were not so, the old system would not have been overthrown and the new system could not have been established. In saying that the socialist relations of production correspond better to the character of the productive forces than did the old relations of production, we mean that they allow the productive forces to develop at a speed unattainable in the old society, so that production can expand steadily and increasingly meet the constantly growing needs of the people. Under the rule of imperialism, feudalism and bureaucrat-capitalism, the productive forces of the old China grew very slowly. For more than fifty years before liberation, China produced only a few tens of thousands of tons of steel a year, not counting the output of the north-eastern provinces. If these provinces are included, the peak annual steel output only amounted to a little over 900,000 tons. In 1949, the national steel output was a little over 100,000 tons. Yet now, a mere seven years after the liberation of our country, steel output already exceeds 4,000,000 tons. In the old China, there was hardly any machine-building industry, to say nothing of the automobile and aircraft industries; now we have all three. When the people overthrew the rule of imperialism, feudalism and bureaucrat-capitalism, many were not clear as to which way China should head – towards capitalism or towards socialism. Facts have now provided the answer: only socialism can save China. The socialist system has promoted the rapid development of the productive forces of our country, a fact even our enemies abroad have had to acknowledge.

But our socialist system has only just been set up; it is not yet fully established or fully consolidated. In joint state–private industrial and commercial enterprises, capitalists still get a fixed rate of interest on their capital, that is to say, exploitation still exists. So far as ownership is concerned, these enterprises are not yet completely socialist in nature. A number of our agricultural and handicraft producers' cooperatives are still semi-socialist, while even in the fully socialist cooperatives certain specific problems of ownership remain to be solved. Relations between production and exchange in accordance with socialist principles are being gradually established within and between all branches of our economy, and more and more appropriate forms are being sought. The problem of the proper relation of accumulation to consumption within each of the two sectors of the socialist economy – the one where the means of production are owned by the whole people and the other where the means of production are owned by the collective – and the problem of the proper relation of accumulation to consumption between the two sectors themselves are complicated problems for which it is not easy to work out a perfectly rational solution all at once. To sum up, socialist relations of production have been established and are in corre-spondence with the growth of the productive forces, but these relations are still far from perfect, and this imperfection stands in contradiction to the growth of the productive forces. Apart from correspondence as well as contradiction between the relations of production and the growth of the productive forces, there is correspondence as well as contradiction between the superstructure and the economic base. The superstructure, comprising the state system and laws of the people's democratic dictatorship and the socialist ideology guided by Marxism-Leninism, plays a positive role in facilitating the victory of socialist transformation and the socialist way of organizing labour; it is in correspondence with the socialist economic base, that is, with socialist relations of production. But the existence of bourgeois ideology, a certain bureaucratic style of work in our state organs and defects in some of the links in our state institutions are in contradiction with the socialist economic base. We must continue to resolve all such contradictions in the light of our specific conditions. Of course, new problems will emerge as these contradictions are resolved. And further efforts will be required to resolve the new contradictions. For instance, a constant process of readjustment through state planning is needed to deal with the contradiction between production and the needs of society, which will long remain an objective reality. Every year our country draws up an economic plan in order to establish a proper ratio between accumulation and consumption and achieve an equilibrium between production and needs. Equilibrium is nothing but a temporary, relative unity of opposites. By the end of each year, this equilibrium, taken as a whole, is upset by the struggle of opposites; the unity undergoes a change, equilibrium becomes disequilibrium, unity becomes disunity, and once again it is necessary to work out an equilibrium and unity for the next year. Herein lies the superiority of our planned economy. As a matter of fact, this equilibrium, this unity, is partially upset every month or every quarter, and partial readjustments are called for. Sometimes, contradictions arise and the equilibrium is upset because our subjective arrangements do not conform to objective reality; this is what we call making a mistake. The ceaseless emergence and ceaseless resolution of contradictions constitute the dialectical law of the development of things.

Today, matters stand as follows. The large-scale, turbulent class struggles of the masses characteristic of times of revolution have in the main come to an end, but class struggle is by no means entirely over. While welcoming the new system, the masses are not yet quite accustomed to it. Government personnel are not sufficiently experienced and have to undertake further study and investigation of specific policies. In other words, time is needed for our socialist system to become established and consolidated, for the masses to become accustomed to the new system, and for government personnel to learn and acquire experience. It is therefore imperative for us at this juncture to raise the question of distinguishing contradictions among the people from those between ourselves and the enemy, as well as the question of the correct handling of contradictions among the people, in order to unite the people of all nationalities in our country for the new battle, the battle against nature, develop our economy and culture, help the whole nation to traverse this period of transition relatively smoothly, consolidate our new system and build up our new state.

II. THE QUESTION OF ELIMINATING
COUNTER-REVOLUTIONARIES

The elimination of counter-revolutionaries is a struggle of opposites as between ourselves and the enemy. Among the people, there are some who see this question in a somewhat different light. Two kinds of people hold views differing from ours. Those with a Right deviation in their thinking make no distinction between ourselves and the enemy and take the enemy for our own people. They regard as friends the very persons whom the masses regard as enemies. Those with a 'Left' deviation in their thinking magnify contradictions between ourselves and the enemy to such an extent that they take certain contradictions among the people for contradictions with the enemy and regard as counter-revolutionaries persons who are actually not. Both these views are wrong. Neither makes possible the correct handling of the problem of eliminating counter-revolutionaries or a correct assessment of this work.

To form a correct evaluation of our work in eliminating counter-revolutionaries, let us see what repercussions the Hungarian incident has had in China. After its occurrence there was some unrest among a section of our intellectuals, but there were no squalls. Why? One reason, it must be said, was our success in eliminating counter-revolutionaries fairly thoroughly.

Of course, the consolidation of our state is not due primarily to the elimination of counter-revolutionaries. It is due primarily to the fact that we have a Communist Party and a Liberation Army both tempered in decades of revolutionary struggle, and a working people likewise so tempered. Our Party and our armed forces are rooted in the masses, have been tempered in the flames of a protracted revolution and have the capacity to fight. Our People's Republic was not built overnight, but developed step by step out of the revolutionary base areas. A number of democratic personages have also been tempered in the struggle in varying degrees, and they have gone through troubled times together with us. Some intellectuals were tempered in the struggles against imperialism and reaction; since liberation many have gone through a process of ideological remoulding aimed at enabling them to distinguish clearly between ourselves and the enemy. In addition, the consolidation of our state is due to the fact that our economic measures are basically sound, that the people's life is secure and steadily improving, that our policies towards the national bourgeoisie and other classes are correct, and so on. Nevertheless, our success in eliminating counter-revolutionaries is undoubtedly an important reason for the consolidation of our state. For all these reasons, with few exceptions our college students are patriotic and support socialism and did not give way to unrest during the Hungarian incident, even though many of them come from families of non-working people. The same was true of the national bourgeoisie, to say nothing of the basic masses – the workers and peasants.

After liberation, we rooted out a number of counter-revolutionaries. Some were sentenced to death for major crimes. This was absolutely necessary, it was the demand of the masses, and it was done to free them from long years of oppression by the counter-revolutionaries and all kinds of local tyrants; in other words, to liberate the productive forces. If we had not done so, the masses would not have been able to lift their heads. Since 1956, however, there has been a radical change in the situation. In the country as a whole, the bulk of the counter-revolutionaries have been cleared out. Our basic task has changed from unfettering the productive forces to protecting and expanding them in the context of the new relations of production. Because of the failure to understand that our present policy fits the present situation and our past policy fitted the past situation, some people want to make use of the present policy to reverse past decisions and to negate the tremendous success we achieved in eliminating counter-revolutionaries. This is completely wrong, and the masses will not permit it.

In our work of eliminating counter-revolutionaries successes were the main thing, but there were also mistakes. In some cases there were excesses and in others counter-revolutionaries slipped through our net. Our policy is: 'Counter-revolutionaries must be eliminated wherever found, mistakes must be corrected whenever discovered.' Our line in the work of eliminating counter-revolutionaries is the mass line. Of course, even with the mass line mistakes may still occur, but they will be fewer and easier to correct. The masses gain experience through struggle. From the things done correctly they gain the experience of how things are done correctly. From the mistakes made they gain the experience of how mistakes are made.

Wherever mistakes have been discovered in the work of eliminating counter-revolutionaries, steps have been or are being taken to correct them. Those not yet discovered will be corrected as soon as they come to light. Exoneration or rehabilitation should be made known as widely as were the original wrong decisions. I propose that a comprehensive review of the work of eliminating counter-revolutionaries be made this year or next to sum up experience, promote justice and counter unjust attacks. Nationally, this review should be in the charge of the Standing Committees of the National People's Congress and of the National Committee of the Political Consultative Conference and, locally, in the charge of the people's councils and the committees of the Political Consultative Conference in the provinces and municipalities. In this review, we must help the large numbers of cadres and activists involved in the work, and not pour cold water on them. It would not be right to dampen their spirits. Nonetheless, wrongs must be righted when discovered. This must be the attitude of all the public security organs, the procurators' offices and the judicial departments, prisons and agencies charged with the reform of criminals through labour. We hope that wherever possible members of the Standing Committee of the National People's Congress, members of the National Committee of the Political Consultative Conference and people's deputies will take part in this review. This will be of help in perfecting our legal system and in dealing correctly with counter-revolutionaries and other criminals.

The present situation with regard to counter-revolutionaries can be described in these words: there still are counter-revolutionaries, but not many. In the first place, there still are counter-revolutionaries. Some people say that there aren't any more left and all is well and that we can therefore lay our heads on our pillows and just drop off to sleep. But this is not the way things are. The fact is, there still are counter-revolutionaries (of course, that is not to say you'll find them everywhere and in every organization), and we must continue to fight them. It must be understood that the hidden counter-revolutionaries still at large will not take things lying down, but will certainly seize every opportunity to make trouble. The US imperialists and the Chiang Kai-shek clique are constantly sending in secret agents to carry on disruptive activities. Even after all the existing counter-revolutionaries have been combed out, new ones are likely to emerge. If we drop our guard, we shall be badly fooled and shall suffer severely. Counter-revolutionaries must be rooted out with a firm hand wherever they are found making trouble. But, taking the country as a whole, there are certainly not many counter-revolutionaries. It would be wrong to say that there are still large numbers of counter-revolutionaries in China. Acceptance of that view would likewise result in a mess.

III. THE QUESTION OF THE COOPERATIVE TRANSFORMATION OF AGRICULTURE

We have a rural population of over 500 million, so how our peasants fare has a most important bearing on the development of our economy and the consolidation of our state power. In my view, the situation is basically sound. The cooperative transformation of agriculture has been successfully accomplished, and this has resolved the great contradiction in our country between socialist industrialization and the individual peasant economy. As the cooperative transformation of agriculture was completed so rapidly, some people were worried and wondered whether something untoward might occur. There are indeed some faults, but fortunately they are not serious and on the whole the movement is healthy. The peasants are working with a will, and last year there was an increase in the country's grain output despite the worst floods, droughts and gales in years. Now there are people who are stirring up a miniature typhoon, they are saying that cooperation is no good, that there is nothing superior about it. Is cooperation superior or not? Among the documents distributed at today's meeting there is one about the Wang Kuo-fan Cooperative in Tsunhua County, Hopei Province, which I suggest you read. This cooperative is situated in a hilly region which was very poor in the past and which for a number of years depended on relief grain from the People's Government. When the cooperative was first set up in 1953, people called it the 'paupers' coop'. But it has become better off year by year, and now, after four years of hard struggle, most of its households have reserves of grain. What was possible for this cooperative should also be possible for others to achieve under normal conditions in the same length of time or a little longer. Clearly there are no grounds for saying that something has gone wrong with agricultural cooperation.

It is also clear that it takes hard struggle to build cooperatives. New things always have to experience difficulties and setbacks as they grow. It is sheer fantasy to imagine that the cause of socialism is all plain sailing and the success comes easily, with no difficulties or setbacks, or without the expenditure of tremendous effort.

Who are the active supporters of the cooperatives? The overwhelming majority of the poor and lower-middle peasants who constitute more than 70 per cent of the rural population. Most of the other peasants are also placing their hopes on the cooperatives. Only a very small minority are really dissatisfied. Quite a number of persons have failed to analyze this situation and to make an overall examination of the achievements and shortcomings of the cooperatives and the causes of these short-comings; instead they have taken part of the picture or one side of the matter for the whole, and consequently a miniature typhoon has been stirred up among some people, who are saying that the cooperatives are not superior.

How long will it take to consolidate the cooperatives and for this talk about their not being superior to wind up? Judging from the experience of the growth of many cooperatives, it will probably take five years or a little longer. As most of our cooperatives are only a little over a year old, it would be unreasonable to ask too much of them. In my view, we will be doing well enough if the cooperatives can be consolidated during the Second Five Year Plan after being established in the First.

The cooperatives are now in the process of gradual consolidation. There are certain contradictions that remain to be resolved, such as those between the state and the cooperatives and those in and between the cooperatives themselves.

To resolve these contradictions we must pay constant attention to the problems of production and distribution. On the question of production, the cooperative economy must be subject to the unified economic planning of the state, while retaining a certain flexibility and independence that do not run counter to the state's unified plan or its policies, laws and regulations. At the same time, every household in a cooperative must comply with the overall plan of the cooperative or production team to which it belongs, though it may make its own appropriate plans in regard to land allotted for personal needs and to other individually operated economic undertakings. On the question of distribution, we must take the interests of the state, the collective and the individual into account. We must properly handle the three-way relationship between the state agricultural tax, the cooperative's accumulation fund and the peasants' personal income, and take constant care to make readjustments so as to resolve contradictions between them. Accumulation is essential for both the state and the cooperative, but in neither case should it be excessive. We should do everything possible to enable the peasants in normal years to raise their personal incomes annually through increased production.

Many people say that the peasants lead a hard life. Is this true? In one sense it is. That is to say, because the imperialists and their agents oppressed and exploited us for over a century, ours is an impoverished country and the standard of living not only of our peasants but of our workers and intellectuals is still low. We shall need several decades of strenuous effort gradually to raise the standard of living of our people as a whole. In this context, it is right to say that the peasants lead a 'hard life'. But in another sense it is not true. We refer to the allegation that in the seven years since liberation it is only the life of the workers that has been improved and not that of the peasants. As a matter of fact, with very few exceptions, there has been some improvement in the life of both the peasants and the workers. Since liberation, the peasants have been free from landlord exploitation and their production has increased annually. Take grain crops. In 1949, the country's output was only something over 210,000 million catties. By 1956, it had risen to more than 360,000 million catties, an increase of nearly 150,000 million catties. The state agricultural tax is not heavy, only amounting to something over 30,000 million catties a year. State purchases of grain from the peasants at standard prices only amount to a little over 50,000 million catties a year. These two items together total over 80,000 million catties. Furthermore, more than half this grain is sold back to the villages and nearby towns. Obviously, no one can say that there has been no improvement in the life of the peasants. In order to help agriculture to develop and the cooperatives to become consolidated, we are planning to stabilize the total annual amount of the grain tax plus the grain purchased by the state at somewhat more than 80,000 million catties within a few years. In this way, the small number of grain-deficient households still found in the countryside will stop being short, all peasant households, except some raising industrial crops, will either have grain reserves or at least become self-sufficient. There will no longer be poor peasants in the countryside, and the standard of living of the entire peasantry will reach or surpass the middle peasants' level. It is not right simply to compare a peasant's average annual income with a worker's and jump to the conclusion that one is too low and the other too high. Since the labour productivity of the workers is much higher than that of the peasants and the latter's cost of living is much lower than that of workers in the cities, the workers cannot be said to have received special favours from the state. The wages of a small number of workers and some state personnel are in fact a little too high, the peasants have reason to be dissatisfied with this, and it is necessary to make certain appropriate adjustments according to specific circumstances.

IV. THE QUESTION OF THE INDUSTRIALISTS AND BUSINESSMEN

With regard to the transformation of our social system, the year 1956 saw the conversion of privately owned industrial and commercial enterprises into joint state–private enterprises as well as the cooperative transformation of agriculture and handicrafts. The speed and smoothness of this conversion were closely bound up with our treating the contradiction between the working class and the national bourgeoisie as a contradiction among the people. Has this class contradiction been completely resolved? No, not yet. That will take a considerable period of time. However, some people say the capitalists have been so remoulded that they are now not very different from the workers and that further remoulding is unnecessary. Others go so far as to say that the capitalists are even better than the workers. Still others ask: if remoulding is necessary, why isn't it necessary for the working class? Are these opinions correct? Of course not.

In the building of a socialist society, everybody needs remoulding – the exploiters and also the working people. Who says it isn't necessary for the working class? Of course, the remoulding of the exploiters is essentially different from that of the working people, and the two must not be confused. The working class remoulds the whole of society in class struggle and in the struggle against nature, and in the process it remoulds itself. It must ceaselessly learn in the course of work, gradually overcome its shortcomings and never stop doing so. Take for example those of us present here. Many of us make some progress each year, that is to say, we are remoulding ourselves each year. For myself, I used to have all sorts of non-Marxist ideas, and it was only later that I embraced Marxism. I learned a little Marxism from books and took the first steps in remoulding my ideology, but it was mainly through taking part in class struggle over the years that I came to be remoulded. And if I am to make further progress, I must continue to learn, otherwise I shall lag behind. Can the capitalists be so good that they need no more remoulding?

Some people contend that the Chinese bourgeoisie no longer has two sides to its character, but only one side. Is this true? No. While members of the bourgeoisie have become administrative personnel in joint state–private enterprises and are being transformed from exploiters into working people living by their own labour, they still get a fixed rate of interest on their capital in the joint enterprises, that is, they have not yet cut themselves loose from the roots of exploitation. Between them and the working class there is still a considerable gap in ideology, sentiments and habits of life. How can it be said that they no longer have two sides to their character? Even when they stop receiving their fixed-interest payments and the 'bourgeois' label is removed, they will still need ideological remoulding for quite some time. If, as is alleged, the bourgeoisie no longer has a dual character, then the capitalists will no longer have the task of studying and of remoulding themselves.

It must be said that this view does not tally either with the actual situation of our industrialists and businessmen or with what most of them want. During the past few years, most of them have been willing to study and have made marked progress. As their thorough remoulding can be achieved only in the course of work, they should engage in labour together with the staff and workers in the enterprises and regard these enterprises as the chief places in which to remould themselves. But it is also important for them to change some of their old views through study. Such study should be on a voluntary basis. When they return to the enterprises after being in study groups for some weeks, many industrialists and businessmen find that they have more of a common language with the workers and the representatives of state ownership, and so there are better possibilities for working together. They know from personal experience that it is good for them to keep on studying and remoulding themselves. The idea mentioned above that study and remoulding are not necessary reflects the views not of the majority of industrialists and businessmen but of only a small number.

V. THE QUESTION OF THE INTELLECTUALS

The contradictions within the ranks of the people in our country also find expression among the intellectuals. The several million intellectuals who worked for the old society have come to serve the new society, and the question that now arises is how they can fit in with the needs of the new society and how we can help them to do so. This, too, is a contradiction among the people.

Most of our intellectuals have made marked progress during the last seven years. They have shown they are in favour of the socialist system. Many are diligently studying Marxism, and some have become communists. The latter, though at present small in number, are steadily increasing. Of course, there are still some intellectuals who are sceptical about socialism or do not approve of it, but they are a minority.

China needs the services of as many intellectuals as possible for the colossal task of building socialism. We should trust those who are really willing to serve the cause of socialism and should radically improve our relations with them and help them solve the problems requiring solution, so that they can give full play to their talents. Many of our comrades are not good at uniting with intellectuals. They are stiff in their attitude towards them, lack respect for their work and interfere in certain scientific and cultural matters where interference is unwarranted. We must do away with all such shortcomings.

Although large numbers of intellectuals have made progress, they should not be complacent. They must continue to remould themselves, gradually shed their bourgeois world outlook and acquire the proletarian, communist world outlook so that they can fully fit in with the needs of the new society and unite with the workers and peasants. The change in world outlook is fundamental, and up to now most of our intellectuals cannot be said to have accomplished it. We hope that they will continue to make progress and that in the course of work and study they will gradually acquire the communist world outlook, grasp Marxism-Leninism and become integrated with the workers and peasants. We hope they will not stop halfway, or, what is worse, slide back, for there will be no future for them in going backwards. Since our country's social system has changed and the economic base of bourgeois ideology has in the main been destroyed, not only is it imperative for large numbers of our intellectuals to change their world outlook, but it is also possible for them to do so. But a thorough change in world outlook takes a very long time, and we should spare no pains in helping them and must not be impatient. Actually, there are bound to be some who ideologically will always be reluctant to accept Marxism-Leninism and communism. We should not be too exacting in what we demand of them; as long as they comply with the requirements laid down by the state and engage in legitimate pursuits, we should let them have opportunities for suitable work.

Among students and intellectuals there has recently been a falling-off in ideological and political work, and some unhealthy tendencies have appeared. Some people seem to think that there is no longer any need to concern themselves with politics or with the future of the motherland and the ideals of mankind. It seems as if Marxism, once all the rage, is currently not so much in fashion. To counter these tendencies, we must strengthen our ideological and political work. Both students and intellectuals should study hard. In addition to the study of their specialized subjects, they must make progress ideologically and politically, which means they should study Marxism, current events and politics. Not to have a correct political orientation is like not having a soul. The ideological remoulding in the past was necessary and has yielded positive results. But it was carried on in a somewhat rough-and-ready fashion and the feelings of some people were hurt – this was not good. We must avoid such shortcomings in future. All departments and organizations should shoulder their responsibilities for ideological and political work. This applies to the Communist Party, the Youth League, government departments in charge of this work, and especially to heads of educational institutions and teachers. Our educational policy must enable everyone who receives an education to develop morally, intellectually and physically and become a worker with both socialist consciousness and culture. We must spread the idea of building our country through diligence and thrift. We must help all our young people to understand that ours is still a very poor country, that we cannot change this situation radically in a short time, and that only through decades of united effort by our younger generation and all our people, working with their own hands, can China be made prosperous and strong. The establishment of our socialist system has opened the road leading to the ideal society of the future, but to translate this ideal into reality needs hard work. Some of our young people think that everything ought to be perfect once a socialist society is established and that they should be able to enjoy a happy life ready-made, without working for it. This is unrealistic.

VI. THE QUESTION OF THE MINORITY NATIONALITIES

The minority nationalities in our country number more than thirty million. Although they constitute only 6 per cent of the total population, they inhabit extensive regions which comprise 50 to 60 per cent of China's total area. It is thus imperative to foster good relations between the Han people and the minority nationalities. The key to this question lies in overcoming Han chauvinism. At the same time, efforts should also be made to overcome local-nationality chauvinism, wherever it exists among the minority nationalities. Both Han chauvinism and local-nationality chauvinism are harmful to the unity of the nationalities; they represent one kind of contradiction among the people which should be resolved. We have already done some work to this end. In most of the areas inhabited by minority nationalities there has been considerable improvement in the relations between the nationalities, but a number of problems remain to be solved. In some areas, both Han chauvinism and local-nationality chauvinism still exist to a serious degree, and this demands full attention. As a result of the efforts of the people of all nationalities over the last few years democratic reforms and socialist transformation have in the main been completed in most of the minority-nationality areas. Democratic reforms have not yet been carried out in Tibet because conditions are not ripe. According to the seventeen-article agreement reached between the Central People's Government and the local government of Tibet the reform of the social system must be carried out, but the timing can only be decided when the great majority of the people of Tibet and the local leading public figures consider it opportune, and one should not be impatient. It has now been decided not to proceed with democratic reforms in Tibet during the period of the Second Five Year Plan. Whether to proceed with them in the period of the Third Five Year Plan can only be decided in the light of the situation at the time.

VII. OVERALL CONSIDERATION AND PROPER ARRANGEMENT

By overall consideration we mean consideration that embraces the 600 million people of our country. In drawing up plans, handling affairs or thinking over problems, we must proceed from the fact that China has a population of 600 million, and we must never forget this fact. Why do we make a point of this? Is it possible that there are people who are still unaware that we have a population of 600 million? Of course, everyone knows this, but when it comes to actual practice, some people forget all about it and act as though the fewer the people, the smaller the circle, the better. Those who have this small-circle mentality abhor the idea of bringing every positive factor into play, of uniting with everyone who can be united with, and of doing everything possible to turn negative factors into positive ones so as to serve the great cause of building a socialist society. I hope these people will take a wider view and fully recognize that we have a population of 600 million, that this is an objective fact, and that it is an asset for us. Our large population is a good thing, but of course it also creates certain difficulties. Construction is going ahead vigorously on all fronts and very successfully too, but in the present transition period of tremendous social change there are still many difficult problems. Progress and at the same time difficulties – this is a contradiction. However, not only should all such contradictions be resolved; they definitely can be. Our guiding principle is overall consideration and proper arrangement. Whatever the problem – whether it concerns food, natural calamities, employment, education, the intellectuals, the united front of all patriotic forces, the minority nationalities, or anything else – we must always proceed from the standpoint of overall consideration, which embraces the whole people, and must make the proper arrangement, after consultation with all the circles concerned, in the light of what is feasible at a particular time and place. On no account should we complain that there are too many people, that others are backward, that things are troublesome and hard to handle, and close the door on them. Do I mean to say that the government alone must take care of everyone and everything? Of course not. In many cases, they can be left to the direct care of the public organizations or the masses – both are quite capable of devising many good ways of handling them. This also comes within the scope of the principle of overall consideration and proper arrangement. We should give guidance on this to the public organizations and the people everywhere.

VIII. ON 'LET A HUNDRED FLOWERS BLOSSOM, LET A HUNDRED SCHOOLS OF THOUGHT CONTEND' AND 'LONG-TERM COEXISTENCE AND MUTUAL SUPERVISION'

'Let a hundred flowers blossom, let a hundred schools of thought contend' and 'long-term coexistence and mutual supervision' – how did these slogans come to be put forward? They were put forward in the light of China's specific conditions, in recognition of the continued existence of various kinds of contradictions in socialist society and in response to the country's urgent need to speed up its economic and cultural development. Letting a hundred flowers blossom and a hundred schools of thought contend is the policy for promoting progress in the arts and sciences and a flourishing socialist culture in our land. Different forms and styles in art should develop freely and different schools in science should contend freely. We think that it is harmful to the growth of art and science if administrative measures are used to impose one particular style of art or school of thought and to ban another. Questions of right and wrong in the arts and sciences should be settled through free discussion in artistic and scientific circles and through practical work in these fields. They should not be settled in an over-simple manner. A period of trial is often needed to determine whether something is right or wrong. Throughout history at the outset new and correct things often failed to win recognition from the majority of people and had to develop by twists and turns through struggle. Often, correct and good things were first regarded not as fragrant flowers but as poisonous weeds. Copernicus's theory of the solar system and Darwin's theory of evolution were once dismissed as erroneous and had to win out over bitter opposition. Chinese history offers many similar examples. In a socialist society, the conditions for the growth of the new are radically different from and far superior to those in the old society. Nevertheless, it often happens that new, rising forces are held back and sound ideas stifled. Besides, even in the absence of their deliberate suppression, the growth of new things may be hindered simply through lack of discernment. It is therefore necessary to be careful about questions of right and wrong in the arts and sciences, to encourage free discussion and avoid hasty conclusions. We believe that such an attitude will help ensure a relatively smooth development of the arts and sciences.

Marxism, too, has developed through struggle. At the beginning, Marxism was subjected to all kinds of attack and regarded as a poisonous weed. This is still the case in many parts of the world. In the socialist countries, it enjoys a different position. But non-Marxist and, what is more, anti-Marxist ideologies exist even in these countries. In China, although socialist transformation has in the main been completed as regards the system of ownership, and although the large-scale, turbulent class struggles of the masses characteristic of times of revolution have in the main come to an end, there are still remnants of the overthrown landlord and comprador classes, there is still a bourgeoisie, and the remoulding of the petty bourgeoisie has only just started. Class struggle is by no means over. The class struggle between the proletariat and the bourgeoisie, the class struggle between the various political forces, and the class struggle between the proletariat and the bourgeoisie in the ideological field will still be protracted and tortuous and at times even very sharp. The proletariat seeks to transform the world according to its own world outlook, and so does the bourgeoisie. In this respect, the question of which will win out, socialism or capitalism, is not really settled yet. Marxists remain a minority among the entire population as well as among the intellectuals. Therefore, Marxism must continue to develop through struggle. Marxism can develop only through struggle, and this is not only true of the past and the present, it is necessarily true of the future as well. What is correct invariably develops in the course of struggle with what is wrong. The true, the good and the beautiful always exist by contrast with the false, the evil and the ugly, and grow in struggle with them. As soon as something erroneous is rejected and a particular truth accepted by mankind, new truths begin to struggle with new errors. Such struggles will never end. This is the law of development of truth and, naturally, of Marxism.

It will take a fairly long period of time to decide the issue in the ideological struggle between socialism and capitalism in our country. The reason is that the influence of the bourgeoisie and of the intellectuals who come from the old society, the very influence which constitutes their class ideology, will persist in our country for a long time. If this is not understood at all or is insufficiently understood, the gravest of mistakes will be made and the necessity of waging struggle in the ideological field will be ignored. Ideological struggle differs from other forms of struggle, since the only method used is painstaking reasoning, and not crude coercion. Today, socialism is in an advantageous position in the ideological struggle. The basic power of the state is in the hands of the working people led by the proletariat. The Communist Party is strong and its prestige high. Although there are defects and mistakes in our work, every fair-minded person can see that we are loyal to the people, that we are both determined and able to build up our mother-land together with them, and that we have already achieved great successes and will achieve still greater ones. The vast majority of the bourgeoisie and the intellectuals who come from the old society are patriotic and are willing to serve their flourishing socialist motherland;

they know they will have nothing to fall back on and their future cannot possibly be bright if they turn away from the socialist cause and from the working people led by the Communist Party.

People may ask, since Marxism is accepted as the guiding ideology by the majority of the people in our country, can it be criticized? Certainly it can. Marxism is scientific truth and fears no criticism. If it did, and if it could be overthrown by criticism, it would be worthless. In fact, aren't the idealists criticizing Marxism every day and in every way? And those who harbour bourgeois and petty-bourgeois ideas and do not wish to change – aren't they also criticizing Marxism in every way? Marxists should not be afraid of criticism from any quarter. Quite the contrary, they need to temper and develop themselves and win new positions in the teeth of criticism and in the storm and stress of struggle. Fighting against wrong ideas is like being vaccinated – a man develops greater immunity from disease as a result of vaccination. Plants raised in hothouses are unlikely to be hardy. Carrying out the policy of letting a hundred flowers blossom and a hundred schools of thought contend will not weaken, but strengthen, the leading position of Marxism in the ideological field.

What should our policy be towards non-Marxist ideas? As far as unmistakable counter-revolutionaries and saboteurs of the socialist cause are concerned, the matter is easy: we simply deprive them of their freedom of speech. But incorrect ideas among the people are quite a different matter. Will it do to ban such ideas and deny them any opportunity for expression? Certainly not. It is not only futile but very harmful to use crude methods in dealing with ideological questions among the people, with questions about man's mental world. You may ban the expression of wrong ideas, but the ideas will still be there. On the other hand, if correct ideas are pampered in hothouses and never exposed to the elements and immunized against disease, they will not win out against erroneous ones. Therefore, it is only by employing the method of discussion, criticism and reasoning that we can really foster correct ideas and overcome wrong ones, and that we can really settle issues.

It is inevitable that the bourgeoisie and petty bourgeoisie will give expression to their own ideologies. It is inevitable that they will stubbornly assert themselves on political and ideological questions by every possible means. You cannot expect them to do otherwise. We should not use the method of suppression and prevent them from expressing themselves, but should allow them to do so and at the same time argue with them and direct appropriate criticism at them. Undoubtedly, we must criticize wrong ideas of every description. It certainly would not be right to refrain from criticism, look on while wrong ideas spread unchecked and allow them to dominate the field. Mistakes must be criticized and poisonous weeds fought wherever they crop up. However, such criticism should not be dogmatic, and the metaphysical method should not be used, but instead the effort should be made to apply the dialectical method. What is needed is scientific analysis and convincing argument. Dogmatic criticism settles nothing. We are against poisonous weeds of whatever kind, but we must carefully distinguish between what is really a poisonous weed and what is really a fragrant flower. Together with the masses of the people, we must learn to differentiate carefully between the two and use correct methods to fight the poisonous weeds.

At the same time as we criticize dogmatism, we must direct our attention to criticizing revisionism. Revisionism, or Right opportunism, is a bourgeois trend of thought that is even more dangerous than dogmatism. The revisionists, the Right opportunists, pay lip-service to Marxism; they too attack 'dogmatism'. But what they are really attacking is the quintessence of Marxism. They oppose or distort materialism and dialectics, oppose or try to weaken the people's democratic dictatorship and the leading role of the Communist Party, and oppose or try to weaken socialist transformation and socialist construction. Even after the basic victory of our socialist revolution, there will still be a number of people in our society who vainly hope to restore the capitalist system and are sure to fight the working class on every front, including the ideological one. And their right-hand men in this struggle are the revisionists.

Literally the two slogans – let a hundred flowers blossom and let a hundred schools of thought contend – have no class character; the proletariat can turn them to account, and so can the bourgeoisie or others. Different classes, strata and social groups each have their own views on what are fragrant flowers and what are poisonous weeds. Then, from the point of view of the masses, what should be the criteria today for distinguishing fragrant flowers from poisonous weeds? In their political activities, how should our people judge whether a person's words and deeds are right or wrong? On the basis of the principles of our Constitution, the will of the overwhelming majority of our people and the common political positions which have been proclaimed on various occasions by our political parties, we consider that, broadly speaking, the criteria should be as follows:

1. Words and deeds should help to unite, and not divide, the people of all our nationalities.
2. They should be beneficial, and not harmful, to socialist transformation and socialist construction.
3. They should help to consolidate, and not undermine or weaken, the people's democratic dictatorship.
4. They should help to consolidate, and not undermine or weaken, democratic centralism.
5. They should help to strengthen, and not shake off or weaken, the leadership of the Communist Party.
6. They should be beneficial, and not harmful, to international socialist unity and the unity of the peace-loving people of the world.

Of these six criteria, the most important are the two about the socialist path and the leadership of the Party. These criteria are put forward not to hinder but to foster the free discussion of questions among the people. Those who disapprove of these criteria can still state their own views and argue their case. However, so long as the majority of the people have clear-cut criteria to go by, criticism and self-criticism can be conducted along proper lines, and these criteria can be applied to people's words and deeds to determine whether they are right or wrong, whether they are fragrant flowers or poisonous weeds. These are political criteria. Naturally, to judge the validity of scientific theories or assess the aesthetic value of works of art, other relevant criteria are needed. But these six political criteria are applicable to all activities in the arts and sciences. In a socialist country like ours, can there possibly be any useful scientific or artistic activity which runs counter to these political criteria?

The views set out above are based on China's specific historical conditions. Conditions vary in different socialist countries and with different Communist Parties. Therefore, we do not maintain that they should or must adopt the Chinese way.

The slogan 'long-term coexistence and mutual supervision' is also a product of China's specific historical conditions. It was not put forward all of a sudden, but had been in the making for several years. The idea of long-term coexistence had been there for a long time. When the socialist system was in the main established last year, the slogan was formulated in explicit terms. Why should the bourgeois and petty-bourgeois democratic parties be allowed to exist side by side with the party of the working class over a long period of time? Because we have no reason for not adopting the policy of long-term coexistence with all those political parties which are truly devoted to the task of uniting the people for the cause of socialism and which enjoy the trust of the people. As early as June 1950, at the second session of the First National Committee of the Political Consultative Conference, I put the matter in this way:

> The people and their government have no reason to reject anyone or deny him the opportunity of making a living and rendering service to the country, provided he is really willing to serve the people and provided he really helped and did a good turn when the people were faced with difficulties and keeps on doing good without giving up halfway.

What I was discussing here was the political basis for the long-term coexistence of the various parties. It is the desire as well as the policy of the Communist Party to exist side by side with the democratic parties for a long time to come. But whether the democratic parties can long remain in existence depends not merely on the desire of the Communist Party but on how well they acquit themselves and on whether they enjoy the trust of the people. Mutual supervision among the various parties is also a long-established fact, in the sense that they have long been advising and criticizing each other. Mutual supervision is obviously not a one-sided matter; it means that the Communist Party can exercise supervision over the democratic parties, and vice versa. Why should the democratic parties be allowed to exercise supervision over the Communist Party? Because a party as much as an individual has great need to hear opinions different from its own. We all know that supervision over the Communist Party is mainly exercised by the working people and the Party membership. But it augments the benefit to us to have supervision by the democratic parties too. Of course, the advice and criticism exchanged by the Communist Party and the democratic parties will play a positive supervisory role only when they conform to the six political criteria given above. Thus, we hope that in order to fit in with the needs of the new society, all the democratic parties will pay attention to ideological remoulding and strive for long-term coexistence with the Communist Party and mutual supervision.

IX. ON THE QUESTION OF DISTURBANCES CREATED BY SMALL NUMBERS OF PEOPLE

In 1956, small numbers of workers or students in certain places went on strike. The immediate cause of these disturbances was the failure to satisfy some of their demands for material benefits, of which some should and could have been met, while others were out of place or excessive and therefore could not be met for the time being. But a more important cause was bureaucracy on the part of the leadership. In some cases, the responsibility for such bureaucratic mistakes fell on the higher authorities, and those at the lower levels were not to blame. Another cause of these disturbances was lack of ideological and political education among the workers and students. The same year, in some agricultural cooperatives there were also disturbances created by a few of their members, and here too the main causes were bureaucracy on the part of the leadership and lack of educational work among the masses.

It should be admitted that among the masses some are prone to pay attention to immediate, partial and personal interests and do not understand, or do not sufficiently understand, long-range, national and collective interests. Because of lack of political and social experience, quite a number of young people cannot readily see the contrast between the old China and the new, and it is not easy for them thoroughly to comprehend the hardships our people went through in the struggle to free themselves from the oppression of the imperialists and Kuomintang reactionaries, or the long years of hard work needed before a fine socialist society can be established. That is why we must constantly carry on lively and effective political education among the masses and should always tell them the truth about the difficulties that crop up and discuss with them how to surmount these difficulties.

We do not approve of disturbances, because contradictions among the people can be resolved through the method of 'unity–criticism–unity', while disturbances are bound to cause some losses and are not conducive to the advance of socialism. We believe that the masses of the people support socialism, conscientiously observe discipline and are reasonable, and will certainly not take part in disturbances without cause. But this does not mean that the possibility of disturbances by the masses no longer exists in our country. On this question, we should pay attention to the following. (1) In order to root out the causes of disturbances, we must resolutely overcome bureaucracy, greatly improve ideological and political education, and deal with all contradictions properly. If this is done, generally speaking there will be no disturbances. (2) When disturbances do occur as a result of poor work on our part, then we should guide those involved onto the correct path, use the disturbances as a special means for improving our work and educating the cadres and the masses, and find solutions to those problems which were previously left unsolved. In handling any disturbance, we should take pains and not use oversimple methods, or hastily declare the matter closed. The ringleaders in disturbances should not be summarily expelled, except for those who have committed criminal offences or are active counter-revolutionaries and have to be punished by law. In a large country like ours, there is nothing to get alarmed about if small numbers of people create disturbances; on the contrary, such disturbances will help us get rid of bureaucracy.

There are also a small number of individuals in our society who, flouting the public interest, wilfully break the law and commit crimes. They are apt to take advantage of our policies and distort them, and deliberately put forward unreasonable demands in order to incite the masses, or deliberately spread rumours to create trouble and disrupt public order. We do not propose to let these individuals have their way. On the contrary, proper legal action must be taken against them. Punishing them is the demand of the masses, and it would run counter to the popular will if they were not punished.

X. CAN BAD THINGS BE TURNED INTO GOOD THINGS?

In our society, as I have said, disturbances by the masses are bad, and we do not approve of them. But when disturbances do occur, they enable us to learn lessons, to overcome bureaucracy and to educate the cadres and the masses. In this sense, bad things can be turned into good things. Disturbances thus have a dual character. Every disturbance can be regarded in this way.

Everybody knows that the Hungarian incident was not a good thing. But it too had a dual character. Because our Hungarian comrades took proper action in the course of the incident, what was a bad thing has eventually turned into a good one. Hungary is now more consolidated than ever, and all other countries in the socialist camp have also learned a lesson.

Similarly, the world-wide campaign against communism and the people which took place in the latter half of 1956 was of course a bad thing. But it served to educate and temper the Communist Parties and the working class in all countries, and thus it has turned into a good thing. In the storm and stress of this period, a number of people in many countries withdrew from the Communist Party. Withdrawal from the Party reduces its membership and is, of course, a bad thing. But there is a good side to it, too. Vacillating elements who are unwilling to carry on have withdrawn, and the vast majority who are staunch Party members can be the better united for struggle. Why isn't this a good thing?

To sum up, we must learn to look at problems from all sides, seeing the reverse as well as the obverse side of things. In given conditions, a bad thing can lead to good results and a good thing to bad results. More than two thousand years ago Lao Tzu said: 'Good fortune lieth within bad, bad fortune lurketh within good.'[1] When the Japanese shot their way into China, they called this a victory. Huge parts of China's territory were seized, and the Chinese called this a defeat. But victory was conceived in China's defeat, while defeat was conceived in Japan's victory. Hasn't history proved this true?

People all over the world are now discussing whether or not a third world war will break out. On this question, too, we must be mentally prepared and do some analysis. We stand firmly for peace and against war. But if the imperialists insist on unleashing another war, we should not be afraid of it. Our attitude on this question is the same as our attitude towards any disturbance: first, we are against it; second, we are not afraid of it. The First World War was followed by the birth of the Soviet Union with a population of 200 million. The Second World War was followed by the emergence of the socialist camp with a combined population of 900 million. If the imperialists insist on launching a third world war, it is certain that several hundred million more will turn to socialism, and then there will not be much room left on earth for the imperialists. It is also likely that the whole structure of imperialism will completely collapse.

In given conditions, each of the two opposing aspects of a contradiction invariably transforms itself into its opposite as a result of the struggle between them. Here, it is the conditions which are essential. Without the given conditions, neither of the two contradictory aspects can transform itself into its opposite. Of all the classes in the world the proletariat is the one which is most eager to change its position, and next comes the semi-proletariat, for the former possesses nothing at all while the latter is hardly any better off. The United States now controls a majority in the United Nations and dominates many parts of the world – this state of affairs is temporary and will be changed one of these days. China's position as a poor country denied its rights in international affairs will also be changed – the poor country will change into a rich one, the country denied its rights into one enjoying them – a transformation of things into their opposites. Here, the decisive conditions are the socialist system and the concerted efforts of a united people.

XI. ON PRACTISING ECONOMY

Here I wish to speak briefly about practising economy. We want to carry on large-scale construction, but our country is still very poor – herein lies a contradiction. One way of resolving it is to make a sustained effort to practise strict economy in every field.

During the movement against the 'three evils' in 1952, we fought against corruption, waste and bureaucracy, with the emphasis on combating corruption. In 1955 we advocated the practice of economy with great success, our emphasis then being on combating the unduly high standards for non-productive projects in capital construction and economizing on raw materials in industrial production. But at that time economy was not yet applied in earnest as a guiding principle in all branches of the national economy, or in government offices, army units, schools and people's organizations in general. This year we are calling for economy and the elimination of waste in every sphere throughout the country. We still lack experience in the work of construction. During the last few years, great successes have been achieved, but there has also been waste. We must build up a number of large-scale modern enterprises step by step to form the mainstay of our industry, without which we shall not be able to turn China into a powerful modern industrial country within the coming decades. But the majority of our enterprises should not be built on such a scale; we should set up more small and medium-sized enterprises and make full use of the industrial base inherited from the old society, so as to effect the greatest economy and do more with less money. Good results have begun to appear in the few months since the principle of practising strict economy and combating waste was put forward, in more emphatic terms than before, by the second plenary session of the Eighth Central Committee of the Communist Party of China in November 1956. The present campaign for economy must be conducted in a thorough and sustained way. Like the criticism of any other fault or mistake, the fight against waste may be compared to washing one's face. Don't people wash their faces every day? The Chinese Communist Party, the democratic parties, the democrats with no party affiliation, the intellectuals, industrialists and businessmen, workers, peasants and handicraftsmen – in short, all our 600 million people – must strive for increased production and economy, and against extravagance and waste. This is of prime importance not only economically, but politically as well. A dangerous tendency has shown itself of late among many of our personnel – an unwillingness to share weal and woe with the masses, a concern for personal fame and gain. This is very bad. One way of overcoming it is to streamline our organizations in the course of our campaign to increase production and practise economy, and to transfer cadres to lower levels so that a considerable number will return to productive work. We must see to it that all our cadres and all our people constantly bear in mind that ours is a large socialist country but an economically backward and poor one, and that this is a very big contradiction. To make China prosperous and strong needs several decades of hard struggle, which means, among other things, pursuing the policy of building up our country through diligence and thrift, that is, practising strict economy and fighting waste.

XII. CHINA'S PATH TO INDUSTRIALIZATION

In discussing our path to industrialization, we are here concerned principally with the relationship between the growth of heavy industry, light industry and agriculture. It must be affirmed that heavy industry is the core of China's economic construction. At the same time, full attention must be paid to the development of agriculture and light industry.

As China is a large agricultural country, with over 80 per cent of its population in the rural areas, agriculture must develop along with industry, for only thus can industry secure raw materials and a market, and only thus is it possible to accumulate more funds for building a powerful heavy industry. Everyone knows that light industry is closely tied up with agriculture. Without agriculture there can be no light industry. But it is not yet so clearly understood that agriculture provides heavy industry with an important market. This fact, however, will be more readily appreciated as gradual progress in the technical transformation and modernization of agriculture calls for more and more machinery, fertilizer, water conservancy and electric power projects and transport facilities for the farms, as well as fuel and building materials for the rural consumers. During the period of the Second and Third Five Year Plans, the entire national economy will benefit if we can achieve an even greater growth in our agriculture and thus induce a correspondingly greater development of light industry. As agriculture and light industry develop, heavy industry, assured of its market and funds, will grow faster. Hence what may seem to be a slower pace of industrialization will actually not be so slow, and indeed may even be faster. In three Five Year Plans or perhaps a little longer, China's annual steel output can be raised to 20,000,000 tons or more, as compared with the peak pre-liberation output of something over 900,000 tons in 1943. This will gladden the people in both town and country.

I do not propose to dwell on economic questions today. With barely seven years of economic construction behind us, we still lack experience and need to accumulate it. Neither had we any experience in revolution when we first started, and it was only after we had taken a number of tumbles and acquired experience that we won nation-wide victory. What we must now demand of ourselves is that we gain experience in economic construction in a shorter period of time than it took us to gain experience in revolution, and not to pay as high a price for it. Some price we shall have to pay, but we hope it will not be as high as that paid during the period of revolution. We must realize that there is a contradiction here – the contradiction between the objective laws of economic development of a socialist society and our subjective cognition of them – which needs to be resolved in the course of practice. This contradiction also manifests itself as a contradiction between different people, that is, a contradiction between those in whom the reflection of these objective laws is relatively accurate and those in whom the reflection is relatively inaccurate; this, too, is a contradiction among the people. Every contradiction is an objective reality, and it is our task to reflect it and resolve it in as nearly correct a fashion as we can.

In order to turn China into an industrial country, we must learn conscientiously from the advanced experience of the Soviet Union. The Soviet Union has been building socialism for forty years, and its experience is very valuable to us. Let us ask: who designed and equipped so many important factories for us? Was it the United States? Or Britain? No, neither the one nor the other. Only the Soviet Union was willing to do so, because it is a socialist country and our ally. In addition to the Soviet Union, the fraternal countries in Eastern Europe have also given us some assistance. It is perfectly true that we should learn from the good experience of all countries, socialist or capitalist: about this there is no argument. But the main thing is still to learn from the Soviet Union. Now there are two different attitudes towards learning from others. One is the dogmatic attitude of transplanting everything, whether or not it is suited to our conditions. This is no good. The other attitude is to use our heads and learn those things which suit our conditions, that is, to absorb whatever experience is useful to us. That is the attitude we should adopt.

To strengthen our solidarity with the Soviet Union, to strengthen our solidarity with all the socialist countries – this is our fundamental policy, this is where our basic interests lie. Then there are the Asian and African countries and all the peace-loving countries and peoples – we must strengthen and develop our solidarity with them. United with these two forces, we shall not stand alone. As for the imperialist countries, we should unite with their people and strive to coexist peacefully with those countries, do business with them and prevent a possible war, but under no circumstances should we harbour any unrealistic notions about them.

WHERE DO CORRECT IDEAS COME FROM?

May 1963

This passage is from the 'Draft Decision of the Central Committee of the Chinese Communist Party on Certain Problems in Our Present Rural Work', which was drawn up under the direction of Comrade Mao Tse-tung. The passage was written by Comrade Mao Tse-tung himself.

Where do correct ideas come from? Do they drop from the skies? No. Are they innate in the mind? No. They come from social practice, and from it alone; they come from three kinds of social practice: the struggle for production, the class struggle and scientific experiment. It is man's social being that determines his thinking. Once the correct ideas characteristic of the advanced class are grasped by the masses, these ideas turn into a material force which changes society and changes the world. In their social practice, men engage in various kinds of struggle and gain rich experience, both from their successes and from their failures. Countless phenomena of the objective external world are reflected in a man's brain through his five sense organs – the organs of sight, hearing, smell, taste and touch. At first, knowledge is perceptual. The leap to conceptual knowledge, i.e., to ideas, occurs when sufficient perceptual knowledge is accumulated. This is one process in cognition. It is the first stage in the whole process of cognition, the stage leading from objective matter to subjective consciousness, from existence to ideas. Whether or not one's consciousness or ideas (including theories, policies, plans or measures) do correctly reflect the laws of the objective external world is not yet proved at this stage, in which it is not yet possible to ascertain whether they are correct or not. Then comes the second stage in the process of cognition, the stage leading from consciousness back to matter, from ideas back to existence, in which the knowledge gained in the first stage is applied in social practice to ascertain whether the theories, policies, plans or measures meet with the anticipated success. Generally speaking, those that succeed are correct and those that fail are incorrect, and this is especially true of man's struggle with nature. In social struggle, the forces representing the advanced class sometimes suffer defeat not because their ideas are incorrect but because, in the balance of forces engaged in struggle, they are not as powerful for the time being as the forces of reaction; they are therefore temporarily defeated, but they are bound to triumph sooner or later. Man's knowledge makes another leap through the test of practice. This leap is more important than the previous one. For it is this leap alone that can prove the correctness or incorrectness of the first leap in cognition, i.e., of the ideas, theories, policies, plans or measures formulated in the course of reflecting the objective external world. There is no other way of testing truth. Furthermore, the one and only purpose of the proletariat in knowing the world is to change it. Often, correct knowledge can be arrived at only after many repetitions of the process leading from matter to consciousness and then back to matter, that is, leading from practice to knowledge and then back to practice. Such is the Marxist theory of knowledge, the dialectical materialist theory of knowledge. Among our comrades there are many who do not yet understand this theory of knowledge. When asked the sources of their ideas, opinions, policies, methods, plans and conclusions, eloquent speeches and long articles, they consider the question strange and cannot answer it. Nor do they comprehend that matter can be transformed into consciousness and consciousness into matter, although such leaps are phenomena of every-day life. It is therefore necessary to educate our comrades in the dialectical materialist theory of knowledge, so that they can orient their thinking correctly, become good at investigation and study and at summing up experience, overcome difficulties, make fewer mistakes, do their work better, and struggle hard so as to build China into a great and powerful socialist country and help the broad masses of the oppressed and exploited throughout the world in fulfilment of our great inter-nationalist duty.

12

TALK ON QUESTIONS
OF PHILOSOPHY

18 August 1964

It is only when there is class struggle that there can be philosophy. It is a waste of time to discuss epistemology apart from practice. The comrades who study philosophy should go down to the countryside. They should go down this winter or next spring to participate in the class struggle. Those whose health is not good should go too. Going down won't kill people. All they'll do is catch a cold, and if they just put on a few extra layers of clothes it'll be all right.

The way they go about it in the universities at present is no good, going from book to book, from concept to concept. How can philosophy come from books? The three basic constituents of Marxism are scientific socialism, philosophy and political economy.[1] The foundation is social science, class struggle. There is a struggle between the proletariat and the bourgeoisie. Marx and the others saw this. Utopian socialists are always trying to persuade the bourgeoisie to be charitable. This won't work, it is necessary to rely on the class struggle of the proletariat. At that time, there had already been many strikes. The English parliamentary inquiry recognized that the twelve-hour day was less favourable than the eight-hour day to the interests of the capitalists. It is only starting from this viewpoint that Marxism appeared. The foundation is class struggle. The study of philosophy can only come afterwards. Whose philosophy? Bourgeois philosophy or proletarian philosophy? Proletarian philosophy is Marxist philosophy. There is also proletarian economics, which has transformed classical economics. Those who engage in philosophy believe that philosophy comes first. The oppressors oppress the oppressed, while the oppressed need to fight back and seek a way out before they start looking for philosophy. It is only when people took this as their starting point that there was Marxism-Leninism, and that they discovered philosophy. We have all been through this. Others wanted to kill me; Chiang Kai-shek wanted to kill me. Thus we came to engage in class struggle, to engage in philosophizing.

University students should start going to the countryside this winter – I am referring to the humanities. Students of natural science should not be moved now, though we can move them for a spell or two. All those studying the humanities – history, political economy, literature, law – must every one of them go. Professors, assistant professors, administrative workers and students should all of them go down, for a limited period of five months. If they go to the countryside for five months, or to the factories for five months, they will acquire some perceptual knowledge. Horses, cows, sheep, chickens, dogs, pigs, rice, sorghum, beans, wheat, varieties of millet – they can have a look at all these things. If they go in the winter, they will not see the harvest, but at least they can still see the land and the people. To get some experience of class struggle – that's what I call a university. They argue about which university is better, Peking University or People's University.[2] For my part I am a graduate of the university of the greenwoods, I learned a bit there. In the past I studied Confucius, and spent six years on the Four Books and the Five Classics.[3] I learned to recite them from memory, but I did not understand them. At that time, I believed deeply in Confucius, and even wrote essays [expounding his ideas]. Later I went to a bourgeois school for seven years. Seven plus six makes thirteen years. I studied all the usual bourgeois stuff – natural science and social science. They also taught some pedagogy. This includes five years of normal school, two years of middle school, and also the time I spent in the library.[4] At that time I believed in Kant's dualism, especially in his idealism. Originally I was a feudalist and an advocate of bourgeois democracy. Society impelled me to participate in the revolution. I spent a few years as a primary school teacher and principal of a four-year school. I also taught history and Chinese language in a six-year school. I also taught for a short period in a middle school, but I did not understand a thing. When I joined the Communist Party I knew that we must make revolution, but against what? And how would we go about it? Of course we had to make revolution against imperialism and the old society. I did not quite understand what sort of a thing imperialism was, still less did I understand how we could make revolution against it. None of the stuff I had learned in thirteen years was any good for making revolution. I used only the instrument – language. Writing essays is an instrument. As for the content of my studies, I didn't use it at all. Confucius said: 'Benevolence is the characteristic element of humanity.' 'The benevolent man loves others.'[5] Whom did he love? All men? Nothing of the kind. Did he love the exploiters? It wasn't exactly that, either. He loved only a part of the exploiters. Otherwise, why wasn't Confucius able to be a high official? People didn't want him. He loved them, and wanted them to unite. But when it came to starving, and to [the precept] 'The superior man can endure poverty', he almost lost his life, the people of K'uang wanted to kill him.[6] There were those who criticized him for not visiting Ch'in during his journey to the West. In reality, the poem 'In the Seventh Month the Fire Star Passes the Meridian' in the *Book of Odes* refers to events in Shensi. There is also 'The Yellow Bird', which talks about the affair in which three high officials of Duke Mu of Ch'in were killed and buried with him on his death.[7] Ssu-ma Ch'ien[8] had a very high opinion of the *Book of Odes*. He said the 300 poems it contains were all written by sages and worthies of ancient times when they were roused. A large part of the poems in the *Book of Odes* are in the manner of the various states, they are the folk songs of the common people, the sages and worthies are none other than the common people. 'Written when they were roused' means that when a man's heart was filled with anger, he wrote a poem!

You sow not nor reap;
How do you get the paddy for your three hundred round bins?
You do not follow the chase;
How do we see the quails hanging in your courtyards?
O that superior man!
He would not eat the bread of idleness![9]

The expression 'to neglect the duties of an office while taking the pay' comes from here. This is a poem which accuses heaven and opposes the rulers. Confucius, too, was rather democratic, he included [in the *Book of Odes*] poems about the love between man and woman. In his commentaries, Chu Hsi characterized them as poems about clandestine love affairs.[10] In reality, some of them are and some of them aren't; the latter borrow the imagery of man and woman to write about the relations between prince and subject. In Shu [present-day Szechwan] at the time of the Five Dynasties and Ten Counties, there was a poem entitled 'The Wife of Ch'in Laments the Winter', by Wei Chuang.[11] He wrote it in his youth, and it is about his longing for his prince.

To return to this matter of going down, people should go beginning this winter and spring, in groups and in rotation, to participate in the class struggle. Only in this way can they learn something, learn about revolution. You intellectuals sit every day in your government offices, eating well, dressing well, and not even doing any walking. That's why you fall ill. Clothing, food, housing and exercise are the four great factors causing disease. If, from enjoying good living conditions, you change to somewhat worse conditions, if you go down to participate in the class struggle, if you go into the midst of the 'four clean-ups' and the 'five antis',[12] and undergo a spell of toughening, then you intellectuals will have a new look about you.

If you don't engage in class struggle, then what is this philosophy you're engaged in?

Why not go down and try it? If your illness gets too severe you should come back – you have to draw the line at dying. When you are so ill that you are on the verge of dying, then you should come back. As soon as you go down, you will have some spirit. *(K'ang Sheng interjects: 'The research institutes in the Departments of Philosophy and Social Science of the Academy of Science should all go down too. At present, they are on the verge of turning into institutes for the study of antiquities, of turning into a fairyland nourishing itself by inhaling offerings of incense. None of the people in the Institute of Philosophy read the Kuang-ming jih-pao.')* I read only the Kuang-ming jih-pao and the Wen-hui pao,[13] I don't read People's Daily, because the People's Daily doesn't publish theoretical articles; after we adopt a resolution, then they publish it. The Liberation Army Daily is lively, it's readable. *(Comrade K'ang Sheng: 'The Institute of Literature pays no attention to Chou Ku-ch'eng,[14] and the Economics Institute pays no attention to Sun Yeh-fang[15] and to his going in for Libermanism, going in for capitalism.')*

Let them go in for capitalism. Society is very complex. If one only goes in for socialism and not for capitalism, isn't that too simple? Wouldn't we then lack the unity of opposites, and be merely one-sided? Let them do it. Let them attack us madly, demonstrate in the streets, take up arms to rebel – I approve all of these things. Society is very complex, there is not a single commune, a single *hsien,* a single department of the Central Committee, which one cannot divide into two. Just look, hasn't the Department of Rural Work been disbanded?[16] It devoted itself exclusively to accounting on the basis of the individual household, and to propagating the 'four great freedoms' – freedom to lend money, to engage in commerce, to hire labour and to buy and sell land. In the past, they put out a proclamation [to this effect]. Teng Tzu-hui had a dispute with me. At a meeting of the Central Committee, he put forward the idea of implementing the four great freedoms.[17]

To consolidate New Democracy, and to go on consolidating it for ever, is to engage in capitalism.[18] New Democracy is a bourgeois-democratic revolution under the leadership of the proletariat. It touches only the landlords and the comprador bourgeoisie, it does not touch the national bourgeoisie at all. To divide up the land and give it to the peasants is to transform the property of the feudal landlords into the individual property of the peasants, and this still remains within the limits of the bourgeois revolution. To divide up the land is nothing remarkable – MacArthur did it in Japan. Napoleon divided up the land too. Land reform cannot abolish capitalism, nor can it lead to socialism.

In our state at present approximately one-third of the power is in the hands of the enemy or of the enemy's sympathizers. We have been going for fifteen years and we now control two-thirds of the realm. At present, you can buy a [Party] branch secretary for a few packs of cigarettes, not to mention marrying a daughter to him. There are some localities where land reform was carried out peacefully, and the land reform teams were very weak; now you can see that there are a lot of problems there.

I have received the materials on philosophy. [*This refers to the materials on the problem of contradictions – note by stenographer.*] I have had a look at the outline, [*This refers to the outline of an article criticizing 'two combine into one'*[19] *– note by stenographer.*] I have not been able to read the rest. I have also looked at the materials on analysis and synthesis.

It is a good thing to collect materials like this on the law of the unity of opposites, what the bourgeoisie says about it, what Marx, Engels, Lenin and Stalin say about it, what the revisionists say about it. As for the bourgeoisie, Yang Hsien-chen talks about it, and Hegel of old talked about it. Such people existed in the olden days. Now they are even worse. There were also Bogdanov and Lunacharsky, who used to talk about deism. I have read Bogdanov's economics. Lenin read it, and it seems he approved of the part on primitive accumulation. (*K'ang Sheng:*

'Bogdanov's economic doctrines were perhaps somewhat more enlightened than those of modern revisionism. Kautsky's economic doctrines were somewhat more enlightened than those of Khrushchev, and Yugoslavia is also somewhat more enlightened than the Soviet Union. After all, Djilas said a few good things about Stalin, he said that on Chinese problems Stalin made a self-criticism.'

Stalin felt that he had made mistakes in dealing with Chinese problems, and they were no small mistakes. We are a great country of several hundred millions, and he opposed our revolution, and our seizure of power. We prepared for many years in order to seize power in the whole country, the whole of the Anti-Japanese War constituted a preparation. This is quite clear if you look at the documents of the Central Committee for that period, including *On New Democracy*. That is to say, you cannot set up a bourgeois dictatorship, you can only establish New Democracy under the leadership of the proletariat, you can only set up a people's democratic dictatorship led by the proletariat. In our country, for eighty years, all the democratic revolutions led by the bourgeoisie failed. The democratic revolution led by us will certainly be victorious. There is only this way out, there is no other way out. This is the first step. The second step will be to build socialism. Thus, *On New Democracy* was a complete programme. It discussed politics, economics and culture as well; it failed to discuss only military affairs. *(K'ang Sheng: 'On New Democracy is of great significance for the world communist movement. I asked Spanish comrades, and they said the problem for them was to establish bourgeois democracy, not to establish New Democracy. In their country, they did not concern themselves with the three points: army, countryside, political power. They wholly subordinated themselves to the exigencies of Soviet foreign policy, and achieved nothing at all.')* These are the policies of Ch'en Tu-hsiu! *(Comrade K'ang Sheng: 'They say the Communist Party organized an army, and then turned it over to others.')* This is useless.

(Comrade K'ang Sheng: 'They also did not want political power, nor did they mobilize the peasantry. At that time, the Soviet Union said to them that if they imposed proletarian leadership, England and France might oppose it, and this would not be in the interests of the Soviet Union.')

How about Cuba? In Cuba they concerned themselves precisely to set up political power and an army, and also mobilized the peasants, as [we did] in the past; therefore they succeeded.

(Comrade K'ang Sheng: 'Also, when they [the Spanish] fought, they waged regular war, in the manner of the bourgeoisie, they defended Madrid to the last.[20] In all things, they subordinated themselves to Soviet foreign policy.')

Even before the dissolution of the Third International, we did not obey the orders of the Third International. At the Tsunyi Conference we didn't obey, and afterwards, for a period of ten years, including the Rectification Campaign and down to the Seventh Congress, when we finally adopted a resolution ('Resolution on Certain Questions in the History of our Party'),[21] and corrected [the errors of] 'Leftism', we didn't obey them at all. Those dogmatists utterly failed to study China's peculiarities; ten-odd years after they had betaken themselves to the countryside, they utterly failed to study the land, property and class relationships in the countryside. You can't understand the countryside just by going there, you must study the relations between all the classes and strata in the countryside. I devoted more than ten years to these problems before I finally clarified them for myself. You must make contact with all kinds of people, in tea houses and gambling dens, and investigate them. In 1925 I was active at the Peasant Movement Training Institute,[22] and carried out rural surveys. In my native village, I sought out poor peasants to ask them about how they lived. Their lives were pitiable, they had nothing to eat. There was one peasant whom I sought out to play dominoes with (the kind with heaven, earth, man, harmony, Mei Ch'ien, Ch'ang Sang and the bench), afterwards inviting him to eat with me. Before, after and during the meal, I talked to him, and came to understand why the class struggle in the countryside was so acute. The reasons he was willing to talk to me were: first, that I looked on him as a human being; second, that I invited him to have a meal; and third, that he could make a bit of money. I kept losing: I lost one or two silver dollars, and as a result he was very well satisfied. I had a friend who came to see me twice after Liberation. Once, in the days before Liberation, he was really in a bad way, and he came looking for me to borrow a dollar. I gave him three, as non-refundable assistance. In those days, such non-refundable assistance was hard to come by. My father took the view that if a man did not look after himself, heaven and earth would punish him. My mother opposed him. When my father died, very few people followed the funeral procession. When my mother died, a great many followed the procession. One time the Ko Lao Hui robbed our family. I said they were right to do so, for people had nothing. Even my mother could not accept this at all.

Once there broke out in Changsha rice riots in which the provincial governor was beaten up. There were some hawkers from Hsiang Hsiang who had sold their broad beans and were straggling back home. I stopped them and asked them about the situation. The Red and Green Gangs in the countryside also held meetings and ate up big families. This was reported in the Shanghai newspapers, and the troubles were only stamped out when troops were sent from Changsha. They did not maintain good discipline, they took the rice of the middle peasants, and so isolated themselves. One of their leaders fled hither and thither, finally taking refuge in the mountains, but he was caught there and executed. Afterwards, the village gentry held a meeting, and killed a few more poor peasants. At that time, there was as yet no Communist Party; these were spontaneous class struggles.

Society pushed us on to the political stage. Who ever thought of indulging in Marxism previously? I hadn't even heard of it. What I had heard of, and also read of, was Confucius, Napoleon, Washington, Peter the Great, the Meiji Restoration, the three distinguished Italian [patriots] – in other words, all those [heroes] of capitalism. I had also read a biography of Franklin. He came from a poor family; afterwards, he became a writer, and also conducted experiments on electricity. *(Ch'en Po-ta: 'Franklin was the first to put forward the proposition that man is a tool-making animal.')*

He talked about man being a tool-making animal. Formerly, they used to say that man was a thinking animal, 'the organ of the heart can think';[23] they said that man was the soul of all creation. Who called a meeting and elected him [to that position]? He conferred this dignity on himself. This proposition existed in the feudal era. Afterwards, Marx put forward the view that man is a tool-maker, and that man is a social animal. In reality it is only after undergoing a million years [of evolution] that man developed a large brain and a pair of hands. In the future, animals will continue to develop. I don't believe that men alone are capable of having two hands. Can't horses, cows, sheep evolve? Can only monkeys evolve? And can it be, moreover, that of all the monkeys only one species can evolve, and all the others are incapable of evolving? In a million years, ten million years, will horses, cows and sheep still be the same as those today? I think they will continue to change. Horses, cows, sheep and insects will all change. Animals have evolved from plants, they have evolved from seaweed. Chang T'ai-yen knew all this. In the book in which he argued about revolution with K'ang Yu-wei, he expounded these principles.[24] The earth was originally dead, there were no plants, no water, no air. Only after I don't know how many tens of millions of years was water formed; hydrogen and oxygen aren't just transformed immediately in any old way into water. Water has its history too. Earlier still, even hydrogen and oxygen did not exist. Only after hydrogen and oxygen were produced was there the possibility that these two elements could combine to give water.

We must study the history of the natural sciences, it won't do to neglect this subject. We must read a few books. There is a great difference between reading because of the necessities of our present struggles, and reading aimlessly. Fu Ying[25] says that hydrogen and oxygen form water only after coming together hundreds and thousands of times; it is not at all a simple case of two combining into one. He was right about this, too; I want to look him up and have a talk. (*Speaking to Lu P'ing*:[26]) You people should not oppose absolutely everything by Fu Ying.

Hitherto, analysis and synthesis have not been clearly defined. Analysis is clearer, but there hasn't been much said about synthesis. I had a talk with Ai Ssu-ch'i.[27] He said that nowadays they only talk about conceptual synthesis and analysis, and do not talk about objective practical synthesis and analysis. How do we analyse and synthesize the Communist Party and the Kuomintang, the proletariat and the bourgeoisie, the landlords and the peasants, the Chinese and the imperialists? How do we do this, for example, in the case of the Communist Party and the Kuomintang? The analysis is simply a question of how strong we are, how much territory we have, how many members we have, how many troops, how many bases such as Yenan, what are our weaknesses? We do not hold any big cities, our army numbers only 1,200,000, we have no foreign aid, whereas the Kuomintang has a great amount of foreign aid. If you compare Yenan to Shanghai, Yenan has a population of only 7,000; adding to this the persons from the [Party and government] organs and from the troops [stationed in Yenan], the total comes to 20,000. There is only handicrafts and agriculture. How can this be compared with a big city? Our strong points are that we have the support of the people whereas the Kuomintang is divorced from the people. You have more territory, more troops and more arms, but your soldiers have been obtained by impressment, and there is opposition between officers and soldiers. Naturally there is also a fairly large portion of their armies which has considerable fighting capacity, it is not at all the case that they will all just collapse at one blow. Their weak point lies here, the key is their divorce from the people. We unite with the popular masses; they are divorced from the popular masses.

They say in their propaganda that the Communist Party establishes community of property and community of wives, and they propagate these ideas right down to the primary schools. They composed a song: 'When Chu Te and Mao Tse-tung appear, killing and burning and doing all kinds of things, what will you do?' They taught the primary school pupils to sing it, and as soon as they had sung it, the pupils went and asked their fathers and mothers, brothers and sisters, thus producing the opposite effect of propaganda for us. There was a little child who heard [the song] and asked his father about it. His father replied: 'You mustn't ask; after you have grown up, you will see for yourself and then you'll understand.' He was a middle-of-the-roader. Then the child asked his uncle. The uncle scolded him, replying: 'What is this about killing and burning? If you ask me again, I'll beat you.' Formerly, his uncle was a member of the Communist Youth League. All the newspapers and radio stations attacked us. There were a lot of newspapers, several dozen in each city, every faction ran one, and all of them without exception were anti-communist. Did the common people all listen to them? Nothing of the kind! We have some experience of Chinese affairs, China is a 'sparrow'.[28] In foreign countries, too, it's nothing else but the rich and the poor, counter-revolution and revolution, Marxism-Leninism and revisionism. You really shouldn't believe that everybody will be taken in by anti-communist propaganda, and join in opposing communism. Didn't we read newspapers at the time? Yet we were not influenced by them.

I have read the *Dream of the Red Chamber* five times, and have not been influenced by it. I read it as history. First I read it as a story, and then as history. When people read the *Dream of the Red Chamber,* they don't read the fourth chapter carefully, but in fact this chapter contains the gist of the book. There is also Leng Tzu-hsing who describes the Jung-kuo mansion, and composes songs and notes. The fourth chapter, 'The Bottle-Gourd Monk', decides the affair of the bottle gourd and talks about the 'Talisman for Officials'. It introduces the four big families:

Shout hip hurrah
For the Nanking Chia!
They weigh their gold out
By the jar.
The Ah-pang Palace
Scrapes the sky,

But it could not house
The Nanking Shih.
The King of the Ocean
Goes along,
When he's short of gold beds,
To the Nanking Wang.
The Nanking Hsueh
So rich are they,
To count their money
Would take all day . . .[29]

The *Dream of the Red Chamber* describes each of the four big families. It concerns a fierce class struggle, involving the fate of many dozens of people, though only twenty or thirty of these people are in the ruling class. (It has been calculated that there are thirty-three [in this category].) The others are all slaves, over three hundred of them, such as Yueh Yang, Ssu-ch'i, Second Sister Yu, Third Sister Yu, etc. In studying history, unless you take a class-struggle view as the starting point, you will get confused. Things can only be analysed clearly by the use of class analysis. More than two hundred years have elapsed since the *Dream of the Red Chamber* was written, and research on the book has not clarified the issues, even down to the present day. From this we can see the difficulty of the problem. There are Yu P'ing-po and Wang K'un-lun, who are both of them specialists.[30] Ho Ch'i-fang[31] also wrote a preface. A fellow called Wu Shih-ch'ang[32] has also appeared on the scene. All this refers to recent research on the *Dream of the Red Chamber,* I won't even enumerate the older studies. Ts'ai Yuan-p'ei's view of the *Dream of the Red Chamber* was incorrect; Hu Shih's was somewhat more correct.[33]

What is synthesis? You have all witnessed how the two opposites, the Kuomintang and the Communist Party, were synthesized on the mainland. The synthesis took place like this: their armies came, and we devoured them, we ate them bite by bite. It was not a case of two combining into one as expounded by Yang Hsien-chen, it was not the synthesis of two peacefully coexisting opposites. They didn't want to coexist peacefully, they wanted to devour you. Otherwise, why would they have attacked Yenan? Their army penetrated everywhere in North Shensi, except in three *hsien* on the three borders. You have your freedom, and we have our freedom. There are 250,000 of you, and

25,000 of us.[34] A few brigades, something over 20,000 men. Having analysed, how do we synthesize? If you want to go somewhere, you go right ahead; we still swallow your army mouthful by mouthful. If we could fight victoriously, we fought; if we could not win, we retreated. From March 1947 to March 1948, one whole army [of the enemy] disappeared into the landscape, for we annihilated several tens of thousands of their troops. When we surrounded I-ch'uan, and Liu K'an came to relieve the city, the commander-in-chief Liu K'an was killed, two of his three divisional commanders were killed and the other taken prisoner, and the whole army ceased to exist. This was synthesis. All of their guns and artillery were synthesized over to our side, and the soldiers were synthesized too. Those who wanted to stay with us could stay, and to those who didn't want to stay we gave money for their travelling expenses. After we had annihilated Liu K'an, the brigade stationed in I-ch'uan surrendered without fighting. In the three great campaigns – Liao-Shen, Huai-Hai and Peking-Tientsin – what was our method of synthesis? Fu Tso-i was synthesized over to our side with his army of 400,000 men, without fighting, and they handed over all their rifles.[35] One thing eating another, big fish eating little fish, this is synthesis. It has never been put like this in books. I have never put it this way in my books either. For his part, Yang Hsien-chen believes that two combine into one, and that synthesis is the indissoluble tie between two opposites. What indissoluble ties are there in this world? Things may be tied, but in the end they must be severed. There is nothing which cannot be severed. In the twenty-odd years of our struggle, many of us have also been devoured by the enemy. When the 300,000-strong Red Army reached the Shen-Kan-Ning area, there were only 25,000 left. Of the others, some had been devoured, some scattered, some killed or wounded.

We must take life as our starting point in discussing the unity of opposites. *(Comrade K'ang Sheng: 'It won't do merely to talk about concepts.')*

While analysis is going on, there is also synthesis, and while synthesis is going on, there is also analysis.

When people eat animals and plants, they also begin with analysis. Why don't we eat sand? When there's sand in rice, it's not good to eat. Why don't we eat grass, as do horses, cows and sheep, but only things like cabbage? We must analyze everything. Shen Nung tasted the hundred herbs,[36] and originated their use for medicine. After many tens of thousands of years, analysis finally revealed clearly what could be eaten and what could not. Grasshoppers, snakes and turtles can be eaten. Crabs, dogs and aquatic creatures can be eaten. There are some foreigners who don't eat them. In North Shensi they don't eat aquatic creatures, they don't eat fish. They don't eat cat there either. One year there was a big flood of the Yellow River, which cast up on the shore tens of thousands of pounds of fish, and they used it all for fertilizer.

I am a native philosopher, you are foreign philosophers.

(*Comrade Sheng: 'Could the Chairman say something about the problem of the three categories?'*)

Engels talked about the three categories, but as for me I don't believe in two of those categories. (The unity of opposites is the most basic law, the transformation of quality and quantity into one another is the unity of the opposites quality and quantity, and the negation of the negation does not exist at all.) The juxtaposition, on the same level, of the transformation of quality and quantity into one another, the negation of the negation, and the law of the unity of opposites is 'triplism', not monism. The most basic thing is the unity of opposites. The transformation of quality and quantity into one another is the unity of the opposites quality and quantity. There is no such thing as the negation of the negation. Affirmation, negation, affirmation, negation . . . in the development of things, every link in the chain of events is both affirmation and negation. Slave-holding society negated primitive society, but with reference to feudal society it constituted, in turn, the affirmation. Feudal society constituted the negation in relation to slave-holding society but it was in turn the affirmation with reference to capitalist society. Capitalist society was the negation in relation to feudal society, but it is, in turn, the affirmation in relation to socialist society.

What is the method of synthesis? Is it possible that primitive society can exist side by side with slave-holding society? They do exist side by side, but this is only a small part of the whole. The overall picture is that primitive society is going to be eliminated. The development of society, moreover, takes place by stages; primitive society, too, is divided into a great many stages. At that time, there was not yet the practice of burying women with their dead husbands, but they were obliged to subject themselves to men. First men were subject to women, and then things moved towards their opposite, and women were subject to men. This stage in history has not yet been clarified, although it has been going on for a million years and more. Class society has not yet lasted 5,000 years. Cultures such as that of Lung Shan and Yang Shao[37] at the end of the primitive era had coloured pottery. In a word, one devours another, one overthrows another, one class is eliminated, another class rises, one society is eliminated, another society rises. Naturally, in the process of development, everything is not all that pure. When it gets to feudal society, there still remains something of the slave-holding system, though the greater part of the social edifice is characterized by the feudal system. There are still some serfs, and also some bond-workers, such as handicraftsmen. Capitalist society isn't all that pure either, and even in more advanced capitalist societies there is also a backward part. For example, there was the slave system in the Southern United States. Lincoln abolished the slave system, but there are still black slaves today, their struggle is very fierce. More than twenty million people are participating in it, and that's quite a few.

One thing destroys another, things emerge, develop and are destroyed, everywhere is like this. If things are not destroyed by others, then they destroy themselves. Why should people die? Does the aristocracy die too? This is a natural law. Forests live longer than human beings, yet even they last only a few thousand years. If there were no such thing as death, that would be unbearable. If we could still see Confucius alive today, the earth wouldn't be able to hold so many people. I approve of Chuang-tzu's approach.[38] When his wife died, he banged on a basin and sang. When people die there should be parties to celebrate the victory of dialectics, to celebrate the destruction of the old. Socialism, too, will be eliminated, it wouldn't do if it were not eliminated, for then there would be no communism. Communism will last for thousands and thousands of years. I don't believe that there will be no qualitative changes under communism, that it will not be divided into stages by qualitative changes! I don't believe it! Quantity changes into quality, and quality changes into quantity. I don't believe that it can remain qualitatively exactly the same, unchanging for millions of years! This is unthinkable in the light of dialectics. Then there is the principle 'From each according to his ability, to each according to his needs'. Do you believe they can carry on for a million years with the same economics? Have you thought about it? If that were so, we wouldn't need economists, or in any case we could get along with just one textbook, and dialectics would be dead.

The life of dialectics is the continuous movement towards opposites. Mankind will also finally meet its doom. When the theologians talk about doomsday, they are pessimistic and terrify people. We say the end of mankind is something which will produce something more advanced than mankind. Mankind is still in its infancy. Engels spoke of moving from the realm of necessity to the realm of freedom, and said that freedom is the understanding of necessity. This sentence is not complete, it only says one half and leaves the rest unsaid. Does merely understanding it make you free? Freedom is the understanding of necessity *and* the transformation of necessity – one has some work to do too. If you merely eat without having any work to do, if you merely understand, is that sufficient? When you discover a law, you must be able to apply it, you must create the world anew, you must break the ground and erect buildings, you must dig mines, industrialize. In the future there will be more people, and there won't be enough grain, so men will have to get food from minerals. Thus it is that only by transformation can freedom be obtained. Will it be possible in the future to be all that free? Lenin said that in the future aeroplanes would be as numerous in the skies as flies, rushing hither and thither. Everywhere they will collide, and what will we do about it? How will we manoeuvre them? And if we do, will things be all that free? In Peking at present there are 10,000 buses; in Tokyo there are 100,000 [vehicles] (or is it 800,000?), so there are more automobile accidents. We have fewer cars, and we also educate the drivers and the people, so there are few accidents. What will they do in Peking 10,000 years hence? Will there still be 10,000 buses? They may invent something new, so that they can dispense with these means of transport, so that men can fly, using some simple mechanical device, and fly right to any place, and land wherever they like. It won't do just to understand necessity, we must also transform things.

I don't believe that communism will not be divided into stages, and that there will be no qualitative changes. Lenin said that all things could be divided. He gave the atom as an example, saying that not only could it be divided, but the electron could, too. Formerly, however, it was held that the atom could not be divided; the branch of science devoted to splitting the atomic nucleus is still very young, only twenty or thirty years old. In recent decades, the scientists have resolved the atomic nucleus into its constituents, such as protons, anti-protons, neutrons, anti-neutrons, mesons and anti-mesons. These are the heavy ones; there are also the light ones. For the most part, these discoveries only got under way during and after the Second World War. As for the fact that one could separate the electrons from the atomic nucleus, that was discovered some time ago. An electric wire makes use of dissociated electrons from the outside of copper or aluminium. In the 300 li of the earth's atmosphere, it has also been discovered that there are layers of dissociated electrons. There, too, the electrons and the atomic nucleus are separated. As yet, the electron has not been split, but some day they will certainly be able to split it. Chuang-tzu said, 'A length of one foot, which is divided in half each day, will never be reduced to zero' *(Chuang-tzu,* chapter [33 G] 'On the Various Schools', quoting Kung-sun Lung). This is the truth. If you don't believe it, just consider. If it could be reduced to zero, then there would be no such thing as science. The myriad things develop continuously and limitlessly, and they are infinite. Time and space are infinite. As regards space, looking at it both macroscopically and microscopically, it is infinite, it can be divided endlessly. So even after a million years scientists will still have work to do. I very much appreciate the article on basic particles in the *Bulletin of Natural Science* by Sakata.[39] I have never seen this kind of article before. This is dialectical materialism. He quotes Lenin.

The weakness of philosophy is that it hasn't produced practical philosophy, but only bookish philosophy.

We should always be bringing forward new things. Otherwise what are we here for? What do we want descendants for? New things are to be found in reality, we must grasp reality. In the last analysis, is Jen Chi-yü[40] Marxist or not? I greatly appreciate those articles of his on Buddhism. There is some research [behind them], he is a student of T'ang Yung-t'ung.[41] He discusses only the Buddhism of the Tang dynasty, and does not touch directly on the Buddhism of later times. Sung and Ming metaphysics developed from the Ch'an School of the Tang dynasty, and it was a movement from subjective idealism to objective idealism.[42] There is both Buddhism and Taoism, and it is wrong not to distinguish between them. How can it be proper not to pay attention to them? Han Yu didn't talk sense. His slogan was, 'Learn from their ideas, but not from their mode of expression.' His ideas were entirely copied from others, he changed the form, the mode of composition of the essays. He didn't talk sense, and the little bit he did talk was basically taken from the ancients. There is little new in writings like the *Discourse on Teachers.* Liu Tzu-hou was different: he knew the ins and outs of Buddhist and Taoist materialism.[43] And yet his 'Heaven Answers' is too short, just a little bit. His 'Heaven Answers' is a product of Ch'u Yuan's 'Heaven Asks.'[44] For several thousand years only this one man has written a piece such as

'Heaven Answers'. What are 'Heaven Asks' and 'Heaven Answers' all about? If there are no annotations to explain it, you can't understand it; you can get only the general idea. 'Heaven Asks' is really fantastic: thousands of years ago it raised all kinds of questions relating to the universe, to nature and to history.

(Regarding the discussion on the problem of two combining into one:) Let Hung Ch'i reprint a few good items, and write a report.

NOTES

INTRODUCTION

1   Along these lines, some Western Marxists attributed Stalinism to the influence of the 'Asiatic mode of production' on Russia, seeing it as a new form of 'Oriental despotism' – the irony being that, for traditional Russians, the exact opposite holds: 'It was always a Western fancy to see Lenin and Stalin as "Oriental" despots. The great Russian tyrants in the eighteenth and the twentieth century were Westernizers' (Lesley Chamberlain, *The Philosophy Steamer*, London, Atlantic Books 2006, p. 270)

2   Emmanuel Lévinas, *Les Imprévus de l'histoire*, Montpellier, Fata Morgana, 1994, p. 172.

3   Martin Heidegger, *Schelling's Treatise on Human Freedom*, Athens, OH, Ohio University Press, 1985, p. 146.

4   G. W. F. Hegel, *Phenomenology of Spirit*, Oxford, Oxford University Press, 1977, p. 288.

5   F. W. J. Schelling, *Die Weltalter. Fragmente. In den Urfassungen von 1811 und 1813*, ed. Manfred Schroeter, Munich, Biederstein, 1979, p. 13.

6   Georgi M. Derluguian, *Bourdieu's Secret Admirer in the Caucasus*, Chicago, The University of Chicago Press, 2005.

7   See below, p. 117.

8   Luc Boltanski and Eve Chiapello, *The New Spirit of Capitalism*, London, Verso, 2005, p. ix.

9   Ibid., p. xvii.

10 See below, p. 87.

11 See below, p. 92.

12 See below, pp. 117–18.

13 Alain Badiou, 'Prefazione all'edizione italiana,' in *Metapolitica*, Naples, Cronopio, 2002, p. 14.

14   See Michael Hardt and Antonio Negri, *Empire*, Cambridge MA, Harvard University Press, 2000 and *Multitude*, London, Hamish Hamilton, 2005.

15   See below, pp. 131, 137.

16   See below, p. 183.

17   See below, pp. 182–8.

18   See below, p. 176.

19   See below, pp. 106–7.

20   Jung Chang and Jon Halliday, *Mao: The Unknown Story*, New York, Knopf, 2005. However, not everything in this work should be taken at face value, see the critique by Andrew Nathan in 'Jade and Plastic', *London Review of Books,* 17 November 2005.

21   Heidegger is also wrong in his letter to Marcuse when comparing the Holocaust to the 1946–47 deportation of Germans from Eastern Europe – Herbert Marcuse was right in his reply: the difference between the fate of Jews and the Eastern European Germans was, at that moment, the thin line that separated barbarism from civilization.

22   See below, p. 181.

23   See below, p. 179, 180.

24   Samuel Beckett, *Trilogy*, London, Calder, 2003, p. 418.

25   See Slavoj Žižek, *Iraq: The Borrowed Kettle*, London, Verso, 2005.

26   See http://www.marxists.org/reference/archive/stalin/works/1938/09.htm

27   Robert Conquest, *The Harvest of Sorrow*, New York, Oxford University Press, 1986, p. 119.

28   Ibid., p. 120.

29   Ibid.

30   No wonder, then, that, when he describes the 'democratic method of resolving contradictions among the people', Mao *has* to evoke his own version of, precisely, 'negation of negation', in the guise of the formula 'unity–criticism–unity': 'starting from the desire for unity, resolving contradictions through criticism or struggle, and arriving at a new unity on a new basis. In our experience this is the correct method of resolving contradictions among the people.' See below, p. 136.

31   See below, pp. 172–73.

32   Jonathan Spence, *Mao*, London, Weidenfeld & Nicolson 1999, pp. xii–xiv.

33   Due to limitations of space, we have chosen to end this selection of texts just before the Cultural Revolution. A second volume of selections from this later period may follow.

34   Alain Badiou, *Logiques des mondes*, Paris, Éditions du Seuil, 2006, pp. 62–70. My translation.

35   Ibid., pp. 543–44.

36   Ibid.

37   G. W. F. Hegel, *Enzyklopädie der philosophischen Wissenschaften*, Hamburg, Franz Meiner Verlag 1959, p. 436.

38   Fredric Jameson, *The Seeds of Time*, New York, Columbia University Press, 1994, p. 89.

39   Ibid., p. 90.

40   Was Che Guevara's withdrawal from all official functions, even from Cuban citizenship, in 1965, in order to dedicate himself to world revolution – this suicidal gesture of cutting the links with the institutional universe – really an *act*? Or was it an escape from the impossible task of the positive construction of socialism, from remaining faithful to the *consequences* of the revolution, namely, an implicit admission of failure?

41   Brian Massumi, 'Navigating Movements', in *Hope*, ed. Mary Zournazi, New York, Routledge, 2002, p. 224.

42   Eyal Weizman, 'Israeli Military Using Post-Structuralism as "Operational Theory" ', available online at www.frieze.com.

43   See below, p. 162.

I. A SINGLE SPARK CAN START A PRAIRIE FIRE

1   [Comrade Fang Chih-min, a native of Yiyang, Kiangsi Province, and a member of the Sixth Central Committee of the Communist Party of China, was the founder of the Red area in north-eastern Kiangsi and of the Tenth Red Army. In 1934 he led the vanguard detachment of the Red Army in marching north to resist the Japanese invaders. In January 1935 he was captured in the battle against the counter-revolutionary Kuomintang troops and in July he died a martyr's death in Nanchang, Kiangsi.]

2   [The subjective forces of the revolution: organized forces of the revolution.]

3   [Lu Ti-ping, a Kuomintang warlord, was the Kuomintang governor of Hunan Province in 1928.]

4   [The war of March–April 1929 between Chiang Kai-shek, the Kuomintang warlord in Nanking, and Li Tsung-jen and Pai Chung-hsi, the Kuomintang warlords in Kwangsi Province.]

5   [The third invasion of the Red Army's base area in the Chingkang Mountains by the Kuomintang warlords in Hunan and Kiangsi lasting from the end of 1928 to the beginning of 1929.]

6   [The quotation is from Mencius, who compared a tyrant who drove his people into seeking a benevolent ruler to the otter which 'drives the fish into deep waters'.]

7   [The Sixth National Congress of the Communist Party of China was held in July 1928. It pointed out that after the defeat in 1927, China's revolution remained bourgeois-democratic in nature, i.e., anti-imperialist and anti-

feudal, and that since the inevitable new high tide in the revolution was not yet imminent, the general line for the revolution should be to win over the masses. The Sixth Congress liquidated the 1927 Right capitulationism of Chen Tu-hsiu and also repudiated the 'Left' putschism which occurred in the Party at the end of 1927 and the beginning of 1928.]

8   [The statement in brackets was added by the author of the letter.]

9   [The regime set up in western Fukien came into being in 1929, when the Red Army in the Chingkang Mountains sallied eastward to build a new revolutionary base area and established the people's revolutionary political power in the counties of Lungyen, Yungting and Shanghang in the western part of that province.]

10   [Stable base areas were the relatively stable revolutionary base areas established by the Workers' and Peasants' Red Army.]

11   [Chiang Po-cheng was then the commander of the Kuomintang peace preservation corps in Chekiang Province.]

12   [Chen Kuo-hui and Lu Hsing-pang were two notorious Fukien bandits whose forces had been incorporated into the Kuomintang army.]

13   [Chang Chen was a divisional commander of the Kuomintang army.]

14   [Chu Pei-teh, a Kuomintang warlord, was then the Kuomintang governor of Kiangsi Province.]

15   [Hsiung Shih-hui was then a divisional commander of the Kuomintang army in Kiangsi Province.]

2. OPPOSE BOOK WORSHIP

1   [See *Confucian Analects*, book III, 'Pa Yi': 'When Confucius entered the Ancestral Temple he inquired into everything.']

2   [Li Kuei was a hero in the well-known Chinese novel *Shui Hu Chuan* (Heroes of the Marshes) which describes the peasant war that occurred towards the end of the Northern Sung dynasty (960–1127). He was simple, outspoken and very loyal to the revolutionary cause of the peasants, but crude and tactless.]

3   [Comrade Mao Tse-tung has always laid great stress on investigation, regarding social investigation as the most important task and the basis for defining policy in the work of leadership. The work of investigation was gradually developed in the Fourth Army of the Red Army on Comrade Mao Tse-tung's initiative. He stipulated that social investigation should be a regular part of the work, and the Political Department of the Red Army prepared detailed forms covering such items as the state of the mass struggle, the condition of the reactionaries, the economic life of the people and the amount of land owned by each class in the rural areas. Wherever the Red

Army went, it first made itself familiar with the class situation in the locality and then formulated slogans suited to the needs of the masses.]

4 [Here 'the mountains' are the Chingkang mountain area along the borders of Kiangsi and Hunan Provinces; the 'plains' are those in southern Kiangsi and western Fukien. In January 1929, Comrade Mao Tse-tung led the main force of the Fourth Army of the Red Army down from the Chingkang Mountains to southern Kiangsi and western Fukien in order to set up two large revolutionary base areas.]

5 [The 'Book of documents' consisted of the resolutions adopted at the Sixth National Congress of the Communist Party of China in July 1928, including the political resolution and the resolutions on the peasant question, the land question, the organization of political power, etc. Early in 1929 the Front Committee of the Fourth Army of the Red Army published these resolutions in book form for distribution to the Party organizations in the Red Army and to the local Party organizations.]

3. ON PRACTICE: ON THE RELATION BETWEEN KNOWLEDGE AND PRACTICE, BETWEEN KNOWING AND DOING

1 V. I. Lenin, 'Conspectus of Hegel's *The Science of Logic*', *Collected Works*, Russian edition, Moscow, 1958, vol. XXXVIII, p. 205.

2 See Karl Marx, 'Theses on Feuerbach', in Karl Marx and Friedrich Engels, *Selected Works*, Moscow, Foreign Languages Publishing House, 1958, vol. II, p. 403, and V. I. Lenin, *Materialism and Empirio-Criticism*, Moscow, Foreign Languages Publishing House, 1952, pp. 134–36.

3 [*San Kuo Yen Yi* (Tales of the Three Kingdoms) is a famous Chinese historical novel by Lo Kuan-chung (written between the fourteenth and early fifteenth centuries).]

4 Lenin, 'Conspectus of Hegel's *The Science of Logic*', p. 161.

5 'In order to understand, it is necessary empirically to begin understanding, study, to rise from empiricism to the universal' (Lenin, 'Conspectus of Hegel's *The Science of Logic*', p. 197).

6 V. I. Lenin, *What Is to Be Done?*, in *Collected Works*, Moscow, Foreign Languages Publishing House, 1961, vol. V, p. 369.

7 Lenin, *Materialism and Empirio-Criticism*, p. 141.

8 J. V. Stalin, 'The Foundations of Leninism', in *Problems of Leninism*, Moscow, Foreign Languages Publishing House, 1954, p. 31.

9 See Lenin, *Materialism and Empirio-Criticism*, pp. 129–36.

4. ON CONTRADICTION

1 V. I. Lenin, 'Conspectus of Hegel's Lectures on the History of Philosophy', *Collected Works*, Russian edition, Moscow, 1958, vol. XXXVIII, p. 249.

2 [In his essay 'On the Question of Dialectics', Lenin said: 'The splitting in two of a single whole and the cognition of its contradictory parts (see the quotation from Philo on Heraclitus at the beginning of Section 3 'On Cognition' in Lassalle's book on Heraclitus) is the essence (one of the "essentials", one of the principal, if not the principal, characteristics or features) of dialectics' (*Collected Works*, Russian edition, Moscow, 1958, vol. XXXVIII, p. 357). In his 'Conspectus of Hegel's *The Science of Logic*', he said: 'In brief, dialectics can be defined as the doctrine of the unity of opposites. This grasps the kernel of dialectics, but it requires explanations and development' (p. 215).]

3 Lenin, 'On the Question of Dialectics', p. 358.

4 [A saying of Tung Chung-shu (179–104 BC), a well-known exponent of Confucianism in the Han dynasty.]

5 Friedrich Engels, 'Dialectics. Quantity and Quality', *Anti-Dühring*, Moscow, Foreign Languages Publishing House, 1959, p. 166.

6 Lenin, 'On the Question of Dialectics', pp. 357–58.

7 Engels, *Anti-Dühring* pp. 166–67.

8 Lenin, 'On the Question of Dialectics', p. 357.

9 Ibid., pp. 358–59.

10 [See 'Problems of Strategy in China's Revolutionary War', *Selected Works*, vol. I, p. 251, n. 10.]

11 [See ibid., p. 249 n.]

12 [Wei Cheng (AD 580–643) was a statesman and historian of the Tang dynasty.]

13 [*Shui Hu Chuan* (Heroes of the Marshes), a famous fourteenth-century Chinese novel, describes a peasant war towards the end of the Northern Sung dynasty. Chu Village was in the vicinity of Liangshanpo, where Sung Chiang, leader of the peasant uprising and hero of the novel, established his base. Chu Chao-feng, the head of this village, was a despotic landlord.]

14 V. I. Lenin, 'Once Again on the Trade Unions, the Present Situation and the Mistakes of Trotsky and Bukharin', *Selected Works*, New York, International Publishers, 1943, vol. IX, p. 66.

15 V. I. Lenin, *What Is to Be Done?*, *Collected Works*, Moscow, Foreign Languages Publishing House, 1961, vol. V, p. 369.

16 Lenin, 'Conspectus of Hegel's *The Science of Logic*', *Collected Works*, vol. xxxviii, pp. 97–98.

17 [*Shan Hai Ching* (Book of Mountains and Seas) was written in the era of the Warring States (403–221 BC). In one of its fables Kua Fu, a superman,

pursued and overtook the sun. But he died of thirst, whereupon his staff was transformed into the forest of Teng.]

18 [Yi is one of the legendary heroes of ancient China, famous for his archery. According to a legend in *Huai Nan Tzu*, compiled in the second century BC, there were ten suns in the sky in the days of Emperor Yao. To put an end to the damage to vegetation caused by these scorching suns, Emperor Yao ordered Yi to shoot them down. In another legend recorded by Wang Yi (second century AD), the archer is said to have shot down nine of the ten suns.]

19 [*Hsi Yu Chi* (Pilgrimage to the West) is a sixteenth-century novel, the hero of which is the monkey god Sun Wu-kung. He could miraculously change at will into seventy-two different shapes, such as a bird, a tree and a stone.]

20 [The *Strange Tales of Liao Chai*, written by Pu Sung-ling in the seventeenth century, is a well-known collection of 431 tales, mostly about ghosts and fox spirits.]

21 Karl Marx, 'Introduction to the Critique of Political Economy', *A Contribution to the Critique of Political Economy*, Chicago, 1904, pp. 310–11.

22 Lenin, 'On the Question of Dialectics', p. 358.

23 [The saying 'Things that oppose each other also complement each other' first appeared in the *History of the Earlier Han Dynasty* by Pan Ku, a celebrated historian in the first century AD. It has long been a popular saying.]

24 Lenin, 'On the Question of Dialectics', p. 358.

25 V. I. Lenin, 'Remarks on N. I. Bukharin's *Economics of the Transitional Period*', *Selected Works*, Russian edition, Moscow-Leningrad, 1931, vol. XI, p. 357.

8. CONCERNING STALIN'S *ECONOMIC PROBLEMS* OF SOCIALISM IN THE USSR

1 [The book at issue in this critique is *Economic Problems of Socialism in the USSR* by J. V. Stalin, Peking, Foreign Languages Press, 1972 (1st edn).]

The date for this document in the 1967 edition of *Selected Works*, volume VI, is 1959. The 1969 edition dates it 1958. There was no Ch'engchou (Chengzhou) Conference in November 1959, but there was one in November 1958. The document almost certainly dates from this earlier time.]

2 [Reply to Comrades A. V. Sanina and V. G. Venzher, included in *Economic Problems*.]

3 [A catty is 1.1 pounds.]

4 [Recipient of Stalin's second letter, included in *Economic Problems*.]

5 [The wage system established in 1953 emphasized predominantly short-

term individual material incentives. It established an eight-grade wage point system ranging from 139 to 390 wage points per month. Similar work in different regions would receive an equal number of work points, but the value of work points varied according to regional costs of living. By 1956, the wage point system had been replaced by a wage system, but the eight-grade structure was retained.]

6   [Experimental fields sought to develop new and advanced techniques, such as close planting, early planting, deep ploughing, etc. If successful in increasing output, the techniques would be popularized throughout China. By increasing production and thus the total wage fund, the experimental field concept could help undermine the ideological base of the graded wage system by demonstrating that specialists could learn from the peasants.]

7   [This is identical, in Chinese, to ownership by the whole people.]

9. CRITIQUE OF STALIN'S *ECONOMIC PROBLEMS OF SOCIALISM IN THE USSR*

1   [Reply to Comrades A. V. Sanina and V. G. Venzher.]

2   [These first four paragraphs comment critically on the entire text. There follows a series of comments criticizing specific sections. Before each comment Stalin's original text is given, as translated for *Jen min ch'u pan she*, 3rd edn, January 1958. (English edition: Peking, Foreign Languages Press, 1972.)]

3   [Mao is here talking about the excessive purchase of grain at the end of 1954 and the consequent rural grain shortages in the spring of 1955. Subsequently, the quota for state purchases was reduced by 7 billion catties and tension in the countryside eased. These occurrences, however, took place in the spring of 1955, not at the end of that year, which was characterized by the continuing high tide of collectivization in China's countryside.]

4   [Material in brackets added from Stalin's text to clarify the point.]

5   [Ch'in Shih Huang Ti (Qin Shi Huangdi), the first emperor, was a king of the state of Ch'in who, between 230 and 221 BC, conquered the neighbouring states and unified China. Under his rule, a feudal system was established, weights and measures and coinage were standardized. The legalist philosophy was the philosophical basis of the Ch'in. The first emperor is remembered for his burning of all non-utilitarian, 'subversive' literature in 213 BC.]

6   [Ts'ao Ts'ao (Cao Cao) was a famous general and chancellor of the latter Han dynasty (AD 25–220) who played a significant role in the wars which finally toppled the Han and led to the epoch of divided empire called the three kingdoms.]

7   [Mencius. Mao seems to mean 'Let's not make a stock villain out of commodity production pedantically'.]

10. ON THE CORRECT HANDLING
OF CONTRADICTIONS AMONG THE PEOPLE

1   Lao Tzu, chapter LVIII.

12. TALK ON QUESTIONS OF PHILOSOPHY

1   In other words (1) Marxist philosophy, that is, dialectical materialism and historical materialism, which deals with the general law of development of the contradictions existing in nature, human society and man's thought; (2) Marxist political economy which elucidates the law governing the development of society's economy and exposes how the capitalist class exploits the working class (the theory of surplus-value); and (3) scientific socialism which shows that capitalist society is bound to develop to a higher stage of society and that the proletariat is the grave-digger of the capitalist system. (For details see Lenin's 'The Three Sources and the Three Component Parts of Marxism'.)]

2   [Peking University, jointly descended from the old Peking University which launched the 4 May Movement in 1919, and from the American-endowed Yenching University, has continued since 1949 to enjoy the highest prestige in China for general intellectual excellence. People's University (*Jen-min ta-hsüeh*), also located in Peking, was specially set up to provide courses more accessible to students from worker and peasant backgrounds.]

3   [Among the Confucian classics, the Four Books represent the core studied by beginners, the Five Classics a somewhat larger corpus.]

4   [Among his varied educational experiences, Mao Tse-tung has long singled out the six months he spent reading in the Hunan Provincial Library, in the winter of 1912–13, as one of the most valuable.]

5   [The first sentence is from the *Doctrine of the Mean,* the second is from *Mencius,* book IV.]

6   [The quotation is from the Confucian *Analects.* The incident in which the people of K'uang detained Confucius and wanted to kill him is referred to in the *Analects.*]

7   [Mao's reasoning is apparently that, whether or not he went there, Confucius had nothing against Ch'in (a state which existed in the first

millennium BC in present-day Shensi, whose ruler ultimately conquered the whole of China and founded the Ch'in dynasty in 221 BC), since he included in the *Book of Odes,* which he is supposed to have edited, a number of poems from that area, including the two mentioned by Mao.]

8 [Ssu-ma Chien (145–90 BC) was China's first great historian, who compiled *shih-chi* (Historical Records) relating the history of China from the origins to his own day.]

9 [The translation of the above poem, and of the titles of the two mentioned previously, are taken from Legge's version of the *Book of Odes.*]

10 [Love poems have traditionally been interpreted by Chinese critics as an allegory for the relations between an official and his prince; Chu Hsi (see below, note 42) held that they should be taken at face value. Mao puts the commonsense view that they should sometimes be taken literally, and sometimes not.]

11 [Wei Chuang (*c*.858–910) was an eminent poet of the late T'ang (618–906) and early Five (907–960) Dynasties. Mao is arguing that the same principles of interpretation should be applied to the *Book of Odes* and to all classical poetry.]

12 [The 'Socialist Education Movement'. launched by Comrade Mao after the Tenth Plenum in the autumn of 1962, was known as the 'four clean-ups' in the countryside, and as the 'five antis' (*wu-fan*) in the cities. The four clean-ups were: socialist rectification in the fields of politics, ideology, organization and economy.]

13 [*Kuang-ming jih-pao*, organ of the China Democratic League, took the lead in criticisms of the Party in April 1957, when the 'blooming and contending' was in full flood. The *Wen-hui pao,* published in Shanghai, was a non-Party organ which had been criticized by Mao for its bourgeois tendencies in 1957. In November 1965, it was to serve as the channel for the opening shot in the Cultural Revolution.]

14 [Chou Ku-ch'eng was the author of numerous works on Chinese and world history. Since 1950 he had been a professor at Futan University in Shanghai. In 1962 he published an article on history and art, in which he expressed ideas on the *Zeitgeist* which were said to be an expression in the realm of aesthetics of Yang Hsien-chen's philosophical theories (see below, note 19).]

15 [Sun Yeh-fang was at this time Director of the Institute of Economics of the Academy of Science; he was dismissed in 1966. As K'ang Sheng's remark indicates, he had adopted the ideas of some Soviet and Eastern European economists with whom he had been in professional contact about the role of the profit motive in a socialist economy.]

16 [In the summer of 1955, just before Mao's speech of 31 July gave a new impetus to the formation of agricultural producers' cooperatives, the Party's Rural Work Department (at the instigation of Liu Shao-ch'i) had disbanded

a number of cooperatives which were said to have been hastily and prematurely formed.]

17 [Teng Tzu-hui (1895–1972) had been head of the Rural Work Department since 1952, though his influence had declined since the late 1950s, because of his share of responsibility for the 'disbanding' or 'weeding-out' of cooperatives in 1955. It would appear, however that he still possessed sufficient status to put his views energetically in opposition to those of Mao when, in the early 1960s, the policies enumerated here by Mao were a subject of dispute within the Party. Both the Rural Work Department and Teng Tzu-hui were severely criticized by Comrade Mao during a debate on cooperative transformation. [For more details see *Selected Works*, vol. V, pp. 224–25.]

[As a symbol to cover this whole spectrum of policies, emphasizing the role of material incentives, private plotting, etc., the expression 'four great freedoms' is less common, in documents published since the beginning of the Cultural Revolution, than *'Sanzi yibao'* ('three freedoms and one fix, or guarantee'). On this concept, which is supposed to sum up the reactionary line of Liu Shao-ch'i and his sympathizers in the countryside, see the article 'Struggle between Two Roads in China's Countryside', *Peking Review,* No. 49 (1967), pp. 11–19.]

18 [A Right opportunist view advocated by Liu Shao-chi' and others. In this connection see Comrade Mao's speech at the Political Bureau meeting of the Central Committee of the CPC 'Refute the Right Deviationist Views that Depart from General Line', *Selected Works*, vol. V, pp. 93–94.]

19 [The view that 'two combine into one' was put forward in the early 1960s by Yang Hsien-chen, who had been, since 1955, President of the Higher Party School. Beginning in July 1964 this formulation was violently attacked in the press on the grounds that it minimized the importance of struggle and contradiction, and contrasted with Mao's view that 'one divides into two', i.e. that struggle, and in particular class struggle, constantly re-emerges, even when particular contradictions have been resolved. The 'outline of an article' referred to in the stenographer's note was presumably a summary of one of the forthcoming attacks on Yang, submitted to the Chairman in advance for his approval.]

20 The defence of Madrid, starting in October 1936, lasted for two years and five months. In 1936, fascist Germany and Italy made use of the Spanish fascist warlord Franco to launch a war of aggression against Spain. The Spanish people, led by the Popular Front Government, heroically defended democracy against aggression. The battle of Madrid, the capital of Spain, was the bitterest in the whole war. Madrid fell in March 1939 because Britain, France and other imperialist countries assisted the aggressors by their hypocritical policy of 'non-intervention' and because divisions arose within

the Popular Front. The point of this criticism is obviously not that the Spanish Republicans fought to the end, but that they failed to grasp the axiom that territorial strong points are not in themselves decisive.

21   [See 'Resolution on Certain Questions in the History of our Party' adopted on 20 April 1945, *Selected Works*, vol. III, pp. 177–225 (1965 edn).]

22   [Mao began his activity at this institute in 1925, but it was in 1926 that he actually served as principal and made his main contribution.]

23   [The quotation is from *Mencius,* book VI, part A, ch. 15.]

24   [This is presumably a reference to Chang Ping-lin's celebrated article, published in 1903, entitled 'A Refutation of K'ang Yu-wei's Letter on Revolution'. In this article, Chang sharply attacked K'ang not only on the issue of revolution versus gradual reform, but on the importance of racial differences between the Chinese and the Manchus, which K'ang tended to minimize. The Manchus, Chang argued, were an alien and decadent race, totally unfit to rule China. It was in this context that he discussed evolution, indicating that the existing racial differences were the product of history.]

25   [Fu Ying is apparently a Chinese scientist who was alive in 1964, since Mao says he wants to look him up.]

26   [Lu P'ing was President of Peking University at this time; he was removed and 'struggled against' in June 1966.]

27   [Ai Ssu-chti (*c.*1910–66) was, at the time of his death, Vice-President of the Higher Party School. He was one of the Party's leading philosophical spokesmen, who had translated works on dialectical materialism from the Russian, and written many books and articles which aimed to make Marxism accessible to the masses. On 1 November 1964 he published an article in *People's Daily* attacking Yang Hsien-chen, the 'bourgeois' philosopher Mao refers to earlier in this talk in connection with the principle of 'two combining into one'.]

28   [The metaphor of 'dissecting a sparrow' is an applied theory and a work method to acquire knowledge and sum up experiences. Instead of attempting to generalize about a vast number of repetitions of a phenomenon, this work method advocates the in-depth analysis, thorough study and investigation of a prototype, and a summing-up experience through such analysis. The slogan is derived from the common saying, 'while a sparrow is small, it contains all the vital organs'. Here, Mao makes the point that, in the broader international context, China as a whole is a microcosm of the problems of revolution in the world today.]

29   [Leng Tzu-hsing discourses on the mansion of the Duke of Jung-kuo in chapter 2 of *The Story of the Stone*. The 'Talisman for Officials' was a list of the rich and influential families in the area which the former novice from the Bottle-Gourd Temple said every official should carry in order to avoid offending them and thereby wrecking his career.]

30 [For Comrade Mao's criticisms on this matter see 'Letter Concerning the *Dream of the Red Chamber*' (*Selected Works*, vol. V, pp. 150–51), 'On Criticising Longloumeng yuanjia' (*Selected Works*, vol. V, pp. 293–94). For Mao's criticism of Yü P'ing-po see 'Letter Concerning the Study of the *Dream of the Red Chamber*', *16 October 1954, Selected Works*, vol. V. Wang K'un-lun was Vice-Mayor of Peking in the 1950s.]

31 [Ho Ch'i-fang (1911–), a lyric poet and powerful figure in the literary world, had defended Yü P'ing-po up to a point at the time of the campaign against him in 1954, saying that Yü was wrong in his interpretation of the *Dream of the Red Chamber*, but politically loyal. He himself came under attack at the time of the Great Leap Forward.]

32 [Wu Shih-ch'ang's work on this subject has been translated into English: *On 'The Red Chamber Dream'*, Oxford, Clarendon Press,1961.]

33 [Mao's statement here concords with the views of Lu Hsün.]

34 [The figures Mao gives here, as he shifts to the present and calls to mind the final showdown with the Kuomintang, are those at the beginning of the Anti-Japanese War rather than those at the beginning of the renewed civil war in 1946, when the People's Liberation Army had grown to at least half a million men.]

35 [In January 1949, General Fu Tso-i, commanding the nationalist garrison in Peiping (as it was then called), surrendered the city without a fight to avoid useless destruction. He subsequently became Minister of Water Conservancy in the Peking government.]

36 [The legendary Emperor Shen Nung is said to have taught the art of agriculture in the third millennium BC, and in particular to have discovered the medicinal properties of plants.]

37 [The Lung Shan and Yang Shao cultures, located respectively in north-eastern and north-western China, were the two most remarkable cultures of the neolithic period. As Mao indicates, they are particularly noted for their pottery.]

38 [The book called the *Chuang-tzu*, which was probably composed only in part by the man of the same name who lived in the second half of the fourth century BC, is not only one of the classic texts of Taoism (with the *Lao-tzu* and the *Book of Changes*), but one of the greatest literary masterpieces in the history of China.]

39 [Sakata Shiyouchi, a Japanese physicist from the University of Nagoya, holds that 'elementary particles are a single, material, differentiated and limitless category which make up the natural order'. An article by him expounding these views was published in *Red Flag* in June 1965.]

40 [Mao is apparently referring to a collection of essays published by Jen Chi-yü in 1963, and reprinted in 1973: *Han T'ang fo-chiao ssu-hsiang lun chi (Collected Essays on Buddhist Thought in the Han and T'ang Dynasties).*

In these studies, he quotes from Lenin at considerable length regarding dialectics.]

41 [T'ang Yung-t'ung (1892–1964), whom Jen Chi-yü acknowledges as his teacher, was the leading historian of Buddhism, who had written on Chinese Buddhism under the Han, Wei, Chin, and Northern and Southern dynasties, on the history of Indian thought, etc. He was Dean of the Humanities at Peking University from 1948 until he fell ill in 1954.]

42 [Under the influence of Ch'an Buddhism (better known under its Japanese name of Zen), Chinese philosophers of the Sung and Ming dynasties, of whom Chu Hsi (1130–1200) is the most famous, developed a synthesis between Confucianism and Buddhism in which a central role is played by the concept *li* (principle or reason), commonly known as Neo-Confucianism. For a Chinese view of the relations between these schools basically similar to Mao's, see Hou Wai-lu, *A Short History of Chinese Philosophy*, Peking, Foreign Languages Press, 1959, pp. 33–51. For an interpretation by a Western specialist, see H. G. Creel, *Chinese Thought from Confucius to Mao Tse-tung*, Chicago, University of Chicago Press, and London, Eyre & Spottiswoode, 1953, Ch. 10.]

43 [Han Yü and Liu Tsung-yüan. Han Yü sought to recreate the simplicity of the classical period, while avoiding excessive archaism. The slogan about 'learning from their ideas' quoted by Mao refers to this aim of seeking inspiration from the ancient Confucian sages, while avoiding outmoded forms of expression. He adopted a critical attitude towards Buddhism, but nonetheless borrowed some ideas from it. Liu Tsung-yüan, whom Mao calls here by his literary name of Liu Tzu-hou, was a close friend of Han Yü.]

44 [Liu Tsung-yüan's essay *T'ien Tui* (Heaven Answers) undertook to answer the questions about the origin and nature of the universe raised by Ch'ü Yüan in his poem *T'ien Wen* (Heaven Asks). The latter is translated under the title 'The Riddles' in Li *Sao and Other Poems of Chu Yuan*. It is, as Mao says, suggestive but extremely obscure.]